The International Ombudsman Yearbook
Volume 8, 2004

The International Ombudsman Yearbook Volume 8, 2004

Edited by

International Ombudsman Institute
Edmonton, Alberta, Canada

and

Linda C. Reif
Professor, Faculty of Law, University of Alberta,
Edmonton, Alberta, Canada

2007

MARTINUS NIJHOFF PUBLISHERS
LEIDEN / BOSTON

A C.I.P. Catalogue record for this book is available from the Library of Congress.

Printed on acid-free paper.

ISSN 1387-1846
ISBN 978-90-04-15692-0

Printed in the Netherlands.

THE INTERNATIONAL OMBUDSMAN INSTITUTE

The International Ombudsman Institute is a non-profit organization whose objects include promotion of the concept of ombudsmanship, encouragement and support of research in the ombudsman field, development of educational programs associated with ombudsmanship, the organization of international ombudsmanship conferences, and provision of a resource center for storage and dissemination of information about the ombudsman institution.

The International Ombudsman Yearbook, published annually by the International Ombudsman Institute and Martinus Nijhoff Publishers, is a multidisciplinary publication devoted to the study of the concept of ombudsmanship and the institution of the ombudsman, either in its classic or adapted form.

Contributions to the body of research and literature in the ombudsman field are welcomed from various disciplines including law, public administration, and political science.

THE INTERNATIONAL OMBUDSMAN YEARBOOK
EDITORIAL ADVISORY BOARD

BOARD OF DIRECTORS
INTERNATIONAL OMBUDSMAN INSTITUTE

Australasia and Pacific

Mr. Bruce Barbour
Regional Vice-President
Ombudsman, New South Wales
Australia
Level 3, 580 George Street
Sydney, N.S.W. 2000, Australia

Mr. Ila Geno
Director
Chief Ombudsman, Papua New Guinea
P.O. Box 852
Boroko, NCD, Papua New Guinea

Europe

Dr. Peter Kostelka
Regional Vice-President
Volksanwaltschaft
Singerstraße 17
AT 1015 Vienna, Austria

Ms. Riitta-Leena Paunio
Director
Parliamentary Ombudsman
Parliament Building Annex
Arkadiankatu 3
FI 00102 Helsinki, Finland

Mr. Rafael Ribó
Director
Sindic de Greuges de Catalunya
Josep Anselm, Clavé, 31
08002 BARCELONA, Spain

Latin America and Caribbean

Mr. José Luis Soberanes Fernández
Regional Vice-President
President, Comisión Nacional de Derechos Humanos, Mexico
Periferiso Sur. No. 3469, 5 piso
Col. San Jeronimo Lidice
C.P. 10200, Mexico D.F.

Dr. Eduardo Rene Mondino
Director
Defensor del Pueblo de la República Argentina
Montevideo 1244
1018 Buenos Aires, Argentina

North America

Mr. André Marin
Regional Vice-President
Ombudsman, Ontario
483 Bay Street
10th Floor, South Tower
TORONTO, Ontario
Canada M5G 2C9

Mr. Gord Button
Director
Ombudsman, Alberta
10303 Jasper Ave, Suite 2800
EDMONTON, Alberta
Canada T5J 5C3

ERRATUM

In the list of the members of the International Ombudsman Institute Board of Directors for 2004-2005 found in the introductory pages of (2003) Volume 7 of The International Ombudsman Yearbook, the name and address of Director Dr. Thomas J. Frawley was mistakenly omitted from the list of Regional Vice-Presidents and Directors for Europe. His name/address should be added as follows:

Dr. Thomas J. Frawley
Northern Ireland Assembly Ombudsman and Commissioner for Complaints
33 Wellington Place
Belfast
Northern Ireland
BT1 6HN

The International Ombudsman Institute apologizes for any inconvenience caused by this omission.

GUIDELINES TO AUTHORS

1. We invite the submission of articles to be considered for publication. In general, articles should not exceed 100 double-spaced, typed pages in length, inclusive of endnotes.
2. Papers to be considered for publication must be sent to the Editor, *The International Ombudsman Yearbook*, International Ombudsman Institute, Faculty of Law, University of Alberta, Edmonton, Alberta T6G 2H5, Canada, <lreif@law.ualberta.ca>. Submission of a paper implies that it comprises original unpublished work. If possible, please submit the paper with a copy on computer diskette or by e-mail attachment. The International Ombudsman Institute uses Wordperfect 6, 7, 8, 9, 10 and 11.
3. Contributors are requested to keep an accurate copy of the manuscript in their possession since the *Yearbook* cannot assume responsibility for the safety of any manuscript sent to it or undertake to return it.
4. Manuscripts (text and endnotes) should be typewritten on one side of the paper only, double-spaced. Endnotes should be placed at the end of the text. All pages should be numbered consecutively. Titles and headings should be short. Extensive quotations in the text should be indented.
5. Cases, statutes, quotations, etc. must be cited accurately. Generally, please see the *Yearbook* for house style. The *Canadian Guide to Uniform Legal Citation* is used for law-related citations. Contributors are responsible for the accuracy of all citations and quotations and are requested to check them with particular care.
6. The Editor reserves the right to make alterations and corrections to conform both with the general style of the publication and accepted rules of grammar and syntax.
7. Galley proofs will be sent to authors and should be corrected clearly and returned to the address given by the date stated.
8. Authors will be provided with one free copy of the *Yearbook* containing their contribution. Authors should supply the address to which the copy of the *Yearbook* should be sent.

THE INTERNATIONAL OMBUDSMAN YEARBOOK (2004) VOLUME 8

TABLE OF CONTENTS

FOREWORD

This publication is the eighth annual volume of *The International Ombudsman Yearbook*, compiled and edited by the International Ombudsman Institute and now produced by Martinus Nijhoff Publishers (formerly Kluwer Law International). During the 1980s and early 1990s, the publication was named *The International Ombudsman Journal* (1981-1994) numbers 1-12, renamed the *International Ombudsman Journal* (1995) for number 13, and was published annually.

The I.O.I. was established in 1978 with its secretariat at the Faculty of Law, University of Alberta, Edmonton, Alberta, Canada. The Board of Directors is comprised of ombudsmen representing all of the regions in the world. By October 2006, the Institutional Membership of the I.O.I. stood at 146 classical and human rights ombudsman offices, illustrative of the popularity of the institution both at national and sub-national levels of government. In 1996 the I.O.I. established a three-language publication policy, establishing English, French, and Spanish as official I.O.I. languages. Where possible, I.O.I. publications are being translated into each of these languages. Although *The International Ombudsman Yearbook* is published mainly in English, each article in the *Yearbook* commences with an abstract of the article printed in the other two languages of the I.O.I.

The development of *The International Ombudsman Yearbook* was a result of the considerable increase in the number of ombudsman offices in the past thirty-five years, with a consequential increase in the interest in research and scholarship on the ombudsman concept. The classical model of the ombudsman office—a general jurisdiction public sector institution established by the legislative branch of government to monitor and regulate the administrative activities of the executive branch—was first established in its modern form in Sweden in 1809, and it then spread through Scandinavia in the first half of the twentieth century. Next, the office was established in Commonwealth and other countries starting in the 1960s and 1970s. The more recent transition to democratic governance in various countries around the world, associated in part with post-Cold War developments, has seen the institution established in many more countries in the past fifteen years, especially in Latin America, Central and East Europe, Africa, and the Asia-Pacific area. The ombudsman model has been established at the international or supranational level of governance—the European Ombudsman was established in the Treaty on European Union (Maastricht Treaty). The ombudsman idea has also been adapted for use in various ways in particular government sectors and in the private sector, such in corporations, industries, colleges, and universities.

The original word for the office—"ombudsman"—can be translated as meaning "representative". Many public and private sector offices around the world have maintained this title. However, a growing number of offices, particularly in the public sector, have adopted new terms to represent the office. These include *Defensor del Pueblo* (e.g. Spain, Argentina, Peru), Public Protector (South Africa), *Médiateur de la République* (e.g. France, Senegal), and Parliamentary Commissioner for Administration (e.g. United Kingdom, Sri Lanka).

The International Ombudsman Yearbook focuses primarily on the public sector ombudsman model. Articles included in the *Yearbook* examine various aspects of the institution from different disciplines, including law, political science, and public administration. The scholarship is both theoretical and practical, as the audience interested in the ombudsman concept is composed of persons directly involved in the establishment and operation of ombudsman offices, scholars, and others who are interested in the theoretical issues in the field.

A list of "Contributors and Titles to *The International Ombudsman Yearbook* and to *The Ombudsman Journal* 1981-2004" can be found at the end of the volume. Copies of the earlier *Journals* can be purchased from the International Ombudsman Institute, Faculty of Law, Law Centre, University of Alberta, Edmonton, Alberta, T6G 2H5, Canada, e-mail: <dcallan@law.ualberta.ca>.

I would also like to thank Mrs. Diane Callan, International Ombudsman Institute Office Manager, and Ms. Heather Grab (LL.B. 2007) for their invaluable assistance in the work of editing and compiling this volume of *The International Ombudsman Yearbook*.

Professor Linda C. Reif
Editor, International Ombudsman Institute
Faculty of Law, University of Alberta

October 18, 2006

THE OMBUDSMAN AND THE RULE OF LAW

John McMillan*

Le respect des lois est le fondement incontournable de tout système législatif et gouvernemental. Bien que l'on mette généralement l'accent sur les aspects judiciaires de ce système, les bureaux des ombudsmans y jouent aussi un rôle important, qui n'est pas toujours suffisamment clair. Prenant l'Australie comme exemple, cet article explique l'importance des ombudsmans pour le respect des lois, et il insiste sur divers aspects de leur travail: défendre les droits des citoyens de soumettre des plaintes au sujet de leur gouvernement, et apporter une solution à celles-ci; mettre l'accent sur le droit à la liberté d'information et sur la protection des dénonciateurs; et trouver de nouvelles solutions pour remédier aux erreurs commises par divers paliers de gouvernement. Cet article pose ensuite la question de savoir si on accorde suffisamment d'importance au rôle joué par les ombudsmans, et s'il ne faudrait pas concevoir cette institution (et tous les organismes de surveillance apparentés) comme une nouvelle branche gouvernementale, chargée de traiter toutes les questions touchant à l'intégrité du système.

****

Una expectativa fundamental en un sistema de gobierno regido por la ley es que dicho sistema se ajuste al imperio de la ley. En general, se concentra en el ámbito judicial el rol de asegurar el cumplimiento de la ley. Las oficinas del Ombusdman también juegan un papel significativo que no siempre se explica cabalmente. Por medio de una discusión de la práctica australiana, esta comunicación explica la importancia de la contribución del ombudsman para asegurar el cumplimiento de la ley. Se señalan diferentes aspectos del papel del

* Australian Commonwealth Ombudsman. This is a revised paper presented at the Annual Public Law Weekend held at the Law Faculty, Australian National University, Canberra, November 5-6, 2004. This paper has also been published in (2005) 44 AIAL Forum 1.

ombudsman tales como : asegurar el derecho del ciudadano de quejarse contra el gobierno, resolver las disputas legales que acontecen en el gobierno, mejorar la libertad de información y proteger a los denunciantes internos; así como también desarrollar soluciones nuevas para los errores del gobierno. Esta comunicación luego cuestiona si la importancia del ombudsman está menoscabada y si debiéramos considerar al ombudsman (y agencias similares de control) como una nueva rama de 'integridad' del gobierno.

> "If the courts do not control these excesses, nobody will."[1]
>
> "[T]he courts are the only defence of the liberty of the subject against departmental aggression."[2]
>
> "[O]fficers or departments of central government [...] are responsible to a court of justice for the lawfulness of what they do, and of that the court is the only judge."[3]
>
> "In the area of refugee law, the Australian judiciary can, quite patently, be the last bastion against executive tyranny for the dispossessed and reviled. At risk is life, liberty and the Rule of Law–not just for the refugee, but for all of us."[4]
>
> "The rule of law is a dry and dusty concept [...] Independent courts, operating according to law, in accordance with fair procedures and resistant to political or public pressure–these are more important to a free society, than democracy."[5]
>
> "Section 75(v) of the Constitution [...is] the means by which the rule of law is upheld throughout the Commonwealth."[6]

Introduction

There can be no doubting the role played by the judiciary in upholding the rule of law in Australia. The political and social history of Australia is replete with examples of landmark instances in which courts have confined the legislature to its constitutional competence and have brought unlawful executive action under control. Bedrock principles that ensure both procedural and substantive fairness in the exercise of governmental power owe their origin to judicial initiative. The development over three decades of a vibrant system of Australian administrative law is studded with instances of judicial creativity and achievement.[7]

This paper does not question the reality and importance of that judicial role. The issue taken up is not whether we have misconstrued the judicial role, but whether we have misstated the way that accountability operates and the rule of law is upheld in the Australian legal system. I will develop this point by looking at the ombudsman's contribution to protecting the rule of law. The same point could as effectively be made by instead looking at a similar contribution made by administrative tribunals—or, for that matter, the media, regulatory agencies, and numerous other non-judicial bodies and processes. In summary, the theme of this paper is that we need to realign the way we portray and understand accountability and the rule of law in Australian law and government.

The quotations given earlier set the context for this paper in presenting a view of the judicial role that, while tendentious, is reflected strongly in Australian legal discourse. Whether it is a mainstream view, it is certainly one that is fashionable and deeply-rooted. As the quotations illustrate—and there are many others of similar tone—it is a view that is consistent both over time and across authors. This view of the judicial role is reinforced in other ways. References to the *rule of law* in legal judgements are now frequent, especially in recent years.[8] Law journal articles on administrative law display an overriding emphasis on the importance of judicial power. Even where a topic is distinctly open to a non-judicial perspective—for instance, whether government agencies should be bound to honor their advice[9]—the usual approach in legal scholarship is for the discussion to look only at doctrines that could be enforceable in the courtroom.

If the theme of this paper is correct—that there is an imbalance in the way that accountability and rule of law issues are addressed in Australian public law—larger issues arise that are taken up at the end of this paper. Two in particular are whether legal scholarship on the protection of individual rights is wrongly focused, and whether traditional thinking about the separation of powers needs adjustment. First, though, it is useful to look at different ways in which the office of ombudsman can make a solid contribution to advancing the rule of law. The analysis begins with a brief discussion of the meaning and scope of the rule of law.

The Rule of Law

Discussion of the rule of law typically acknowledges that it is a protean concept, invoked for effect as much as for meaning. There is, nonetheless, some common ground.[10]

The focus of the rule of law is upon controlling the exercise of official power by the executive government. The foundational principle is that agencies and officers of government, from the minister to the desk official, require legal authority for any action they undertake, and must comply with the law in discharging their functions. Government is not above the law, but is subject to it. This contrasts with the position of members of the public: they too are subject to the law, but are free to engage in any activity that is not specifically prohibited. Unlike government, individuals need not point to a source of law in order to move and operate in the world.

Because of that essential difference between government and the governed, the relationship between the two is a key element of the rule of law. This is borne out in many areas of law. One such area is the principles of statutory construction, which require government to have express statutory authorization—"a clear expression of an unmistakable and unambiguous intention"[11]—for activities that are coercive, punitive, intrusive, or threatening in nature. To like effect are legal doctrines that allow any member of the public aggrieved by government action to institute proceedings for declaratory, injunctive, and compensatory remedies. Administrative law plays a similar role, by prescribing as a condition of the validity of executive action that it is authorized, performed by an authorized officer, made for an authorized purpose, not based on impermissible considerations, and takes account of the adverse impact that official action can have on those to whom it applies.

Some definitions of the rule of law go much further and stipulate minimum standards of fairness and justice to which legal rules must conform. It is unnecessary in this paper to enter that debate. Suffice to say that the rule of law, on any definition, is concerned at one level or another with safeguarding individual liberty and integrity against government oppression.

For that safeguard to be a reality there must be a legal mechanism by which the rule of law can be upheld. Specifically, there must be a forum to which disputes can be taken about the validity of government action. The forum—or dispute resolution body—must have sufficient independence, integrity, and professionalism that it can reach an unbiased decision that will be accepted by others and implemented. Support and respect for the dispute resolution body should permeate government and society.

The body that best fits that description is, unquestionably, the judiciary. In the exercise of judicial power, courts are able to reach a conclusive finding on any issue of law.[12] There is a duty upon others, also enforceable by judicial order, to respect and implement a judicial decree. Moreover, there is a strong tradition in Australia of judicial independence and impartiality, bolstered at the federal level by the constitutional separation of powers. Not surprisingly, most rule of law theory is heavily focused—at times exclusively so—on the role of courts. Discussion of the rule of law in Australian legal and academic circles often has more to say about the role of courts than about the true focus of the doctrine, which is the behavior and thinking of governments.

Are courts the only mechanism that fulfils rule of law objectives? And, in terms of practical steps to safeguard the rule of law, are there gaps that courts and judicial power cannot fill?

The Ombudsman Contribution to Upholding the Rule of Law

The following discussion will point to ways in which the office of ombudsman plays a forceful role in safeguarding the rule of law in Australia. There are admittedly distinct limitations on the role, meaning that the ombudsman can only ever complement and not supplant the judicial role. As is well-known, the ombudsman cannot make a declaration of invalidity, and must rely on recommendation, persuasion, and publicity to effect change.[13] Nor can the ombudsman injunct an agency, command action, or award compensation for defective administration. There are also significant jurisdictional limitations on what the ombudsman can investigate: notable exclusions are ministerial actions and decisions, the conduct of security intelligence bodies such as the Australian Security Intelligence Organisation (ASIO), and employment action in the public service.[14]

Those limitations are important, but they too easily assume center-stage in discussion of what the ombudsman is able to do. Following are some aspects of the ombudsman's role that can contribute to safeguarding the rule of law.

Dealing With Complaints Against Government

Ombudsman offices have now been established for thirty years in Australia, handling complaints against every tier of government—national, state, territory, and local. The number of complaints handled each year is an impressive total. The Commonwealth Ombudsman, for example, received 17,496 complaints and 9,036 other inquiries in 2003-04[15] (the respective totals for the previous year were 19,850 and 11,178). Across Australia, the public sector ombudsmen receive in excess of 60,000 complaints each year against government.

That total is important in its own right, as an indication of the frequency with which people turn to the ombudsman for assistance and the number of queries and grievances against government that are addressed each year. In jurisprudential terms the total is significant in another way. It signifies that, through the mechanism of the ombudsman, the notion is now embedded in Australia that people have a right to complain against government, to an independent agency, without hindrance or reprisal, and to have their complaint resolved on its merits according to the applicable rules and the evidence. Acceptance of this notion permeates both popular thinking and the practice of government.

From a rule of law perspective, complaint handling by the ombudsman bolsters the notion that government is bound by rules and that there can be an independent evaluation of whether there has been compliance with the rules. Government accountability and the right to complain go hand in hand. That this notion is taken for granted in Australia should not overshadow the importance of the fact that it can be taken for granted. The example of other countries in which the struggle for democracy is still vigorous provides a reminder that public disagreement with government decisions is a disputed right in many parts of the world. Recognition of the right can be an important marker of whether democracy and the rule of law are being practiced.

Another sign of institutional acceptance of the right to complain in Australia is the spread of the ombudsman model in the private sector. Major utilities and public services are subject to oversight by—to name a few—the Telecommunications Industry Ombudsman, Banking and Financial Services Ombudsman, Energy and Water Ombudsman (N.S.W. and Victoria), Private Health Insurance Ombudsman, Public Transport Industry Ombudsman (Victoria), and, soon, a Postal Industry Ombudsman. In the last year alone, proposals have been made by parliamentary committees, political leaders and public commentators for the creation of an aviation ombudsman,[16] children's ombudsman,[17] small business ombudsman,[18] aged-care ombudsman,[19] media ombudsman,[20] arts ombudsman,[21] franchising ombudsman,[22] and sports ombudsman.[23]

The spread of the ombudsman model internationally over the last thirty years has been just as great. Whereas fewer than twenty jurisdictions had an ombudsman in 1970, over 100 countries have now established an office by one name or another. It is perhaps the fastest growing (or widely copied) institution in the modern era. Viewed in that light, the establishment of a large number of ombudsman offices in Australia is part of a global trend that crosses political, cultural, and language barriers.

Resolving Legal Issues

The rule of law is especially concerned with whether there is legal compliance by government. Ostensibly this is the only issue of concern to a court undertaking judicial review. What of the ombudsman?

Before that question is addressed specifically, it is useful to place it in context by recalling that issues of law, fact, procedure, discretion, and judgement often shade imperceptibly into each other. A study of judicial review cases undertaken by the author and a colleague showed that two of the legal grounds most likely to be argued by applicants and accepted by courts were failure to take a relevant consideration into account and breach of natural justice.[24] While those are legal errors that can invalidate a decision, they are also administrative shortcomings that are not unlike the errors that are routinely the focus of ombudsman investigations. A similar observation holds true for immigration cases in Australian courts, in which probably the single most common line of attack by applicants is against the analysis of evidence by tribunals in their reasons for decision.

Turning more specifically to the ombudsman's role in ensuring legal compliance, it is undoubtedly the case (as noted later in this paper) that complaints to the ombudsman are more about matters of administrative style and fact-finding than about legal errors. Nevertheless, the law is never far from the sphere of investigation. This point was made in my annual report for 2003-04 in relation to debt recovery by Centrelink, which was the largest single source of complaints for that year. After observing that legislation authorized Centrelink to recover debts, the report observed that "[t]he focus of our concern is that debt recovery policies and procedures developed and implemented by Centrelink are not only authorised by those laws, but also have regard to the position of special needs of Centrelink customers and are not heavy handed."[25]

The same point can be illustrated many times over, in relation to taxation, immigration, child support, law enforcement, and countless other areas. A common cause of the complaints that people have against government is that legislative schemes of entitlement and regulation are nowadays detailed, complex, specific, and sometimes rigid and harsh. The rule of law is as much concerned with explaining to a person why an adverse decision was made and is unimpeachable as it is with examining whether a decision was legally proper. A chief responsibility of the ombudsman's office is to discharge that mixture of functions in an integrated fashion.

There are occasions too when the office plays a role that is indistinguishable, at least as to the result, from the role played by courts. A recent example was action taken by my office to ensure payment of the $600 child bonus family payment to some parents who were eligible but had not received the payment.[26] The Department of Family and Community Services had initially taken the view that some parents were not eligible at that stage because of the terms of the family assistance legislation. My office had a different view as to how the legislation should be construed, and this view was ultimately accepted by the Department. Significantly, too, the legal entitlement enforced in this example resulted in a payment to a large number of people and did not require initiation of legal proceedings by any one or more of them.

As that example illustrates, the ombudsman is often well-placed to resolve legal issues affecting a large number of people, in circumstances where cost, complexity, or lack of information inhibit the commencement of legal proceedings.[27] Another recent example is of action taken by an Australia Capital Territory (ACT) government agency to repay a camera-detected speeding penalty to approximately 470 motorists when doubts about the adequacy of traffic warning signs were raised by my office in the course of an own-motion investigation into traffic infringement notices.[28]

A different facet of the legal compliance role the ombudsman can play is in drawing attention to gaps and anomalies in the legal framework. An example taken once again from the annual report for 2003-04 concerns an aspect of the migration legislation that can result in unfair and unreasonable consequences for individuals.[29] The problem exposed was that a student studying in Australia may not, for reasons beyond their control, be able to meet the time limit for renewing their student resident visa, and unavoidably will have to leave the country to lodge a fresh visa application. We took the issue up with the government, which agreed to legislative change affecting nineteen visa subclasses that came into operation in December 2004.

Other Accountability Functions of the Ombudsman

The traditional and still the core function of the ombudsman is to investigate, on complaint or on the ombudsman's own motion, whether there has been defective administrative action. Over the years a number of other functions have been conferred on the office that are significant from a rule of law perspective.

Many ombudsmen in Australia have been designated with a special role under whistleblower protection and freedom of information (FOI) legislation. The thrust of both legislative schemes is to ensure transparency and accountability in government: whistleblower protection does so by providing legal protection to a person who discloses information about unlawful or improper official action, and FOI does so by providing a right of public access to government documents. My own office (in its guise as ACT Ombudsman) has a lead role under section 13 of the *Public Interest Disclosure Act 1994* (ACT) as a "proper authority" to which protected disclosures can be made and investigated.[30] FOI legislation also makes special mention of the ombudsman's role in investigating complaints about denial or processing of FOI requests.[31] The office has always proclaimed a special interest in FOI matters, which has included the conduct of own-motion investigations into FOI administration by Commonwealth agencies.[32]

Another example of a special role discharged by the Commonwealth Ombudsman is under the new anti-terrorism legislation. That legislation confers powers that enable joint action by the Australian Security Intelligence Organisation (ASIO) and police to enter and search property and to detain people for questioning.[33] The legislation precludes judicial review of the exercise of those powers, while expressly preserving the role of the ombudsman and the Inspector-General of Intelligence and Security in investigating complaints against, respectively, the police or ASIO.[34] My own office has developed protocols with other agencies to ensure that a detainee can contact our office's Law Enforcement Team twenty-four hours per day.

One of the more significant but less known roles of the ombudsman is to monitor compliance by the Australian Federal Police and the Australian Crimes Commission with legislation authorizing telecommunications interception and controlled operations.[35] Police activity of that nature can only be undertaken in accordance with tightly-written statutory requirements that impose specific and demanding obligations upon police concerning authorization of the interception or entrapment activity, the duration of the activity, preservation and destruction of records, and reporting to ministers and the parliament. The rigorous legislative code can be traced to concerns expressed by courts, royal commissions and members of the public generally about unlawful telephone interception and police entrapment.[36]

Judicial review of police compliance with these statutory requirements is still an option, but in practice will be intermittent and fractional. Instead, the legislation confers upon the Ombudsman a more systematic role of periodically inspecting the police records to ensure compliance with the legislation and to report the findings to the Minister and the Parliament. My own experience is that compliance auditing of this kind is a highly effective and low cost mechanism for ensuring strict compliance with statutory procedures that are grounded in the ideals of rule of law and rights protection. Importantly, too, I have seen how the systematic nature of this oversight has induced a culture of compliance within the law enforcement agencies; this is now anchored in the development of internal procedures for rigorous quality assurance and legal compliance, and in active support shown by senior law enforcement managers for the Ombudsman's oversight role.

Four other examples from the past year illustrate how the legal compliance and monitoring role of the Ombudsman is developing and poised for further expansion. First, on the recommendation of the Senate Standing Committee on Scrutiny of Bills, my office recently undertook a sample audit of the use by the Australian Taxation Office of its entry and search powers.[37] It is likely that this audit will be done periodically. Secondly, an own-motion investigation of change of assessment decisions by the Child Support Agency looked *inter alia* at the criteria applied by decision makers in calculating parental income.[38] An interesting and disquieting finding was that there are regional differences in the criteria being applied, meaning that on the same facts a parent's liability or entitlement under the child support legislation can potentially vary according to the state in which the parent lives. Thirdly, legislation enacted in 2004 requires annual inspection by the Ombudsman of the records of the Building Industry Taskforce, concerning its exercise of coercive powers to inspect building and industrial activity in Australia.[39] A recent decision of the Federal Court, warning that the notices issued by the Taskforce requiring the production of documents must not be "foreign to the workplace relations of civilised societies, as distinct from undemocratic and authoritarian states," is a reminder of the need for effective oversight of the exercise of coercive powers.[40] Finally, the *Surveillance Devices Act 2004* (Cth.) confers a new role on the Ombudsman of inspecting the records that law enforcement authorities are required to compile when using surveillance devices in criminal investigations and the location and safe recovery of children.[41]

Adapting to Change

A perpetual challenge for all administrative law bodies is to adapt their function to cope with changes in the structure of government and the delivery of public services. The change that has attracted considerable attention and comment in recent years is the corporatization, privatization, and contracting out of government functions and service delivery.[42] The statutory jurisdiction of administrative law bodies was mostly devised in an earlier age when there was a sharper distinction between the public and private sectors. The jurisdictional concepts embodied in legislation have not kept pace with changes in government, and in varying degrees constrain administrative law review bodies from reviewing administrative conduct that was formerly within jurisdiction. Many critics have complained that this has undermined accountability and the rule of law.

Administrative tribunals have probably had the least room to move in adjusting to this change. The decisions that are reviewable by tribunals are specified in legislation; outsourcing the function will sometimes remove the function from a tribunal's jurisdiction.

Judicial review has had mixed fortunes. On the one hand, courts exercising common law jurisdiction have been prepared on occasions to apply judicial review principles (notably natural justice) to decision-making by non-government bodies.[43] There was, on the other hand, considerable caution displayed by the High Court in *Neat Domestic Trading Pty Ltd. v. AWB Ltd.* [44] in holding that a public law remedy did not lie against a non-government body exercising a statutory veto on wheat export (in place, essentially, of a function formerly discharged within government). There has similarly been a reluctance by courts to sanction judicial review of government decision-making that is commercial in nature.[45]

The Ombudsman has often drawn critical attention to the impact that recent trends in the changing structure of government have on the limited jurisdiction conferred by section 5 of the *Ombudsman Act 1976* (Cth.), to investigate complaints against a "department" or "prescribed authority" (essentially, a body established by legislation for a public purpose).[46] The difficulties are real, and legislative amendment to close the growing gap in the Ombudsman's jurisdiction has been recommended by the Administrative Review Council and the Joint Committee of Public Accounts and Audit[47] and accepted by the government. Even so, there has been more adaptation of the Ombudsman's role than the public debate might suggest. This is significant in rule of law terms in showing that in some respects at least the Ombudsman has greater flexibility than other administrative law agencies to extend accountability principles to non-government activity. One example of this point is that a private company manages immigration detention facilities, but that does not absolve the Department of Immigration from its responsibility to respond to an Ombudsman complaint about the operation of a detention facility. Another example is the own-motion investigation undertaken by my office in 2003 of complaint handling in the Job Network.[48] The jurisdictional focus of that investigation was the Department of Employment and Workplace Relations, but the purpose of the investigation was to ensure that the non-government contracted service providers—who essentially are discharging a public function—adhere to accepted public sector standards in complaint handling.

Another trend in government to which I drew attention in the *Annual Report 2003-04* is the use (seemingly, a growing use) of executive power rather than legislation to establish schemes of entitlement and assistance.[49] Two examples are the General Employee Entitlements and Redundancy Scheme (GEERS) administered by the Department of Employment and Workplace Relations, and an executive scheme for disaster assistance administered by Centrelink. Decisions made under an executive rather than statutory scheme are not subject to review by a tribunal or under the *Administrative Decisions Judicial Review Act 1977* (*Cth.*) (*ADJR Act*). Nor is there a right to obtain a statement of reasons under the *ADJR Act*. And yet the executive decisions are indistinguishable, in nature and importance for those affected, from social support decisions made under legislation. The only avenue of administrative law review still available to a person aggrieved by action taken under an executive scheme is a complaint to the Ombudsman. This right has proved important, including from a rule of law perspective. To take one example, in 2003-04 my office received roughly 120 complaints about decisions made under the GEERS scheme. Issues that we took up with the Department (with a favorable reception) were denials of natural justice in decision-making, inadequate statements of reasons, inadequate investigation upon internal review of decisions, and inadequate notification of the scheme to those eligible to apply under it.[50]

Finding a Remedy for Governmental Error

A standard comment made about the ombudsman, in legal literature in particular, is that its effectiveness is undermined by its absence of determinative powers. The description "toothless tiger" is often applied.[51]

There is no denying that that restriction inhibits the ability of the ombudsman to provide relief as easily or assuredly as a court or tribunal could. Recognizing that point, the office will often suggest to a complainant that an issue in dispute can more appropriately be addressed in judicial or tribunal review; sometimes the office will decline to investigate on that basis.[52] Nevertheless, the significance of this restriction in evaluating the effectiveness of ombudsman review is too easily overstated.

Examples given earlier in this paper illustrate that agencies are prepared to accept a reasoned argument that a decision or agency practice is contrary to law and should be altered. Indeed, nearly all formal recommendations made by the ombudsman are accepted by agencies;[53] my experience is that there is a similarly high rate of acceptance of other suggestions and less formal recommendations. Even in urgent situations where a coercive judicial remedy might be thought more appropriate, there is a preparedness by agencies (as to some decisions at least) to accede to an ombudsman request that implementation of a decision be deferred pending investigation of a complaint. For example, on a number of occasions the Defence Force has accepted an Ombudsman request to suspend impending executive action to discharge a member of the Defence Force until completion of an investigation. Another recent example was a decision by a maritime authority to defer demolition of a structure that was the subject of a heritage dispute until a fuller investigation could be conducted.

A further point as to remedies is that the ombudsman style of investigation, resting largely on inquisitorial method and consultation with agencies, is amenable to resourcefulness in deciding how best to resolve a problem. Not infrequently, the difficulties that people encounter with government can be approached from different angles: the remedy that will satisfy a person is not necessarily the remedy they had in mind in lodging a complaint. A foremost example of this point is that compensation for administrative error is a remedy commonly adopted under the government-approved scheme for Compensation for Detriment Caused by Defective Administration (CDDA). The Ombudsman's office played a key role in the development of this scheme, which currently provides that a recommendation by the Ombudsman for payment of compensation is a sufficient basis for making a payment.[54]

A recent example of a payment made under the scheme illustrates the flexibility it offers for finding a fitting remedy for governmental error. An agency had declined on legal and administrative grounds to discharge a debt owed to the agency by a member of the public. Later, the agency accepted that an administrative lapse played a part in the debt being incurred, and the agency agreed to make a CDDA payment to the person of an equivalent amount, thus effectively extinguishing the debt.

The same flexibility can be used in other areas to circumvent legal obstacles. For example, a vexed administrative problem is whether a decision can be remade if it appears there was a legal or factual error in the original decision. The law on this topic is not altogether clear or easy to apply, resting as it does on concepts such as whether the allegedly defective decision was a nullity, was infected by jurisdictional error, or was a decision without legal effect under the statute under which it was purportedly made.[55] Although the Ombudsman's office has to work within that doctrinal framework, we are often in a position to prompt an agency to approach the legal problem in a different way. I gave a couple of examples in my *Annual Report 2003-04* of how we had persuaded an agency to take executive action to revise an obvious error or misnomer in a person's application, so as to validate the intent of the applicant and the legislation.[56] This effectively circumvented the problem initially raised by the agency, that it lacked statutory authority to revise its initial decision to reject the person's application.

It is important also to remember that the problems people have with government are more commonly about procedural justice than about the substantive correctness of decisions.[57] The prevalent issues raised in complaints to the ombudsman are matters such as delay, misleading advice, inexplicable reasons, lost paperwork, and discourtesy. Rarely will the remedy for such a grievance be the reversal of a decision by a determinative decree or a declaratory, mandatory, or injunctive order of the kind granted in judicial review. Oftentimes the more appropriate and accepted remedy is an explanation or an apology. Those remedies do not find a niche in rule of law theory, but nor should their importance be overlooked in evaluating how to civilize a system of government and make it attuned to its accountability and responsibility to the public.

Other Steps in Legal Compliance

I have noted elsewhere that the effectiveness of judicial review of administrative decision-making rests in part on a blend of faith and assumption.[58] The reason is that we have scant empirical data or scientific understanding as to what happens after a court reaches a finding that a government decision is invalid. There is no published record to which one can turn to find the ultimate outcome. There is no procedure for reporting what occurs following a court decision nor does any official have the function of monitoring the outcome of a court decision to ensure it is implemented as between the particular parties, or that its principles are applied in other similar cases considered by the agency.

The situation is probably not as dire on the ground as that observation suggests. Two empirical studies undertaken jointly by the author with Professor Creyke revealed both a high level of support among executive officers for court and tribunal review of decision-making, and a high rate of implementation of court decisions both in individual cases and across the board.[59] However, the studies also showed that there is room for improvement in agency processes in implementing the lessons to be learnt from external review. One is left too with the fact that there is a lack of institutional mechanisms for ensuring that judicial review fulfils the rule of law benefits that are often claimed for it.

The ombudsman model is more attuned to this issue. It is conventional for the office to define its role as one concerned as much with systemic problems in public administration as with transitory malfunctions in administrative decision making. It is normal for the office to follow through and examine whether recommendations have been implemented and assurances have been honored. Particularly through own-motion investigations and publications on decision making,[60] the office has both a functional and educative role in improving public administration, including legal compliance.

Of special importance has been the role of the office over three decades in stimulating the creation within agencies of internal complaint handling units.[61] Many of these units (such as Australian Taxation Office complaints) are well-resourced and professional units that handle a substantially larger number of inquiries than the Ombudsman's office. This development is significant in rule of law terms. The integration of these units with the program work of the agencies, and the sponsorship and support the units often receive from agency management and the legal section, are influential in ensuring that within the agency there is a higher level of transparency, responsiveness, objectivity, and legal compliance than might otherwise be the case.

A final point worth making has to do with the composition of ombudsman offices. A criticism sometimes made of judicial review is that the sense of justice and community values that it imparts is at risk of being culturally specific. There is a high proportion of males holding judicial office and a comparable narrowing in other qualifications for judicial appointment. The same narrowing trend has been occurring in appointments to some tribunals.[62] To my mind, a particular strength of ombudsman offices is the diversity of qualifications, skills, experience, and gender of the staff. The staffing profile of my office in June 2004 was fifty-seven women and thirty-five men, including twenty-two men and nineteen women in the executive level and Senior Executive Service (SES) band. Without laboring the point, my own experience is that the perspective the office brings to issues of legal compliance and government accountability reflects the diversity of the staff composition and is all the better for it.

A New Context

An underlying premise of this paper is that legal scholarship too often presents a mistaken view of how accountability operates and the rule of law is upheld in the Australian legal system. The argument could stop there with a call for a different presentation in legal writing. But deeper questions can be posed about how we define accountability and the rule of law in the contemporary setting of Australian government. Two issues taken up in the following discussion concern the mechanisms for human rights protection and the constitutional placement of ombudsman offices and other integrity institutions.

Human Rights Protection in the Australian Legal System

There is a growing emphasis in Australia on improving the legal mechanisms for human rights protection. A common strain in academic legal discourse is that we need to develop a fresh approach to this challenge. Options often mentioned are the enactment of a bill of rights, incorporation of international human rights principles into Australian domestic law, and giving greater prominence to a human rights dimension in judicial review principles and constitutional doctrines. The argument for better human rights protection is often framed as an argument for enhancing respect for the rule of law.

Without entering that general debate about whether there is adequate protection of human rights in Australia, I would observe that the proponents for greater protection frequently overlook the established and effective human rights role currently played by ombudsman offices and other elements of the administrative law system. The meters of books about human rights on law library shelves rarely mention the ombudsman as a human rights agency. The focus overwhelmingly is upon bills of rights, courts, and international instruments. Yet, an implicit theme in this paper is that complaint investigation by the ombudsman is directly concerned with human rights issues, in areas as diverse as law enforcement, withdrawal of social security benefits, detention of immigrants, treatment of young children, imposition of taxation penalties, and the exercise of government coercive power. Furthermore, both symbolically and at a practical level, the ombudsman's office captures what is arguably the most fundamental of all human rights, namely the right to complain against and to challenge the government in an independent forum.

Recent developments in the Australian Capital Territory (ACT) on the human rights front illustrate my concern. In 2004 the Legislative Assembly of the ACT enacted the *Human Rights Act 2004*. It is doubtless true that the Act has an important potential to direct attention to human rights criteria in ACT law and government. Yet there is a discernible risk that the legal effect of the new statute will be overstated. For example, I disagree that the ACT is "the first Australian jurisdiction to formally incorporate rights into its legislation."[63] There are countless examples of statutes enacted decades earlier that formally protect the rights of members of the public in their dealings with government: an apt example is the large body of Commonwealth and state anti-discrimination and human rights legislation that establishes a procedure for complaint investigation and adjudication applying human rights criteria that are not dissimilar to those in the ACT *Human Rights Act*.[64] Most features of that *Act*—such as the obligation cast on legislative scrutiny bodies and executive agencies to have regard to the rights listed in the *Act*—have a parallel in established elements and doctrines of Australian public law. Perhaps the main innovation in the ACT statute is the jurisdiction it confers on the Supreme Court pursuant to section 32 to make an advisory declaration that an ACT statute is inconsistent with one of the rights declared in the *Act*.

To overstate the change wrought by the *Act* is at the same time to understate the efficacy of the established mechanisms for human rights protection in the ACT. A deficiency of that kind preceded the enactment of the *Human Rights Act*, in the report in 2003 of the Bill of Rights Consultative Committee. In evaluating the existing mechanisms to protect human rights in the ACT, the Committee made no mention of the ACT Ombudsman or of administrative law.[65] There is a worry that that misrepresentation of the present public law system will be compounded. For example, a recent article on the ACT statute foreshadows that it will "encourage a culture of respect for rights within [the] branches of government," but warns that "[t]he considerable effort which it takes to comprehensively change public service and executive government culture to one that is conscious and respectful of human rights should not be underestimated."[66]

Assessments of that kind carry little weight unless there is solid empirical evidence to substantiate them. My own view is that the limited empirical evidence that is available suggests that institutions such as the ombudsman, together with other innovations in administrative law and government, have had a marked impact over three decades in developing a new culture in public administration that is more attuned to the rights of members of the public.[67] If so, those innovations—which are now strongly rooted in Australian public law—deserve more attention in any discussion about enhancing respect for the rule of law in Australia.

The Integrity Branch of Government

In a recent address, Chief Justice Spigelman of the N.S.W. Supreme Court proposed that we should recognize "an integrity branch of government as a fourth branch, equivalent to the legislative, executive, and judicial branches."[68] The same argument has been made by an American constitutional scholar, Professor Ackerman, that "a separate "integrity branch" should be a top priority for drafters of modern constitutions."[69]

This idea may seem novel to anyone schooled in the trinitarian separation of powers, but the developments in Australian law and government over the past thirty years are sufficiently momentous to raise questions about the durability of constitutional models and thinking that date from a far earlier age.

There are now a great many independent statutory agencies that perform an important accountability and integrity function in the legal system. The list includes auditors-general, ombudsmen, administrative tribunals, independent crime commissions, privacy commissioners, information commissioners, human rights and anti-discrimination commissions, public service standards commissioners, and inspectors-general of taxation, security intelligence, and military discipline. The function they discharge embraces legal compliance, good decision-making, and improved public administration. But the shared concern of these agencies goes further to embrace institutional integrity. Chief Justice Spigelman explains:

> Institutional integrity goes beyond a narrow concept of illegality to encompass at least two additional considerations. First, the maintenance of fidelity to the public purposes for the pursuit of which an institution is created. Secondly, the application of the public values, including procedural values, which the institution was excepted and/or required to obey.
>
> This focus on fidelity to purpose and on applicable public values...distinguish[es] the integrity function from other governmental functions, including most executive, legislative and judicial decision-making, which are concerned with the quality of outcomes.[70]

The constitutional practice in Australia has been to classify these accountability or integrity agencies as being part of the executive branch of government. When the classification seems strained, unsatisfactory hybrid categories such as *quasi-judicial* have been coined (more particularly for adjudicative tribunals). But is the tension now too great?

It is misleading to classify many of these agencies as "executive"; both their independence and the watchdog role they play in government differentiate them from other agencies in the executive branch. The alternative, as Chief Justice Spigelman suggests, is to rethink their classification by taking stock of the enormous change that has occurred in the framework of government. It is premature to spell out a new constitutional philosophy of government, but a few pointers may help.

The conventional way of altering the structure of government is to embody the change in a constitutional document. That is not a promising option as regards the framework of national government because of the difficulty of formal constitutional change under the referendum procedure in section 128 of the *Constitution*. The difficulty is not so great at the state level. Already, for example, in Victoria, the Ombudsman, Auditor-General, and Electoral Commissioner are recognized in the *Constitution*.[71]

Transformation of the structure or conventions of government can be achieved as well by non-constitutional means. In Queensland, the Ombudsman, Auditor-General, and Crime and Misconduct Commission are grouped together as an integrity branch for the purposes of their appearance before parliamentary estimates committees.[72] Statutory requirements—on matters such as parliamentary oversight, annual reporting, and appointment and removal of statutory office holders—also play a role in characterizing an agency within the structure of government. An example in point is the N.S.W. *Ombudsman Act 1974* that establishes a joint committee of both houses of the legislature, called the Committee on the Office of the Ombudsman and the Police Integrity Commission. The functions of the Committee include the exercise of a power of veto over the proposed appointment of a person as Ombudsman, the examination of the reports of the Ombudsman, and monitoring and keeping the legislature informed on the operations of the Ombudsman.[73]

The terminology and classifications that are used in describing a system of government are also an important element of that system. Here it is noteworthy that the concept of "integrity" is increasingly being used both to describe and to evaluate the health of governmental systems. One example is the inaugural *Global Integrity Report* prepared in 2004 by the Washington-based Center for Public Integrity. Interestingly, the ombudsman framework in Australia was an influential factor in Australia being ranked third among twenty-five democracies on the index.[74]

Another relevant Australian development was the publication in 2004 of a *National Integrity System* report by an Australian Research Council funded project conducted jointly over five years by Transparency International Australia and Griffith University's Key Centre for Ethics, Law, Justice and Governance.[75] The report was the first such attempt to "map" a single country's integrity system. A large number of recommendations were made for improving Australia's integrity framework, including the creation of a national independent statutory authority to investigate and prevent corruption and misconduct, and also to promote integrity and accountability in government; the creation in each Australian jurisdiction of a governance review council, including representatives of agencies such as the Ombudsman, Auditor-General, public service head, parliamentary standards commissioner, and community representatives; the creation of a parliamentary committee to oversee the core integrity institutions; the imposition of a statutory duty on public sector agencies to prepare an organizational code of conduct; the creation of better consultative and other links between the core integrity institutions; and the development of accredited training on integrity, accountability, and ethics requirements in public and private sector agencies.

Those proposals illustrate the fertile possibilities for conceiving of "integrity" as a function or even a branch of government. As a concept it does not replace more traditional legal concepts such as the rule of law and separation of powers in defining the fundamentals of the system of law and government. On the other hand, the emergence of novel concepts and ways of looking at government are a reminder of the need for traditional concepts to be revisited from time to time to take account of other changes in government and society.

Endnotes

1. *Paradise Projects Pty. Ltd. v. Gold Coast City Council* [1994] 1 Qd. R. 314 at 322.

2. *Dyson v. Attorney-General* [1911] 1 K.B. 410 at 424.

3. *Inland Revenue Commissioners v. National Federation of Self-Employed and Small Businesses* [1982] A.C. 617 at 644. Note also the observation of Lord Roskill at 663 that the role of the U.K. Parliamentary Commissioner was "to redress administrative wrongs, not remediable in the courts."

4. M. Crock, "Refugees in Australia: of Lore, Legends and the Judicial Process" (paper presented to the Judicial Conference of Australia, Seventh Colloquim, May 30, 2003) <www.jca.asn.au>.

5. M. Costello, "Don't blame the courts for Bali trip-ups" *The Australian* (August 27, 2004) 13.

6. *Re Carmody; Ex parte Glennan* (2000) 173 A.L.R. 145 at para. 2-3 [Carmody]. Gauudron J. observed similarly in *Re Patterson; Ex parte Taylor* (2001) 207 C.L.R. 391 at para. 64 that s. 75(v) "provides the mechanism by which the Executive is subjected to the rule of law." Cf. Gleeson C.J. in *Plaintiff S157/2002 v. Commonwealth* (2003) 211 C.L.R. 476 at para. 5 noting of s. 75(v) only that "it secures a basic element of the rule of law."

7. For examples see the entries on "Administrative Law" and related topics in T. Blackshield, M. Coper & G. Williams, *The Oxford Companion to the High Court of Australia* (Melbourne: Oxford University Press, 2001).

8. For example, High Court cases between 2000-04 that mention the rule of law include *Fejzullahu* (2000) 74 A.L.J.R. 830; *Carmody supra* note 6; *Coal and Allied* (2000) 203 C.L.R. 194; *Enfield* (2000) 199 C.L.R. 135; *Jia* (2001) 205 C.L.R. 507; *Yusuf* (2001) 206 C.L.R. 323; *Patterson* (2001) 207 C.L.R. 391; *Allan* (2001) 208 C.L.R. 167; *Plaintiff S157/2002* (2003) 211 C.L.R. 476; *Eastman* (2003) 198 A.L.R. 1; *Palme* (2003) 201

A.L.R. 327; *Dossett* [2003] H.C.A. 69; *Appellant S395/2002* (2003) 203 A.L.R. 112; *Behrooz* [2004] H.C.A. 36; *Electrolux* [2004] H.C.A. 40; *Al-Kateb* [2004] H.C.A. 37. See also *infra* note 10 for the more frequent treatment of the issue in legal papers.

9. This topic is invariably addressed as one to be resolved by the development of a public law doctrine of estoppel. Providing a remedy for incorrect agency advice is a major focus of ombudsmen, as illustrated by some own-motion reports of the Commonwealth Ombudsman: *Issues Relating to Oral Advice: Clients Beware* (1997), *Balancing the Risks* (1999), and *To Compensate or Not to Compensate* (1999).

10. Contemporary essays discussing the rule of law include K. Mason, "The Rule of Law" in P. Finn, ed., *Essays on Law and Government*, Vol. 1, Principles and Values, (Sydney: Law Book, 1995) 114; D. Dyzenhaus, ed., *Recrafting the Rule of Law: the Limits of Legal Order* (Oxford: Hart Publishing, 1999); C. Saunders & K. Le Roy, *The Rule of Law* (Annandale, N.S.W.: Federation Press, 2002); M. Gleeson, "Courts and the Rule of Law" in Saunders & Le Roy, *ibid*; Spigelman C.J., "Rule of Law: Human Rights Protection" (Conference Address, December 10, 1998) [unpublished].

11. *Coco v. R.* (1994) 179 C.L.R. 427 at 437.

12. *Brandy v. Human Rights and Equal Opportunity Commission* (1995) 183 C.L.R. 245.

13. *Ombudsman Act 1976* (Cth.), ss. 12(3), 15, 16.,

14. *Ibid.,* s. 5(2).

15. Commonwealth Ombudsman, *Annual Report 2003-04* at 15.

16. House of Representatives Standing Committee on Transport and Regional Services, *Making Ends Meet: Regional Aviation and Island Transport Services* (2003) at 207.

17. Senate Community Affairs Committee, *Forgotten Australians: A Report on Australians Who Experienced Institutional or Out-of-Home Care as Children* (2004) at 8.146, 8.167.

18. A. Gome, "Labor Names its Targets" *Business Review Weekly* (February 19, 2004) 38 (policy proposal by ALP).

19. S. Maher, "Latham Plans 3000 More Aged Beds – Election 2004 " *The Australian* (October 2, 2004) (election policy proposal by ALP).

20. M. Wenham, "Premier Gives the Media a Bad Review" *The Courier-Mail* (October 1, 2004).

21. J. Rankin-Reid, "Warning Bell: A Vision Ignored at Our Peril" *The Sunday Tasmanian* (October 3, 2004).

22. P. Switzer, "An Ombudsman Would Ensure Fair Play For All" *The Australian* (September 7, 2004).

23. R. Messenger, "Sports Drug Agency "Incompetent"" *Canberra Times* (March 23, 2004) at 3.

24. R. Creyke & J. McMillan "Judicial Review Outcomes – An Empirical Study" (2004) 11 Aust. J. of Admin. Law 82 at 97. In the nearly 300 cases analyzed in this study, failure to consider relevant matters was argued in 48.3% of cases and upheld in 35.3%, and breach of natural justice was argued in 38.5% and upheld in 34.2%. The more common ground was error of law (including misinterpretation of legislation) which was argued in 49.3% and upheld in 42.3% of cases.

25. *Supra* note 15 at 39.

26. See Commonwealth Ombudsman, "Families Should Get $600 Per Child Bonus Payment Sooner" Press Release, (August 2, 2004) <www.ombudsman.gov.au>.

27. For other examples see D. Pearce, "The Ombudsman and the Rule of Law" (1994) 1 A.I.A.L. Forum 1.

28. This will be reported in the 2004-05 annual report of the ACT Ombudsman. A similar example is given by the Queensland Ombudsman in his *Annual Report 2003-04* at 17 of action taken by a local council at the ombudsman's instigation to repay to residents more than $53,000 in licensing fees that had been imposed without legal authority.

29. *Supra* note 15 at 51.

30. The role of ombudsman offices in whistleblower protection legislation is discussed in N.S.W. Ombudsman, *Adequacy of the Protected Disclosures Act to Achieve its Objectives,* Issues Paper (2004).

31. See *Freedom of Information Act 1982* (Cth.), s. 57. The FOI Act as originally enacted conferred a larger role on the Ombudsman, which included an advocacy role in the Administrative Appeals Tribunal on behalf of FOI applicants (Pt. V.A.). These provisions of the Act were later repealed at the Ombudsman's suggestion because the function was not separately resourced. In Queensland, the function of Information Commissioner is conferred on the Ombudsman: *Freedom of Information Act 1992* (Qld.), s. 61(2). See also the annual audit of FOI reporting by agencies conducted by the N.S.W. Ombudsman, for example, *Audit of FOI Annual Reporting 2002-2003.*

32. Commonwealth Ombudsman, *Needs to Know: Own Motion Investigation into the Administration of the Freedom of Information Act 1982 in Commonwealth Agencies* (1999). The office is currently conducting another own-motion investigation, from which results should be published in early 2005.

33. See *Australian Security Intelligence Organisation 1979* (Cth.), Div. 3.

34. *Ibid.*, ss. 34E, 34F (preserving Ombudsman's role), s. 34X (excluding judicial review).

35. See *Telecommunications (Interception) Act 1979* (Cth.), s. 84; *Crimes Act 1914* (Cth.), Part 1AB. A *controlled operation* is a covert police operation, to obtain evidence of criminal conduct that involves police engaging in conduct that might itself be unlawful were it not authorized under a controlled operations certificate (e.g., drug importation).

36. Telephone interception legislation was enacted following incidents such as the *Age tapes* and the Stewart Royal Commission into Unlawful Telephone Interception: see E. Whitton, *Can of Worms* (Sydney: The Fairfax Library, 1986) at 158. The controlled operations legislation followed the decision of the High Court in *Ridgeway v. R.* (1995) 184 C.L.R. 19, in which the High Court condemned police entrapment activity undertaken without a statutory basis.

37. Commonwealth Ombudsman, *Use of Access Powers by the Australian Taxation Office* (2004).

38. Commonwealth Ombudsman, *Child Support Agency Change of Assessment Decisions—Administration of Change of Assessment Decisions Made on the Basis of Parents' Income, Earning Capacity, Property and Financial Resources*, Report No. 1 of 2004.

39. *Workplace Relations Act 1996* (Cth.), s. 88AI.

40. *Thorson v. Pine* [2004] F.C.A. 1316 at para. 40.

41. *Surveillance Devices Act 2004* (Cth.), s. 55.

42 For example, see two reports by the Administrative Review Council, *Government Business Enterprises and Commonwealth Administrative Law*, Report No. 38 (1995), and *The Contracting Out of Government Services*, Report No. 42 (1998).

43. For example, *R. v. Panel on Take-overs and Mergers; ex parte Datafin plc* [1987] 1 Q.B. 815. Cf. *Forbes v. New South Wales Trotting Club* (1979) 143 C.L.R. 242 and *Dorf Industries Pty. Ltd. v. Toose* (1994) 127 A.L.R. 654, 666. See generally, M. Aronson, B. Dyer & M. Groves, *Judicial Review of Administrative Action,* 3d ed. (Sydney: LBC, 2004) at ch. 3.

44. (2003) 198 A.L.R.179. See A. Buckland & J. Higgison, "Judicial Review of Decisions by Private Bodies" (2004) 42 A.I.A.L. Forum 37.

45. For example, *General Newspapers Pty. Ltd. v. Telstra Corporation* (1993) 45 F.C.R. 164; *Australian National University v. Burns* (1982) 43 A.L.R. 25. Cf. *MBA Land Holdings Pty. Ltd. v. Gungahlin Development Authority* [2000] A.C.T.S.C. 89.

46. See A. Stuhmcke, "Privatisation and Corporatisation: What Now for the Commonwealth Ombudsman?" (2004) 11 Aust. J. of Admin. Law 101; and K. Del Villar, "Who Guards the Guardians? Recent Developments Concerning the Jurisdiction and Accountability of Ombudsmen" (2003) 36 *A.I.A.L. Forum* 25; rep. in (2002) 6 *Int. Omb. Yrbk*. 3.

47. Administrative Review Council, *The Contracting Out of Government Services*, Report No. 42 (1998) at ch. 4; Joint Committee of Public Accounts and Audit, *Contract Management in the Australian Public Service*, Report 379 (2000).

48. Commonwealth Ombudsman, *Own Motion Investigation into Complaint Handling in the Job Network* (2003).

49. *Supra* note 15 at 89.

50. *Ibid*. at 65.

51. To like effect is the distinction drawn by H. Schoombee, "Administrative Law: Choice of Remedies" (1995) 6 A.I.A.L. Forum 9 at 9: "One of the first questions to be considered is whether recourse should be had to "sharp-edged remedies" such as review or appeal, or whether "softer" remedies such as the ombudsman [...] should be utilized."

52. *Supra* note 13, s. 6(3).

53. For example, *supra* note 15 at 15, noting that all but one of thirty-one formal recommendations in reports were accepted that year. Agency preparedness to change decisions after administrative law review was also confirmed in a study of judicial review cases undertaken jointly by the author, which found that close to 80% of favorable judicial review decisions were followed by a reversal of the original agency decision, *supra* note 24 at 87.

54. Clause 21 of the CDDA guidelines, available on the website of the Department of Finance and Administration. See also the Ombudsman's own-motion report, *To Compensate or Not to Compensate: Own Motion Investigation of Commonwealth Arrangements for Providing Financial Redress for Maladministration* (1999).

55. For example, *Minister for Immigration and Multicultural Affairs v. Bhardwaj* (2002) 209 C.L.R. 597. See also the Full Federal Court decisions in *Comptroller-General of Customs v. Kawasaki* (1991) 103 A.L.R. 661 and *Jadwan Pty. Ltd. v. Secretary, Department of Health and Aged Care* (2004) 204 A.L.R. 55.

56. *Supra* note 15 at 87.

57. See J. Howieson, "The Justice of Court-Connected Mediation" *VCAT Mediation Newsletter*, No. 6 (November 2002) 24: "psycho-legal researchers have... identified that it is *procedural justice* (the perception that the procedure is fair), rather than *distributive justice* (the perception that the outcome is fair), that is the most important factor in shaping disputants' overall perceptions of fairness, and in determining disputants' satisfaction with legal dispute resolution procedures."

58. *Supra* note 24 at 82. See also R. Creyke & J. McMillan, "Executive Perceptions of Administrative Law – An Empirical Study" (2002) 9 Aust. J. of Admin. Law 163.

59. *Ibid.*

60. For example, Commonwealth Ombudsman, *A Good Practice Guide for Effective Complaint Handling* (2nd ed, 1999). Manuals on effective decision-making published by State Ombudsmen include: *Good Conduct and Administrative Practice* and *Effective Complaint Handling*, published by the N.S.W. Ombudsman, <www.nswombudsman.gov.au>; *An Easy Guide to Good Administrative Decision-Making*, published by the Queensland Ombudsman <www.ombudsman.qld.gov.au>; and *The Ombudsman's Guidelines for Conducting Administrative Investigations*, published by the W.A. Ombudsman, <www.ombudsman.gov.au>.

61. See also Administrative Review Council, *Internal Review of Agency Decision Making*, Report No. 44 (2000).

62. For example, the annual reports of the Refugee Review Tribunal (RRT) and Migration Review Tribunal (MRT) for 2002-03 showed that 56% of RRT members and 72% of MRT members had a degree in law; 78% of the eighteen new members appointed to the RRT in 2003 had a degree in law.

63. C. Evans, "Responsibility for Rights: The ACT *Human Rights Act*" (2004) 32 Fed. L. Rev. 291 at 309.

64. For example, the *Human Rights and Equal Opportunity Commission Act 1986* (Cth.) confers a right to complain about breach of one of the standards in many of the leading international human rights conventions that are contained in Schedules to the Act (such as the International Covenant on Civil and Political Rights).

65. ACT Bill of Rights Consultative Committee, *Towards an ACT Human Rights Act* (2003) 30-32.

66. *Supra* note 63 at 300.

67. That was the clear conclusion in two empirical studies I jointly undertook: see two articles by Creyke & McMillan, *supra* notes 24 and 58. The annual reports of the Commonwealth Ombudsman also describe the steps taken by agencies to improve their systems in response to complaints from members of the public. Similarly, for an explanation of how the creation of an accountability and integrity framework within the executive branch of government transformed the Queensland Police Service (in the view of the Queensland Ombudsman) "from a corrupt institution at the highest levels to a professional and respected organisation" see D. Bevan, "Queensland's Public Accountability Framework: Effective Regulation or Effectively Over-Regulated?" in M. Barker, ed., *Appraising the*

Performance of Regulatory Agencies (A.I.A.L., 2004) 228 [Bevan].

68. The Hon. J. J. Spigelman, "Jurisdiction and Integrity" (Second Lecture in the 2004 National Lecture Series of the Australian Institute of Administrative Law, August 5, 2004) [unpublished].

69. B. Ackerman, "The New Separation of Powers" (2000) 113 Harv. L. Rev. 633 at 694.

70. *Supra* note 68.

71. *Constitution Act 1975* (Vic.), ss. 94A, 94E, 94F. A similar proposal was made in Queensland by the Queensland Constitutional Review Commission for constitutional recognition of certain statutory office holders, but this recommendation was not accepted by the Government. See Legal, Constitutional and Administrative Review Committee, *The Queensland Constitution: Specific Content Issues*, Report No. 36 (2002) 48-53.

72. Generally, see Bevan, *supra* note 67.

73. *Ombudsman Act 1974* (N.S.W.), ss. 6A, 31B, 31BA. See also in Queensland the *Ombudsman Act 2001,* s. 89, which confers an oversight role on a parliamentary committee and the *Public Sector Ethics Act 1994*, which creates the position of Queensland Integrity Commissioner (s. 26) and defines "integrity" as one of the five "ethics principles... fundamental to good public administration" (s. 4).

74. See J. Uhr, "Australia: Integrity Assessment" in M. Camerer ed., *Global Integrity Report* (2004), Centre for Public Integrity, online: <www.publicintegrity.org>.

75. *Chaos or Coherence: Strengths, Challenges and Opportunities for Australia's National Integrity Systems*, draft report (November 2004), online: <www.griffith.edu.au/centre/kceljag/nisa>.

THE ROLES OF ADMINISTRATIVE COURTS AND OMBUDSMEN IN FRANCE AND MALTA: A REVIEW OF TWO CONTRASTING SYSTEMS

Ivan Mifsud and Cécile Plaidy*

Cet article analyse deux pays–la France et Malte–dont les développements politiques, constitutionnels, juridiques et administratifs ont suivi des voies contrastées au cours des siècles derniers. Mais pourquoi la France? et pourquoi Malte?

D'un côté, le rôle dominant de la France et de la Révolution française dans le développement des structures politiques, juridiques et institutionnelles européennes modernes est largement reconnu. De l'autre côté, Malte a été pendant un siècle et demi une forteresse militaire britannique, et l'impact de la tradition britannique sur son système juridique et administrative est resté fort. Il donc n'est pas étonnant que les voies suivies par la France et par Malte dans le domaine de la justice contrastent amplement, notamment en ce qui concerne la

* Ivan Mifsud, lawyer, Office of the Ombudsman of Malta. Cécile Plaidy, French lawyer, currently working for national public administration in Brussels. The authors would like to thank the Hon. Dr. Carmelo Mifsud Bonnici, Parliamentary Secretary, Ministry of Justice, the Hon. Dr. Joseph Brincat, Joël Arnould, Judge at the *Tribunal Administratif* of Lyon, and Matthieu Plaidy, Judge assistant at the Administrative Court of Appeal of Lyon, for discussing the topic at length with the authors. The authors also thank the former Maltese Ombudsman Mr. Joseph Sammut and Dr. Anthony Vassallo, Consultant to Mr. Sammut, for suggestions on improvement of the text and M. Michel Sironneau, Office of the French *Médiateur*, for providing requested documentation. Finally, the authors would like to thank Mr. Michael Sant, Maltese Ombudsman Office Manager.

responsabilité des gouvernements vis-à-vis des droits et des intérêts des citoyens. L'examen comparatif qui suit permet une analyse approfondie de ces différences.

****

En esta comunicación se tratan dos países-Francia y Malta-cuyos desarrollos políticos, constitucionales y judiciales así como sus tradiciones administrativas y públicas han seguido muy distintos y contrastivos caminos en los últimos dos o tres siglos. Esto lleva a preguntarse:¿Por qué Francia? y ¿por qué Malta?

El papel dominante de Francia y la Revolución Francesa es reconocido ampliamente en el desarrollo de las estructuras políticas, legales e institucionales europeas. Por su parte, Malta pasó a ser una fortaleza militar bajo el régimen de Gran Bretaña en 1800. Como resultado, aunque Malta se independizó en 1964, la tradición británica tiene una fuerte presencia en campos como el de la justicia y de la administración pública. Por lo tanto, no es sorprendente que en el área de la justicia, especialmente en lo que se refiere a la revisión judicial y administrativa, los caminos seguidos por Francia y Malta contrasten mucho. En particular, existen diferencias en los casos que conciernen la responsabilidad del gobierno frente a los derechos e intereses de los ciudadanos. Esta revisión comparativa presenta un análisis de tales diferencias.

Introduction

This paper provides a comparative study of the systems adopted for the solution of administrative issues between citizens and their respective governments in two European countries with strikingly contrasting backgrounds. This paper is about two countries—France and Malta—whose political, constitutional, and judicial developments as well as their administrative and public service traditions in the last two or three centuries have followed sharply different and contrasting paths.

France is one of the largest founding members of the European Union, with an area of some 544,000 km^2 and a population of 60 million while Malta, in the centre of the Mediterranean and some 100 km south of Sicily, is merely 320 km^2 and has 0.4 million inhabitants. Although, for some time late in the eighteenth century the two countries seemed to be moving towards each other, this process stopped abruptly and contacts between them in subsequent years became virtually non-existent.

The dominant role of France and the French Revolution in the development of modern European political, legal, and institutional structures is widely recognized. On the other hand, Malta's role throughout the centuries was determined by its geo-strategic position in the central Mediterranean. After some two and one-half centuries of rule by the Knights of Malta, the island was captured by Napoleon in 1798 and passed under the rule of Great Britain as a military island fortress in 1800. This long association with the United Kingdom had lasting effects on the island's political, economic, educational, and administrative systems. As a result, although this influence eased when Malta became independent in 1964, the impact of British tradition in fields such as justice and public administration in Malta remained strong.

It is therefore not surprising that in the area of justice with special reference to judicial and administrative review, the paths followed by France and Malta contrast sharply. The link between the two countries in this particular sector was short-lived and had no major consequences and explains the different outlook between them where governmental liability vis-à-vis the rights and interests of citizens is concerned.

The brief presence of the French in Malta (1798-1800) was characterized by the short, momentous stay of Napoleon on the island. During these six days, Napoleon announced the right of the Maltese to be considered as French citizens while in his first order on June 13, 1798 he decreed that the island should be governed "by a Commission of Government...entrusted with all acts of government" which had "...without delay [to] organize the civil and criminal courts, on lines similar as far as possible to those of France."[1]

In July 1798, the Commission issued instructions on the reorganization of the whole judicial system in Malta including the duties and functions of the law courts with a civil and criminal jurisdiction. This marked the introduction of the *Civil Code* in Malta, a code based on continental civil law, with its roots traceable to Roman Law as codified under Emperor Justinian I in the sixth century A.D. This is as close as Malta ever came to a wholesale application of a legal framework in the field of civil law based on a continental European model.

In subsequent years, as Malta came under the increasingly dominant influence of Great Britain, its legal system followed the principles and practice of British public law regarding relations between government administrative and executive action and Maltese citizens. This was reflected in the jurisdiction of the ordinary courts of the country except where, in line with the British-style system of administrative tribunals, *ad hoc* tribunals were set up in Malta under particular laws, rules, and regulations as described elsewhere in this paper. This in turn explains why the administration in Malta does not have any courts of its own in contrast with the legal system in continental Europe where the concept of the separation of powers led to the setting up of structures that allow a country's administration to assume responsibility for its own affairs even in judicial matters.

This comparative review of the operation of institutions for the solution of administrative grievances and of their respective roles and relevance in two societies with a different tradition in the field of administrative law is particularly interesting. It allows a critical analysis of different procedures, rules, and systems in institutions for the settlement of administrative issues in two countries with contrasting systems for administrative redress in the context of accountability, standards of good governance, and the protection of citizen rights.

Administrative Courts and the Ombudsman Institution in Malta

Introduction to the Maltese Legal System

Maltese law is very much a hybrid of various legal systems. While Maltese civil law is of continental European lineage, constitutional law and administrative law in the country tend to follow largely the British system. Thus, just to give one example, the Maltese law of tort has nothing to do with the British interpretation and understanding of the principles of tort law liability in its various areas but bears a distinct similarity to the French notion.

When a person in Malta has a grievance against the Maltese government, he must resort to one of the vast array of *ad hoc* tribunals set up by law or take the matter to court—obviously depending on the case. This is because the system in Malta is somewhat different from that on the European mainland. Maltese law has created about one hundred different tribunals to review decisions of different administrative bodies; and these tribunals may be considered as the nearest existing Maltese counterparts to the administrative court system in France. In terms of separation of powers, these tribunals form part of the executive arm of government. Where none of these has jurisdiction over a particular situation, the courts enjoy a residual power of review under section 469A of the *Code of Organisation and Civil Procedure*,[2] as shall be explained later in further detail. When it comes to other grievances against the government that do not involve review of administrative action, such as actions in tort against the government, these are dealt with by the courts, namely the Court of Magistrates in its civil capacity or the First Hall Civil Court.[3]

It is therefore to be made clear from the outset that administrative courts as understood on the European continent in the sense of a "specialist corps of judges who sit in special courts"[4] do not exist in Malta. There are however "administrative courts" in the wider sense of tribunals providing an administrative remedy, with the myriad of *ad hoc* tribunals set up by law that may collectively be equated with an "administrative court", since they amount to a mechanism whereby the executive arm of government can reviews its own decisions, just like administrative courts in the continental sense, leaving the civil courts with a somewhat residual jurisdiction at least as far as review of administrative action is concerned.

Procedures Adopted By the Tribunals and Courts

(a) A Description of the Maltese Legal Framework With Particular Reference to its Main Characteristics and Organization

(i) The Planning Appeals Board

As stated earlier, the Maltese legislator has created a wide array of tribunals under various laws, providing for the review of particular administrative decisions. This process of review, revealing Malta's Anglo-Saxon roots, is usually referred to as a "right of appeal" and many of the tribunals are actually called "appeals boards". Appeals however are the review by the competent tribunal of the administrative decision brought before it.[5] There is no doubting that, irrespective of nomenclature, these bodies are tribunals[6] since they are independent of the administrative bodies whose decisions they review, they reach binding decisions, their decisions are reached by a panel of members, procedures tend to be very similar to those of a court, and they enjoy a permanent existence.

Since it is not possible to discuss here in any detail all the tribunals that exist under Maltese primary and secondary legislation, it may perhaps be appropriate to give coverage to one such body that enjoys a certain amount of prominence in the country at large in view of its role in physical development and planning control. This is the Planning Appeals Board set up under the *Development Planning Act.*[7] In view of its features and characteristics that are typical of other similar bodies, this tribunal may be considered as highly representative of other tribunals that operate in the country.

The Planning Appeals Board consists of a lawyer who presides, a "person versed in planning and another person each of whom shall be appointed by the President, acting on the advice of the Minister."[8] Its role is to hear and determine appeals from decisions taken by the Malta Environment and Planning Authority[9] on development control, including the enforcement of such control. These appeals may be lodged either by applicants for development planning permission or by interested third parties and individuals affected by enforcement action commenced by the Authority. The Planning Appeals Board also has the final say when disagreement arises between the minister responsible for development planning in the Maltese Islands and the Authority over the issue of subsidiary plans and certain planning policies. Furthermore, since recent amendments to the *Environment Protection Act*,[10] it also hears appeals from environment-related decisions.[11]

(ii) The Courts

Sections 95 and 99 of the Maltese *Constitution* refer respectively to the Superior Courts and to the Inferior Courts.[12] Whereas the Superior Courts are presided over by judges, the Inferior Courts are presided over by magistrates.

There are nine different Superior Courts and two Inferior Courts under the Maltese legal system. In Gozo, Malta's sister island, the set-up is somewhat different but, for the purposes of this study, we shall set aside the differences between the Maltese and the Gozitan courts and refer merely to the First Hall Civil Court with general jurisdiction,[13] the Courts of Appeal, and the Court of Magistrates dealing with civil matters. While the First Hall Civil Court is composed of one judge and the Court of Magistrates is composed of one magistrate, the Courts of Appeal are presided over by three judges when dealing with appeals from the First Hall but are composed of only one judge when considering appeals from the Inferior Courts.

It is the *Code of Organisation and Civil Procedure* that establishes the nature of cases that are to be dealt with by the Superior Courts and by the Inferior Courts. This *Code* lays down that the Inferior Courts are to hear and determine all claims of an amount not exceeding Lm5,000[14] against persons residing or having their ordinary abode in Malta except for causes involving questions of ownership of immovable property or relating to easements, burdens, or other rights annexed to such property, even though the claim does not exceed Lm5,000.[15]

(b) The Institution of Proceedings Before the Different Adjudicatory Bodies

(i) The Planning Appeals Board

All appeals to the Planning Appeals Board are by application and submissions should include reasoned grounds based on planning considerations to justify the appeal. Appeals must be made within thirty days from the date of the decision of the Authority that is being complained of and a copy of the appeal is to be served on the Authority itself, which then has to file its reply within another thirty days of service upon it of the application. The reply must also be served upon the appellant.

During hearings held by the Planning Appeals Board, the appellant appears before the Board either in person or represented by an agent. He makes his submissions and produces evidence. The Board also allows the Authority the opportunity to make its submissions and produce evidence in justification of its decisions. The Board confirms, revokes, or alters the decision appealed against and gives such direction as it may deem appropriate. All the hearings of the Board are held in public. The law also states that, subject to the Third Schedule to section 15 of the *Development Planning Act*,[16] the Board regulates its own procedures throughout its hearings.

The decisions of the Planning Appeals Board are final and delivered in public. They are drafted in the same style and layout as court judgements and include references to the proceedings and the reasons on which they are based. No appeal is allowed from the decision, except on a question of law. In the event that the appellant or the Authority itself are dissatisfied with any point of law decided by the Board, an appeal may be made by filing an application to the

Court of Appeal in its Inferior Jurisdiction.

(ii) The Courts

Proceeding before Maltese courts having a civil jurisdiction requires that a number of conditions be met. Detailed rules of procedure must be followed.

First, a plaintiff filing a judicial act must possess the requisite legal capacity and, as a rule, minors, persons who are mentally retarded, or persons who are not vested with administration of the rights to which the action refers cannot institute court proceedings.[17] Furthermore, the plaintiff must possess sufficient juridical interest in the cause.[18] Thirdly, the action must clearly fall within the jurisdiction of the courts—this matter is regulated by section 742(1) of the *Code of Organisation and Civil Procedure*.[19] These requirements apply to all actions, whether instituted before the Superior Courts or the Inferior Courts and whether the action is instituted against the government or against a private individual.

The *Code of Organisation and Civil Procedure* lays down that proceedings in the Inferior Courts are to be instituted by writ of summons whereas those in the Superior Courts are also to be instituted by writ of summons except where the law stipulates expressly that such proceedings are to be made by application.[20] The writ of summons in proceedings before the Superior Courts must be in writing and must be served on the defendant.

Once the defendant is served, he has twenty days from the date of service to file his statement of defense or a note of admission if he intends to admit to the claim. This is served on the plaintiff or his lawyer through the court registry. With the filing of the statement of defense or on the lapse of the twenty days mentioned earlier, whichever comes first, written procedures are deemed to be closed. The causes are then set for trial by the Court Registrar who serves the parties with a notice of the day and time of the hearing.

Once the stage of written pleadings is concluded, hearings are to commence and "shall be brought to a conclusion as expeditiously as possible."[21] The *Code* also states that the court should plan all the sittings that are to be held as well as the anticipated date of judgement. At this stage the *Code of Organisation and Civil Procedure* lays down a wide range of detailed rules that are to come into play which, for example, concern the pleas that can be raised and at what stage of the proceedings, the production of evidence, the admissibility of evidence, and respect due to the court.

Once hearings are concluded, the judgement is delivered by the judge or magistrate before whom the cause has been tried. Whereas, when passing judgement in the Superior Courts judges must restrict themselves to the claims made in court, magistrates in the Inferior Courts may adjudge on a right that "...does not fall precisely within the terms of the claim as originally framed"[22] although this is only possible at first instance.

In a court consisting of more than one member, the decision of the majority forms the judgement of the whole court. The judgement must include the reasons on which the decision of the court is based and must also include a reference to the proceedings, the claims of the plaintiff, and the pleas of the defendant while every declaration intended by the court to be conclusive or binding must be included in the operative part of the judgement. Judgements are executive titles and, as a rule, may be enforced two days from when the judgement becomes final.[23]

The law stipulates the mode of procedure before an appellate court. This can be done by an application that the judgement appealed from or any part thereof be reversed or varied together with detailed reasons on which the appeal is entered. An appeal may be entered by any party and once the application of appeal has been served, the party against whom the appeal is directed shall, within twenty days, file a reply containing the reasons why the appeal should be dismissed. Requests may be made to have these time limits reduced in urgent cases.

As stated earlier, action against the government other than on constitutional matters is instituted before the Civil Courts. The rules of procedure apply to government as they do to any other defendant although the government may be considered to enjoy a number of "privileges" in court over other defendants including:

- the obligation of plaintiffs to serve the government with a judicial letter, in which the demand claimed or right sought is clearly stated, ten days before filing court proceedings;

- the provision whereby causes to which the Maltese government is a party shall be heard before any other cause "unless the court shall deem it necessary, on grounds of urgency...to try other causes;"[24]

- the classification of a substantial number of government documents as "exempt";[25]

- the prohibition of the issue of precautionary warrants of seizure or garnishee orders in security of any right or claim against the government; and

- the limitation for the institution of court proceedings into the validity of any administrative act to a period of six months from the date when

> the interested person becomes aware or could have become aware of the administrative act, whichever is earlier.

c) Jurisdiction and Competence of the Different Adjudicatory Bodies

(i) The Planning Appeals Board

Only the Malta Environment and Planning Authority falls under the Planning Appeals Board's jurisdiction. The competence of the Planning Appeal Board is discussed above in section (a)(i) of this paper.

(ii) The Courts

The jurisdiction of the courts is regulated by section 742(1) of the *Code of Organisation and Civil Procedure*. This section states that:

> the civil courts of Malta shall have jurisdiction to try and determine all actions, without any distinction or privilege, concerning the persons hereinafter mentioned:
>
> (a) citizens of Malta, provided they have not fixed their domicile elsewhere;
> (b) any person as long as he is either domiciled or resident or present in Malta;
> (c) any person, in matters relating to property situate or existing in Malta;
> (d) any person who has contracted any obligation in Malta, but only in regard to actions touching such obligation and provided such person is present in Malta;
> (e) any person who, having contracted an obligation in some other country, has nevertheless agreed to carry out such obligation in Malta, or who has contracted any obligation which must necessarily be carried into effect in Malta, provided in either case such person is present in Malta;
> (f) any person, in regard to any obligation contracted in favour of a citizen or resident of Malta or of a body having a distinct legal personality or association of persons incorporated or operating in Malta, if the judgment can be enforced in Malta;
> (g) any person who expressly or tacitly, voluntarily submits or has agreed to submit to the jurisdiction of the court.

With regards to competence of the courts, insofar as review of administrative action is concerned, this is limited by law to "the following cases:

> (a) where the administrative act is in violation of the Constitution;
> (b) when the administrative act is ultra vires on any of the following grounds:
> (i) when such act emanates from a public authority that is not authorised to perform it; or
> (ii) when a public authority has failed to observe the principles of natural justice or mandatory procedural requirements in performing the administrative act or in its prior deliberations thereon; or
> (iii) when the administrative act constitutes an abuse of the public authority's power in that it is done for improper purposes or on the basis of irrelevant considerations; or
> (iv) when the administrative act is otherwise contrary to law."[26]

The courts' powers of review are further limited by section 469A(4) which states that review of administrative action by the courts is not permissible "where the mode of contestation or of obtaining redress, with respect to any particular administrative act before a court or tribunal is provided for in any other law."[27] In other words, matters falling within the competence of any one of the various *ad hoc* tribunals set up by law cannot be dealt with in court. Thus, in *Victor Attard v. Chairman, Planning Authority in representation of the same*,[28] a case instituted in connection with failure by the Authority to issue development permits and give reasons for such failure, it was held that proceedings were wrongly instituted since the First Hall lacked jurisdiction and the plaintiffs should have filed an appeal in the first place to the Planning Appeals Board. There are other cases where the courts have adopted a similar position.

Review by the courts is also limited by the fact that section 469A of the *Code of Organisation and Civil Procedure* does not apply to issues related to government employment.[29]

The Ombudsman Institution

(a) The Origin, Characteristics, and Organization of the Ombudsman

Malta's first Commissioner for Administrative Investigations called the Ombudsman was appointed by virtue of the *Ombudsman Act 1995*.[30] Since then, the post of University Ombudsman has been created,[31] appointed by the Parliamentary Ombudsman, and a Commissioner for Children[32] has been established who is effectively a children's ombudsman. However, for the purposes of this paper, reference is made exclusively to the Parliamentary Ombudsman.

The Ombudsman is an Officer of the Maltese Parliament appointed to hold office for a term of five years by the President of the Republic acting in accordance with a resolution of the House of Representatives supported by the votes of not less than two-thirds of all members of the House. The Ombudsman is eligible for appointment for one consecutive term of five years.

The *Ombudsman Act* lays down that the function of the Maltese Ombudsman is "to investigate any action taken by or on behalf of the Government and other authority, body or person to whom...(the Act)...applies, being taken in the exercise of their administrative functions."[33] This includes investigating any failure by Maltese public authorities to take the necessary action in their day-to-day operations.

The *Ombudsman Act* is applicable to government ministries and departments and other public authorities, statutory bodies, partnerships, and other bodies in which the Government has a controlling interest or over which it holds effective control. Local councils also fall under the jurisdiction of the Ombudsman. In Part A of its First Schedule, the *Act* also lists a number of persons and bodies to whom the *Act* does not apply. These include the President of the Republic, the House of Representatives, the cabinet, the judiciary, and any tribunal constituted by or under any law.

The Second Schedule to the *Act* lists various matters that are not subject to investigation. These include any matter certified by the Prime Minister to affect the internal or external security of Malta, actions which affect relations between the Maltese Government and any other government or any international organization of states or governments, action taken by the Government under the *Extradition Act*, and the conduct of civil or criminal proceedings before any court of law or any tribunal in Malta.

(b) Admissibility of Complaints

The Ombudsman investigates written complaints against a public body. He may also conduct any investigation on his own initiative. According to the *Ombudsman Act*, any committee of the House of Representatives may at any time to refer for the Ombudsman's consideration matters that are within his or her jurisdiction. The *Act* also allows the Prime Minister at any time to refer to the Ombudsman for investigation and report any matter which the Prime Minister considers should be investigated by the Ombudsman.[34] In the exercise of his or her functions, the Ombudsman is impartial and enjoys security of tenure.

Section 13(2) of the *Ombudsman Act* states that the Ombudsman may conduct an investigation upon receiving a written complaint from "any person" who claims to have been aggrieved by an act of maladministration.[35] That person must have "a sufficient personal interest in the subject-matter of the complaint." What constitutes "sufficient personal interest" is not defined in the law. The Ombudsman has given a wide interpretation to this requirement, but has excluded complaints lodged "in the public interest". On the other hand, the

Ombudsman has conducted "own initiative" investigations into matters he considered to be of a public interest.

The Ombudsman insists on being furnished with written evidence that a complainant has sought to exhaust ordinary remedies before resorting to the Ombudsman. This position is based on section 13(3) of the *Act* which allows the Ombudsman to decline to investigate a complaint "where adequate means of redress are or have been available to the complainant under any other law." This includes availing oneself of internal complaints handling procedures. Where these do not exist, individuals with a grievance must first write to the head of the organization concerned in a bid to resolve the issue and allow a reasonable time in which to receive a reply. If after a reasonable period of time the individual does not receive a reply, or does not receive a satisfactory reply, he or she may approach the Ombudsman for assistance.

When a person decides to institute proceedings in court, this is considered to be an "extraordinary" remedy. The Ombudsman does not consider instituting court proceedings to be a course of action to be resorted to before approaching him, but the *Ombudsman Act* precludes the Ombudsman from launching an investigation into any complaint where the subject-matter is being dealt with or has already been dealt with by a court or tribunal.[36] However, since filing a judicial protest or an official letter does not amount to instituting court proceedings, a person does not lose the right to seek recourse to the Ombudsman's assistance by resorting to such measures. Nor does a person lose the right to go to the Ombudsman if, for instance, after instituting court proceedings, the individual then decides to stop the case.

Section 14(2) of the *Ombudsman Act 1995* states that "a complaint shall not be entertained under this *Act* unless it is made not later than six months from the day on which the complainant first had knowledge of the matters complained about" unless the Ombudsman considers that there are special circumstances which make it proper for the Ombudsman to investigate a case notwithstanding the lapse of the six-month time limit.

(c) Formalities Involved When Resorting to the Ombudsman

The Maltese Ombudsman seeks to keep the rules and formalities to a minimum so that the service offered will be as user-friendly as possible. Most complainants submit complaints in writing. Illiterate and inarticulate persons have their complaints written for them, usually by the Ombudsman's Public Relations Officer. Section 16(1) of the *Ombudsman Act* states that oral complaints are to be put in writing as soon as practical.

Letters to the Ombudsman are not expected to follow any specific format. Nor are they required to be written or countersigned by a legal person or by any other professional person. They may be written either in English or Maltese, must be signed by the complainant—who must always provide identification—and must be accompanied by supporting documentation.

(d) Proceedings Once Complaints Are Accepted for Investigation

New complaints that are lodged with the Ombudsman are immediately acknowledged. When complaints are not accepted for investigation, the complainant is so informed in writing. The Ombudsman must state the reasons behind his or her decision. On the other hand, in grievances where the Ombudsman decides to launch an investigation, complainants are informed that "preliminary investigations" are being undertaken as a first step. These preliminary inquiries serve to determine whether or not there exists a *prima facie* case. In the absence of a *prima facie* case, inquiries are discontinued forthwith and reasons are provided to the complainant.

The investigation of complaints includes inspecting documents, gathering evidence and information, and interviewing public officials and other individuals connected with the case under review. If considered necessary, meetings with complainants and on-site inspections are also held. Direct confrontation of the parties that are involved is avoided.

The *Ombudsman Act 1995* allows the Ombudsman to hear and obtain information from any such persons and to make such enquiries as he or she thinks fit. No person is entitled as of right to be heard by the Ombudsman at this stage, and the Ombudsman is fully empowered to regulate his or her procedures in a manner thought to be fitting.

Once investigations are completed, a preliminary report is prepared containing information about the main thrust of the complaint, the facts as established by the investigations, the findings, the basis of the Ombudsman's considerations, as well as conclusions and recommendations. A copy of the preliminary report is sent either to the public body involved in the event that the complaint is considered to be justified and should be upheld or to the complainant if, in the alternative, the complaint is not upheld. There have also been instances when complaints were partially justified and the preliminary report was sent to both parties. The party to whom the preliminary report is sent is allowed a time limit, laid down by the Ombudsman, within which to reply to the preliminary report.

After giving the necessary consideration and attention to the reactions that are submitted to the preliminary report, the Ombudsman is then generally in a position to draw up the final opinion that is made available to all the parties that are involved in the issue. In the event that the complaint has not been upheld, the case is closed;[37] whereas if some form of remedial action has been recommended, the Ombudsman will follow up the case with a view to getting the recommendation(s) implemented by the public body concerned.

In this regard it should be pointed out that the *Ombudsman Act* does not grant the Ombudsman any executive power to ensure that his or her recommendations are implemented. Section 22(4) of the *Act* lays down the procedures that are to be followed in similar cases. It states that if, within a reasonable time after the Ombudsman's final report is made, no action is taken which seems to be adequate and appropriate to implement the recommendations, the Ombudsman may at his or her discretion send a copy of the report and recommendations to the Prime Minister. The Ombudsman may also thereafter submit any such report on the issue to the House of Representatives as he or she thinks fit.

Administrative Courts and the Ombudsman Institution in France

Introduction to the French Legal System

Whereas, on the one hand, the main concern of a country's administration is to safeguard the overriding national interest and to respect the fundamental rights and freedoms of the individual, on the other hand, the State can also, through the might of its administration and the extent of resources at its disposal, be seen to pose a threat to the individual rights and freedoms of its citizens. In such a case, conflicts and mistrust are likely to arise between the national administration and its citizens. It is therefore the responsibility of the State to put into place appropriate systems and mechanisms in order to control the administration and to allow citizens to defend their rights whenever these are breached by the administration. These systems are the administrative courts and the ombudsman. The latter in France is called *Médiateur de la République*.[38]

Procedures Adopted by the Administrative Courts

The description below is not intended to be exhaustive and is limited to the elements that support the analysis and reflections that appear in subsequent sections of this paper.

(a) The Origin, Characteristics, and Organization of Administrative Courts in France

French administrative law gives the administration overriding powers and privileges in order to protect the general interest. As a result, administrative action is not governed by the country's *Civil Code* but by special rules[39] and specific courts with jurisdiction to review the acts of the administration. These specific courts are known as the administrative courts. The possibility to submit an application to an administrative court against an administrative act allows the citizen the opportunity to contest the prerogatives of the administration. The administrative courts in turn ensure that the administration acts in compliance with the law, and even sanction the administration if there is evidence that it has acted illegally or has caused damage to citizens.

Since the laws of August 16 and 24, 1790 were enacted, the French judicial system has been based on a dual system. Whereas judicial courts have jurisdiction to deal with conflicts between private parties, administrative courts are entrusted with responsibility to oversee and to control the decisions and the functioning of the administration on the basis of the provisions of the country's administrative laws. The Court of Arbitration was set up in 1872 to solve conflicts whenever an administrative court and a judicial court assert or decline their jurisdiction over a particular case.

The administrative courts may be specialized to deal with conflicts arising within a specific sector, such as sports federations and professional associations. Administrative courts with a general jurisdiction are charged with the review of other types of cases and are classified as described hereunder. Firstly, the *tribunaux administratifs*,[40] of which there are thirty-seven, are the ordinary courts deciding in first instance. They are divided into chambers specialized in specific subject matters. Each chamber is composed of a president, a government commissioner, two chief clerks, and a court registrar service. Since the *Decree of June 24, 2003*, these *tribunaux administratifs* have jurisdiction as courts of first and final instance in relation to some cases.[41] In such cases, the decisions of these *tribunaux administratifs* can be subject to judicial review proceedings but cannot be challenged before an administrative court of appeal.

There are seven administrative courts of appeal.[42] They were set up by the *Law of December 31, 1987* and are resorted to either by the applicant or the administration itself who disagrees with the judgement given by the *tribunaux administratifs* in first instance. Their jurisdiction has been progressively extended and they can now receive most appeals lodged against the judgements of the *tribunaux administratifs*. In principle both the *tribunaux administratifs* and administrative courts of appeal are constituted collegially except in some cases where they are constituted by a single judge.[43]

Lastly, the *Conseil d'État* is the supreme administrative court. It mainly intervenes in the context of judicial review proceedings, reviewing the extent of conformity with the law of judgements given by administrative courts of appeal and by the *tribunaux administratifs* when the latter give judgements as courts of first and final instances. The *Conseil d'État* can annul the judgement of the lower courts and either refer the case to another lower court or give a new judgement on the substance of the case. The *Conseil d'État* also has jurisdiction to act in first and last instances in appeals lodged against national regulations, such as decrees and orders in council, and can give opinions regarding new questions of law that are provided by lower courts and that raise serious difficulties. Therefore, the *Conseil d'État* ensures a uniform interpretation and application of the rule of law and contributes to a definition of the scope of the jurisdiction of administrative courts.

(b) Conditions for the Presentation of an Application

In order to be admissible, an application lodged against the administration must meet several conditions concerning the nature of the administrative act that is being contested, the legal status of the applicant, the time limit for the submission of an application, and the formal requirements.

First, applications can only be lodged against an administrative decision, explicit or implicit, which is unilateral and which affects the applicant adversely. Such applications cannot concern judgements, acts of government,[44] contracts,[45] internal measures, and preparatory acts. Applicants must first request the administration to repair the damage suffered and only if not satisfied with the reply given by the administration can they institute proceedings.

Second, the applicant must be a natural person or a legal person and should possess the legal capacity to make an application. A natural person should be of the legal age of majority and should not be deprived of his right to be a party to legal proceedings. For legal persons, the rules are more complex. For instance, one of the conditions for an association or a company to make an application consists of the preliminary authorization from the General Assembly. Similarly, a mayor needs the authorization of his or her Municipal Council.

Third, as a general rule, the prescriptive time limit for the submission of an application to court is two months after the administrative act has been published or the applicant has received notification thereof.[46] However, this time limit can vary in disputes arising in connection with various matters. For instance, there is no such time limit for disputes in relation to public works.

Fourth, with regard to the formalities required, the applicant should submit a written memorial to the court. This document should include the applicant's name and domicile, the decision that is expected from the court, as well as legal and factual pleas. The applicant should also pass on to the court a copy of the decision that is being challenged. Following the suppression of the stamp duty of €15 by the *Ordinance of December 22, 2003*, applicants need no longer pay this duty. In principle, a lawyer should represent an applicant who is requesting the refund of payments made to the administration but there are exceptions, in particular in relation to various applications made to *tribunaux administratifs*. Moreover, an applicant can lodge a *recours pour excès de pouvoir*[47] without the services of a lawyer.

c) Jurisdiction

The jurisdiction of administrative courts is determined by the definition of an "administration" which is considered as being vested with the special prerogatives of public authorities. As a result, apart from public organizations, even some private organizations may fall under the jurisdiction of administrative courts because of the nature of the functions which they exercise in particular circumstances.

(d) Powers of Administrative Courts

Administrative courts do not have the power to give a judgement *ultra* and *extra petita*. They are limited in their powers to deciding the request made by the applicant in his written memorial. Except for pleas of public policy,[48] the courts cannot review an administrative decision on the basis of pleas of facts and law other than those stated in the applicant's memorial.

Administrative courts consider whether any defects exist that affect the legality of an administrative act. These defects may affect the administrative act either internally[49] or externally.[50] In the process, administrative courts enjoy very wide powers. They can require from the administration the factual and legal reasons that support the decision being challenged. They can also view any documents that may be useful for their judgements.[51] The courts may also require expert advice on particular topics, undertake site inspections, put questions to witnesses, and verify the authenticity of documents. Refusal by an administration to comply with a request leads the courts to consider that the applicant's claim is substantiated.

An applicant may seek the annulment of an administrative act by lodging a *recours pour excès de pouvoir*. He may ask for damages by lodging a *recours en plein contentieux*.[52] In the case of a *recours pour excès de pouvoir*, the court can annul the administrative act partially or totally in cases when the unlawful disposition is not severable from the rest of the act. Any such annulment has the absolute authority of a final judgement: the applicant cannot abandon the benefit of the judgement and the act is annulled for all including third parties and the courts. Moreover, the judgement has a retroactive effect as the annulled act is treated as if it never existed. The administration must therefore conduct itself as if the act had never been adopted. At the same time, in respect of a *recours en plein contentieux*, the court has broader power in the sense that it can order the administration to compensate the damage suffered by an applicant. It can also amend directly a decision of the administration in cases of disputes that concern specific issues such as taxes or elections.

Law N° 95-125 of February 8, 1995 amended the *Code of Administrative Courts and Tribunals.*[53] It granted to *tribunaux administratifs* and administrative courts of appeal powers of injunction and authority to inflict penalties. Administrative courts can therefore order enforcement of their judgements within a time limit and subject to the payment of penalties. They can also ask the administration to take the necessary action arising from their judgements that are based on annulment of an administrative act. *Law N° 95-125* therefore introduced a derogation to the principle stated by case law that administrative courts cannot issue injunctions to the administration and it also gave the courts the means to ensure the execution of their judgements by the administration. In this respect there are further proceedings at the disposal of the courts such as proceedings of enforcement following which the courts can impose penalty payments on the administration or proceedings which enable the courts to condemn directly the person(s) responsible for failure to execute its judgement.

Moreover, *Law N° 2000-597* of June 30, 2000, on summary applications to administrative courts, makes it easier for the courts to order the suspension of an administrative act by simplifying procedures in case of urgency. The law therefore introduces provisions aimed at easing compliance by the administration with the judgement on the merits that follow the summary judgement.

Finally, *Law N° 86-14* of January 6, 1986 states that *tribunaux administratifs* can exercise a function of conciliation. However, the *tribunaux* cannot be made to exercise this function and refusal cannot be appealed. Exercise of this function of conciliation has to be accepted by all the parties involved. It appears that, so far, *tribunaux administratifs* have not often exercised these conciliatory functions. This may partly be explained by the fact that judicial conciliation does not suspend the preclusive time limit of two months to make an application to the court. Moreover, the law gives very few rules on the way in which the courts shall exercise conciliation.

The Ombudsman Institution

(a) The Origin, Characteristics, and Organization of the *Médiateur*

The *Médiateur* in France was instituted by means of *Law N° 73-6* of January 3, 1973.[54] This law confers to a third and independent party the task of receiving complaints from citizens against their administration and, whenever these complaints are found to be justified, to encourage the administration to change its attitude in order to resolve conflict. This institution in France was inspired by foreign examples such as the Swedish Ombudsman and the British Parliamentary Commissioner.

The law of 1973 was amended on various occasions. *Law N° 76-1211* of December 24, 1976[55] recognizes in particular the principle of "equity" as a key principle governing the actions of the ombudsman institution and vests the *Médiateur* with the power to propose legislative and regulatory reforms. *Law N° 89-18* of January 13, 1989[56] gave the *Médiateur* the status of an independent authority and substituted the title *Médiateur* with *Médiateur de la République*. *Law N° 92-125* of February 6, 1992[57] enables legal persons to lodge complaints with the *Médiateur* while *Law N° 2000-321* of April 12, 2000[58] enables foreign ombudsmen and the European Ombudsman to forward cases to the *Médiateur*. *Law N° 2000-321* also gives legal status to delegates of the *Médiateur*, allows the *Médiateur* to propose reforms on his own-motion, and requires the *Médiateur* to present his annual report to the two assemblies.

The French *Médiateur* is appointed by the country's executive power for a six year mandate that cannot be renewed. The appointment is at the discretion of the President of the French Republic and is made by a decree of the President adopted in the Council of Ministers. In general, successive *Médiateurs* were chosen from among persons who enjoyed a high public profile. As a result, over the years the institution has come to be strongly identified by the public at large with the person selected to fill the post of *Médiateur*. Consequently, the standing enjoyed by the *Médiateur* is considered to be an important feature for the continued success of the institution.

In a decision of July 10, 1981,[59] the Council of State qualified the

Médiateur as an "administrative authority". The *Médiateur* is therefore an independent authority and, as such, is neither under the hierarchy nor under the guardianship of the executive power. The holder of the post does not receive any instructions from any authority.[60] Moreover, the *Médiateur* benefits from statutory guarantees that ensure his independence *vis-à-vis* the executive power. The *Médiateur* enjoys civil and criminal immunity for his actions and cannot be arrested or judged for the opinions that he formulates in the exercise of his functions, even after the end of his mandate.[61] The *Médiateur* also enjoys security of tenure, because he can be removed from office only under very strict conditions that are defined by the *Decree of March 9, 1973*.[62] The Law also defines various matters which are incompatible with the functions of the *Médiateur* and which he cannot perform. In particular, the *Médiateur* cannot be a Member of Parliament and he or she cannot serve as a general or as a municipal advisor. Finally, the financial control on the budget of the *Médiateur* is exercised only by the Court of Auditors and not by the Ministry of Finance.

The *Médiateur* has at his or her disposal central services called *médiature* and has discretion to choose his collaborators. Also, since 1978, he has external assistants in the administrative districts called *délégués départementaux*.[63] These persons are designated by the *Médiateur* and they act in his name; they inform citizens of the functions of the *Médiateur* and give them advice and indications on the admissibility of their complaints. In 2003, the *Médiateur* had 282 *délégués*.

Law N°2000-321 of April 12, 2000 gives a legal basis to *délégués départementaux* and vests them with power to solve conflicts at a local level. They only refer a complaint to the *Médiateur* when the complaint is lodged against the central administration or when it is lodged against a local administration but is particularly difficult to resolve. Furthermore, *Law N° 2003-591* of July 2, 2003 authorizes the Government to adopt by ordinance all necessary measures in relation to *délégués départementaux*. Finally, *Ordinance N° 2004-281* of March 25, 2004[64] amended Article 6 of the *Law* and laid down that *délégués* must exercise their activity without making any profit and can only receive compensation for their expenses.

The *Médiateur* also has correspondents in ministries and organizations with a public service mission. These correspondents serve as intermediaries in the dialogue between the *Médiateur* and the administration.

(b) Admissibility of Complaints

The action of the *Médiateur* is generally limited to the investigation of complaints received. Regarding the nature of administrative actions against which a complaint may be lodged, Article 1 of the *Law* stipulates that a complaint may be lodged against the functioning of the administration in its relationships with citizens. Moreover, Article 6 states that the complaint shall be issued by "a physical or moral person which considers that one of the organizations designated in Article 1 has not complied with its public service mission."[65] Article 7 states that a complainant should have exhausted all the necessary means to find an amicable solution to a grievance with the administration before lodging the complaint.

A complainant has to be a natural person or a legal person, French or foreign, and resident in France or in a foreign country. Moreover, the complainant should have a direct personal interest in the matter being complained about.

A complainant cannot directly approach the *Médiateur* except to request a reform of the law. Otherwise, complainants are required first to bring their complaints to a Member of Parliament[66] who has discretionary power to decide whether to send the case to the *Médiateur*. The Member of Parliament may consider that the complaint is inadmissible. However, on the other hand, if he or she considers that a complaint is admissible, the Member of Parliament can then send the matter either directly to the *Médiateur* or to a *délégué départemental*. The latter may then either deal with the case directly or forward it to the *Médiateur*.

Members of Parliament can also approach the *Médiateur* directly on their own initiative. Moreover, the Presidents of the Senate and of the Chamber of Deputies can send a petition to the *Médiateur* although any such petition must be signed by one of the six permanent commissions of the two assemblies.

When the *Médiateur* receives a complaint, the grievance is forwarded to the relevant section of the Office's central services to assess its admissibility. When a complaint is considered to be inadmissible, the *Médiateur* sends a reply to the Member of Parliament or to the complainant explaining the reasons for its inadmissibility and, when appropriate, making further suggestions. For instance, when a complainant lodges a grievance directly with the *Médiateur*, the *Médiateur* may suggest that the complainant bring his case first to a *délégué départemental* in order to gather more information about the grievance and then to send the complaint to a Member of Parliament.[67] When the *Médiateur* considers that the complaint is admissible, an enquiry is launched.

There is no time limit for the lodging of a complaint with the *Médiateur*. Complaints are made free of charge and without any formalities. It is enough for a citizen to mention on a signed letter that he wants to lodge a complaint with the *Médiateur*, what he expects from the *Médiateur*, and his arguments, and then to ask a Member of Parliament to transmit his file to the *Médiateur*. If a complainant has difficulty in putting his or her complaint in writing, the complainant may explain the complaint orally to a *délégué départemental* who will help to prepare a written complaint.

(c) Jurisdiction of the *Médiateur*

The jurisdiction of the *Médiateur* is wide in the sense that the institution may receive complaints concerning the functioning of the central, regional, and local administrations, public organizations, and other agencies and authorities entrusted with a public service mission.[68] This excludes parliamentary commissions and their services, the government, and other constitutional bodies. However, the actions of legal persons governed by private law and entrusted with the management of a public service, public undertakings, industrial and commercial public undertakings, and administrative public undertakings fall within the field of action of the *Médiateur*.

Article 1 of the *Law* lays down that complaints by citizens shall concern their relationships with the administration and shall concern the execution of the public service mission of the organizations mentioned above.[69] The notion of public service has been widely interpreted by the *Médiateur*. In principle, the *Médiateur* considers that an organization has a public service mission when its task is to satisfy the general interest or when it is controlled by the administration. Internal matters of the administration such as conflicts between the administration and its civil servants[70] or conflicts between private parties are therefore excluded.

(d) The Powers of the *Médiateur*

The *Law* grants the *Médiateur* a limited range of power of inquiry to scrutinize a case. For instance, the *Médiateur* does not have the power to force a witness to come forward and testify in the way that a judge would do in court. However, the *Law* obliges Ministers and public authorities to collaborate with the *Médiateur* in the context of an investigation[71] and to put their employees at the disposal of the *Médiateur*. They shall send to the *Médiateur* the documents that he or she requests even when these are confidential. Exceptions are made for confidential documents on matters of national defence, state security, and external policy. Furthermore, the *Law* requires the *Conseil d'État* and the Court of Auditors to collaborate with the *Médiateur* by drafting the studies that he or she requests.

When the *Médiateur* receives a complaint, the extent to which the action of the administration complies with the law is reviewed. The *Médiateur* also assesses whether the administration acted in compliance with the principle of equity and with the good sense necessary to ensure the proper functioning of the public service.[72]

The *Law* sets the conditions for the *Médiateur* to rule on the basis of the principle of equity. Thus, for instance, the consequences that are apparently inequitable in the text applied by the administration shall not be voluntarily foreseen by the authors of the text; the recommendation(s) of the *Médiateur* shall not affect the rights of third parties; the inequity shall be clearly established, i.e. damages must be sufficiently substantial; the measure proposed by the *Médiateur* shall be materially applicable by the administration;[73] and a solution based on equity cannot create a precedent.

On the basis of these principles the *Médiateur* adopts recommendations. The *Médiateur* can recommend that the administration change its behavior when a complaint is considered to be admissible and justified, since the *Médiateur* has no power to impose his or her recommendation(s) up on the administration. The *Médiateur* cannot annul or modify an administrative act and can in fact take individual decisions only in relation to his or her own employees. The *Médiateur*'s recommendations are purely persuasive and the administration is not compelled to follow them. However, the administration cannot remain silent and shall inform the *Médiateur* of their follow-up on the recommendations. If the *Médiateur* does not receive any reply from the administration, the *Médiateur* can publish these recommendations in the annual report.[74]

Complaints alert the *Médiateur* to the malfunctioning of an administrative department or the inadequacy of a regulation or a law and the *Médiateur* can in turn make proposals on the basis of these complaints to suggest amendments to the regulation or law concerned. The *Médiateur* can also propose adaptations to the working methods of the administration.[75] In addition, *Law N° 2000-321* of April 12, 2000 on citizens' rights in their relationships with the administration allows the *Médiateur* to propose reforms on his or her own initiative.

The *Médiateur* also has a power of injunction in the event that a *res judicata* judgement has not been implemented by the administration.[76] The *Médiateur* can order the administration to comply with the judgement within a time limit. If the administration does not comply with the order, the *Médiateur* can draft a special report addressed to the President of the Republic and to Parliament and have it published in the *Official Journal*.[77] Finally, the *Médiateur* also has disciplinary power and in the event that the administration fails to sanction a public official who has been found to be at fault,[78] the *Médiateur* may initiate judicial proceedings, for instance, by informing the disciplinary board.

Administrative Courts and the Ombudsman Institution—Analysis of Procedures

An Analysis of Maltese Procedures

The common thread that links all the institutions and systems under discussion is that they all aim at ensuring that, in their own way, justice prevails and is seen to prevail at the end of the day. In this process there is the overriding need to ensure that the principles of natural justice are observed although from a procedural point of view the Ombudsman has little to do with the other institutions under discussion.

Clearly, the most fundamental difference between the institutions is that whereas the role of the Ombudsman is eminently of an investigative nature, the role of the courts and tribunals is purely adjudicatory. The Ombudsman is entrusted with the task of receiving complaints by disgruntled citizens and launching investigations into these grievances on the basis of documentary and other factual and circumstantial evidence which are collected in the course of investigations. The Ombudsman is free to discuss and to listen to the views of both the complainant and the public body against which the grievance has been lodged and reaches a position on the basis of the evidence.

On the other hand, the courts and tribunals have no such investigative functions but consider the arguments that are brought forward by the parties that are involved, hear witnesses and the facts that emerge during any cross-examinations that may take place, weigh the evidence that is presented, and pass judgement on the basis of the facts that are put before them throughout the proceedings. The Ombudsman may therefore be considered to possess a more direct and exploratory role and to be able to adopt a freer and more flexible approach than the courts in the Ombudsman's efforts to investigate grievances.

This greater latitude that is enjoyed by the Ombudsman can perhaps best be encapsulated by the way in which evidence that is available is handled. Whereas under court procedures it is up to the parties involved to list the witnesses who are to be summoned in court and for these parties to examine and cross-examine the witnesses,[79] the Ombudsman decides on the persons who are to be summoned (if at all) in connection with a complaint that is in hand and will question the witnesses personally in order to gather details and background information that can shed more light on the grievance in question.

It is also widely recognized that whereas court and tribunal procedures tend to promote an adversarial culture, the procedures that are adopted by the Ombudsman are not based on confrontation but are aimed primarily at promoting solutions that are based on safeguarding the right of citizens to administrative justice. For instance, in court a case is brought by a plaintiff against a defendant and the system is generally geared towards rewarding the side which presents the better case from a legal perspective and which can put forward the best legal arguments. On the other hand, in proceedings before the Ombudsman, although an aggrieved citizen will consider the executive government to be the main adversary and the source of his or her concerns and worries, the Ombudsman's interest will be to resolve the administrative issue that lies at the root of the problem under consideration and to ensure that the citizen's right to good public administration is respected. Any recommendations put forward by the Ombudsman are therefore meant to restore the administrative balance that may have been upset and to serve as a means whereby the country's administrative authorities will remedy a situation in the public administration sector that is likely to give rise to similar concerns.[80]

Another distinction concerns the way in which proceedings are organized. Parties to court cases are named, hearings are open to the public, and judgements are delivered in public too. Generally speaking, this also applies to *ad hoc* tribunals. The Ombudsman's position is completely different. Proceedings before the Ombudsman are confidential and any information that is gathered by the Ombudsman and his staff throughout investigations or for the purpose of an investigation is not disclosed except in connection with a report that is published under the *Ombudsman Act* for distribution to the parties involved. Furthermore, the *Act* lays down that the Ombudsman and members of his staff shall not be called upon to give evidence in any proceedings of matters coming to their knowledge in the course of an investigation.

This veil of confidentiality that covers the Ombudsman's work is only partly lifted when the identity of complainants and the essence of their complaints are revealed to the public body against which the grievance has been raised—and, clearly, it cannot be otherwise. There have been occasions, however, when the Ombudsman did not even reveal the identity of the complainant to the public body that was involved.

Quite unlike proceedings in court and tribunals, the Ombudsman does not hold public hearings but only holds closed meetings with the parties that are involved as well as with witnesses and experts, if this is considered necessary. Similarly, the Ombudsman's decisions and final recommendations are only conveyed to the complainant and the public bodies involved.

Documents and papers that form part of the Ombudsman's files throughout investigations are kept under confidential cover both while investigations are under way and even after cases are concluded. This ensures that confidentiality is at all times maintained. On the other hand, however, files pertaining to court and tribunal cases are archived and, in the case of the courts, available to whoever wishes to see them for whatever reason.

In this connection it is of interest to point out that the Office of the Ombudsman in Malta issues a biannual publication called *Case Notes* which gives coverage to some of the most interesting cases which the Office comes across in its work to protect citizens from maladministration. These publications are meant to provide an insight into the reasoning that underlies the recommendations of the Ombudsman and to serve as lessons to Maltese public authorities and to employees in the public service about the way in which citizens are to be treated by public officials. All the cases which feature in this publication are given in anonymized form and the identities of complainants are withheld while the names of the localities where these cases occur are also purposely changed since in a small island community such as Malta special care has to be taken to ensure that the real identities of complainants are effectively masked. The same system is adopted in the *Annual Report of the Office of the Ombudsman* which normally includes a section that gives coverage to the most interesting aspects of cases dealt with by the Office during the year under review.

The *Code of Organisation and Civil Procedure* emphasizes the presence of both plaintiffs and defendants during court sittings and their absence without valid justification could have serious repercussions. Thus, for instance, in special summary proceedings failure by the defendant to appear could lead to the court passing judgement in favour of the plaintiff,[81] whereas in ordinary sittings failure by the plaintiff to appear could lead the court to order the cancellation of the cause at the plaintiff's expense.[82] On the other hand, if the defendant fails to appear, the court may proceed according to law on the acts available and may hear the evidence that is available before it notwithstanding the default of appearance by the defendant.[83] In contrast, the Ombudsman does not hold any meetings in order to confront the parties that are involved and instead holds closed meetings on an individual basis.

Court proceedings in Malta, as elsewhere, entail considerable expense to the parties that are involved. The whole process from beginning to end is very formal and follows a set of procedures that are very well defined. Formalities include writs of summons, applications, notes, and other documents which should be drafted according to particular formats while court sittings are required to proceed in a particular way. Furthermore, parties in court have to respect an established dress code and men cannot appear before a judge or a magistrate without a jacket and a tie.

In contrast, the Ombudsman operates on very different lines. Complainants who submit their grievances to the Ombudsman are not required to pay for this service while formalities are kept to a minimum to the extent that even oral complaints are accepted although, as indicated earlier, these complaints have to be put in writing as soon as practical. Complainants are free to submit their own grievances without requiring any representation although complaints that are submitted by legal advisors, etc., on behalf of their clients are also accepted.

The Ombudsman holds no formal sittings or hearings. Meetings with complainants and with representatives and officials of public bodies take place in an informal setting and without the constraints that may result from formal proceedings. There is no particular dress code for persons who call at the Office of the Ombudsman and there are no defined rules regulating matters such as the method of summons, serving of documents, etc. Furthermore, when the Ombudsman reaches the stage where he or she has to form an opinion and possibly make recommendations, the Ombudsman is not bound by any rules such as those which bind the court. For instance, the Ombudsman can go into matters that were not raised and did not even feature in the complainant's original submission.

Court proceedings in Malta tend to be time-consuming and lengthy. It is not unheard of for court cases to drag on for many years. In recent years, the Government has adopted various measures aimed at shortening court proceedings and cutting down on the heavy backlog of outstanding court cases. Other legislative measures are planned to be taken in hand in the coming months to further expedite matters in court.[84]

Compared with the traditional slow pace at which the Maltese legal system operates, the Office of the Ombudsman is known to offer a speedy service to complainants and has gained a reputation throughout the country of resolving cases expeditiously and fairly. The *Annual Report 2003* of the Office of the Ombudsman in fact states that while 595 complaints were completed during 2003, there were another 128 open complaints at the end of the year; of these, eighty-eight grievances (69%) were less than three months old, fifteen cases (12%) had been pending between four to six months, while only another fifteen cases had been open for more than six months.

An obviously common link between the institutions concerns their impartiality, independence, and fairness towards the public which makes use of their services. Thus, section 4(3) of the *Ombudsman Act* of Malta bars the Ombudsman from holding "...any position which is incompatible with the correct performance of his official duties or with his impartiality and independence or with public confidence therein." The Ombudsman also enjoys security of tenure in the sense that removal or suspension of the Ombudsman from office by the President of the Republic needs to be supported by the votes of not less than two-thirds of all the members of the House of Representatives. Furthermore he may only be removed from office on the grounds of infirmity of body or mind or proved misbehavior. The *Ombudsman Act* also allows for the appointment of a Temporary Additional Ombudsman in the event that the Ombudsman considers it necessary not to conduct any particular investigation himself.

The *Constitution of Malta* makes similar provisions for the security of tenure and independence of judges and magistrates[85] while the *Code of Organisation and Civil Procedure*[86] caters for the challenge or abstention of judges or magistrates. These provisions typify the formalities that are a characteristic feature of court proceedings; not only are the grounds of challenge or abstention laid down but the *Code* goes into details of how a judge may make his declaration of abstention, who decides when a judge or magistrate is challenged, etc.

The Ombudsman also observes the second rule of natural justice[87] in many ways such as, for instance, by allowing the public body concerned ample time to reply to the allegations raised by complainants, by listening to all those who are involved in a complaint, by holding meetings with complainants to discuss their grievances, by sending preliminary opinions, and by inviting comments on this preliminary document before reaching a final decision and issuing the final recommendation(s).

Clearly, this basic principle is also fully respected while court proceedings are under way. Both parties must be served with copies of all relevant documentation and are expected to be present while court sittings are in progress. Furthermore, both parties are allowed ample opportunity to present their case and also to challenge the case presented by the other side. The *Code of Organisation and Civil Procedure*[88] in fact states that breach of the *audi alteram partem* principle could lead to a retrial while section 39 of the *Constitution* lays down a number of provisions in order to ensure a fair, independent, and impartial hearing, and to guarantee the civil rights of the parties appearing before the court.

The wide range of tribunals and other administrative appeals boards set up under particular laws tend to operate and be guided by procedures, norms, and regulations that lie somewhere between those that regulate the courts and the Office of the Ombudsman. However, the extent to which any particular tribunal operates in a formal way, costs involved, and the speed and effectiveness of its operations—all these issues depend on the tribunal that an aggrieved individual happens to be dealing with.

Again using the Planning Appeals Board as a benchmark, this Board tends to take after the court in the sense that its operations are guided by the provisions of the *Code of Organisation and Civil Procedure*. Thus, for instance, in appeal reference 339/95E/KA, the Board abstained from further hearing of an appeal that was not lodged within the stipulated time limits by raising *ex officio* its lack of jurisdiction and applying the provisions of section 774 of the *Code of Organisation and Civil Procedure*.[89] Also possibly due to the fact that a lawyer heads this Board, its procedures are very formal and the Board is known to regulate its procedures on the basis of the provisions appearing in the *Code of Organisation and Civil Procedure*. The lodging of appeals is also subject to the payment of fees by applicants—and by Maltese standards this is recognized as quite an expensive process.[90]

A comparison of the average length of proceedings before this Board reveals also that this process is not as expeditious as when complaints are submitted to the Ombudsman and cases are known to have lasted months and, in some instances, even years.[91] In this connection it should also be pointed out that just like the courts, the Appeals Board proceeds in a public manner and is, of its very nature, adversarial.

An Analysis of French Procedures

The setting up of the institution of the *Médiateur* in France served not only to help administrative courts deal with an increasing number of complaints lodged by citizens against the administration but also to fill a gap. The need was felt to create an institution that could protect citizens against administrative unfairness in situations where administrative courts are not suitable forums for citizens to legitimately defend their rights. As a result, from a procedural perspective, legislation clearly distinguishes the institution of the *Médiateur* from the institution of administrative courts in order to make the former more easily accessible and more approachable by citizens. Besides the procedural differences existing in the conditions to lodge a complaint and the scope of power of each institution, the law has limited the powers of the *Médiateur* in relation to court proceedings.

In order to make the institution of the *Médiateur* an easily available and approachable institution for citizens, the legislator ensured that conditions to lodge a complaint with the *Médiateur* are simple, straightforward, flexible, and easy to follow. Moreover, the law introduces flexibility and a certain amount of latitude in the definition of the jurisdiction of the *Médiateur* so as to enable the latter to deal with a large number of cases that may not fall within the jurisdiction of the courts and which involve defence of the rights of citizens against the administration.

Conditions governing the admissibility of a complaint submitted to the *Médiateur* differ from those governing the admissibility of an application made to administrative courts; and the former conditions are in general more flexible, less complex, less formal, and less expensive. Thus, for instance, insofar as the nature of an administrative act that gives rise to a grievance is concerned, conditions of admissibility required by the courts have led to complex case law and subtle distinctions such as the distinction between internal measures that cannot be appealed and regulatory circulars that can be appealed. On the other hand, the conditions that are required to lodge a complaint with the *Médiateur* are drafted in a wide manner and some articles of the law provide for clear conditions of admissibility.

The procedural flexibility of the *Médiateur* is also demonstrated by the absence of a time limit for the lodging of a complaint. In fact a grievance may be referred to the *Médiateur* at any stage of a dispute between a citizen and the administration whereas an application to an administrative court must be made within two months from the publication or notification to the applicant of the administrative decision being challenged.[92]

The formal requirements governing the admissibility of a claim submitted to the *Médiateur* are also more flexible and less burdensome than those that are required for an application in the administrative courts. In the latter case, the citizen has to file with the court a written memorial stating in full the judgement expected from the court as well as the legal and factual pleas. Procedures in court and the arguments of the parties may be complex for the average citizen who has little knowledge of the law. As a result, even in cases where representations by a lawyer are not compulsory, an applicant may need to engage the services of a lawyer.[93] The resulting cost is generally on the high side and may increase as a result of the expertise that may be required and of the costs that may be imposed on the applicant in a judgement in favour of the administration.

On the contrary, the submission of a complaint to the *Médiateur* only requires the complainant to send a preliminary registered letter to the administration concerned and to file the complaint with a Member of Parliament. Lodging a complaint with the *Médiateur* is therefore generally inexpensive and easier than making an application to the administrative courts despite the filtering of complaints by Members of Parliament.

With regards to jurisdiction, the institutions are competent to deal with cases that relate to similar subject matters since the jurisdiction of the *Médiateur* is not limited to subject matters which do not fall within the jurisdiction of administrative courts. The jurisdiction of the *Médiateur* is in fact wider than the jurisdiction of administrative courts. For instance, the *Médiateur* has jurisdiction to review the acts of any organization with a public service mission—and the concept of organizations with a public service mission is undoubtedly wide. On the other hand, the courts are bound by the definition of an "administration" as being vested with the special prerogatives of public authorities in order to have any jurisdiction over such an administration. In addition, the field of action of the *Médiateur* covers not only legal acts taken by the administration but any activities by the administration concerning the functioning of the public service.[94]

The powers of the *Médiateur* are different in many aspects from those that belong to administrative courts. Insofar as preliminary enquiries are concerned, administrative courts have more power than the *Médiateur*. Thus, whereas on the one hand administrative courts can run their own enquiries and enjoy extended powers of investigation, on the other hand the power of preliminary inquiry of the *Médiateur* is exercised through the administration and eventually depends on the goodwill of the latter. The requests of the *Médiateur* are not legally binding and the *Médiateur* can only give coverage to a refusal from an administration in his annual report in the event that the administration refuses to cooperate.

The powers of the *Médiateur* are more flexible and wider in scope than the power of the courts. Thus, for instance, the *Médiateur* can make a recommendation *ultra petita* and is not limited by the requests and pleas raised by complainants. On the other hand, administrative courts are in principle limited by the requests and pleas that are stated in the written memorial of the applicant. The *Médiateur* can also prompt the administration to review acts that are contrary not only to law but also to good sense and to the principle of equity. He can propose reforms to legal texts that may be in conflict with the principle of equity. When deciding on a case, administrative courts may rely on the principle of equity[95] although this principle is not the main basis underlying their judgements and remains a residual consideration.

Another example of the flexibility of the power of the *Médiateur* lies in the fact that the latter assesses the solution of a conflict without reference to any precedents. The *Médiateur* determines whether the administration has acted in compliance with the principles of good sense and equity on a case-by-case basis. On the other hand, although precedents do not bind administrative courts, they are more likely to be inclined towards relying on precedent, as their interpretation of the law is circumscribed by the need to ensure consistency in the practice of the institution.

Insofar as the effects of their decisions are concerned, the judgements of administrative courts have a stronger force than the decisions of the *Médiateur* in the sense that court judgements have a *res judicata* force whereas the recommendations of the *Médiateur* have only a persuasive value and the *Médiateur* cannot compel the administration to act upon his or her request. If the administration does not comply with a recommendation or an injunction of the *Médiateur*, the latter can only publish the refusal in the annual report. On the contrary, administrative courts have various procedures and means at their disposal to compel the administration to enforce their judgements.

The law prevents the *Médiateur* from intervening directly in the course of proceedings lodged with an administrative court to alter proceedings or to influence judgement.[96] However, when a complaint is first lodged with the *Médiateur* and afterwards with a court, the *Médiateur* does not have to decline jurisdiction. The *Médiateur* can still address recommendations to the administrative body involved to propose solutions although the court may later give a judgement that would contradict the recommendations of the *Médiateur*.

However, if the *Médiateur* solves a conflict that is pending before a court by obtaining the withdrawal of the contested act, the judge may in turn dismiss the application. The *Médiateur* can also deal with a case that had already been judged in the administrative courts provided he or she does not review the legality of the judgement. A judgement in favor of the administration does not prevent the *Médiateur* from making a recommendation in favor of the complainant on the grounds of equity since the *Médiateur's* recommendation does not affect the judgement and is placed in a non-legal context. For instance, a citizen has lodged a claim with the *Médiateur* and in parallel with the administrative court regarding a tax carryover that the administration had refused to grant. The administrative court adopted a judgement in favor of the administration on the basis that the latter had complied with the law. However, the *Médiateur* issued a recommendation in favor of the citizen on the basis of equity. The administration agreed to comply with the recommendation of the *Médiateur* and renounced to the benefit of the judgement.[97]

Administrative Courts and Ombudsman Institutions—Differences and Risk of Overlap

Reflections on the Situation in Malta

The organs of executive government that fall under the Ombudsman's jurisdiction also fall under the jurisdiction of the courts as well as of tribunals which handle cases involving the executive arm of civil government.

The Ombudsman's mandate is clear and well defined in section 13(1) of the *Ombudsman Act 1995* which states that the functions of the Ombudsman are "...to investigate any action taken by or on behalf of the Government, or other authority, body or person to which this *Act* applies, being action taken in the exercise of their administrative functions." Section 22(1) of the *Act* in turn lays down the criteria on which an administrative decision, recommendation, or omission that is the subject-matter of an investigation may be judged by the Ombudsman. The Ombudsman may, for instance, consider that any such action is:

- contrary to law;
- unreasonable, unjust, oppressive, or improperly discriminatory or in accordance with a law or a practice that is or may be unreasonable, unjust, oppressive or improperly discriminatory;
- based wholly or partly on a mistake of law or fact; or,
- wrong.

Following investigations, the Ombudsman may also reach an opinion that "a discretionary power has been exercised for an improper purpose or on irrelevant grounds or on the taking into account of irrelevant considerations, or that, in the case of a decision made in the exercise of any discretionary power, reasons should have been given for the decision."[98]

In the event that any of these circumstances occur, in accordance with subsection 22(3) of the *Act,* the Ombudsman may be of the opinion:

> (a) that the matter should be referred to the appropriate authority for further consideration; or
> (b) that the omission should be rectified; or
> (c) that the decision should be cancelled or varied; or
> (d) that any practice on which the decision, recommendation, act, or omission was based should be altered; or
> (e) that any law on which the decision, recommendation, act, or omission was based should be reconsidered; or
> (f) that reasons should have been given for the decision; or
> (g) that any other steps should be taken.

These provisions confer on the Ombudsman a function that is similar to that of the courts when adjudicating on actions that are instituted under section 469A of the *Code of Organisation and Civil Procedure*.

This shared ability to review administrative action should, however, be viewed in its proper perspective. Thus, whereas the Ombudsman may only issue recommendations and has no executive authority to ensure that they are implemented, the courts' decisions are executive orders which have to be put into practice in accordance with well-defined and specific targets. At the same time, however, the provisions of law dealing with judicial review of administrative action[99] place certain limitations on the court's powers of review that are not placed on the Ombudsman. In particular, section 469A of the *Code of Organisation and Civil Procedure* precludes the courts from reviewing discretionary powers conferred on public authorities whereas section 22 of the *Ombudsman Act* allows the Ombudsman to review any administrative decision or omission including the exercise of discretionary powers.

Furthermore, the Ombudsman in Malta has interpreted his mandate in a way that has led him to take on other matters and this has prompted claims by his critics that he has overstepped his mandate and gone beyond the functions that are assigned to him by the *Act*. In this respect, *Case No. C 275* is considered as a classic example.

This case concerned a complaint that was lodged with the Ombudsman by a youth who was driving his car after sunset on a deserted country road and who drove his vehicle into an unprotected open ditch. When this person complained to the council of the locality where this accident happened that the road had been left in utter darkness and that no precautions had been taken to prevent the accident from taking place, he also requested a refund of the expenses which he had incurred to repair his vehicle. The local council, however, did not even bother to reply to his letter. Feeling aggrieved by this lack of response by the local council, the driver presented his case to the Ombudsman.

The Ombudsman's initial reaction was to inform the local council that in the interest of good administration the council should reply to the issue that had been raised by the complainant. Resistance by the council prompted the Ombudsman to investigate the matter further and in due course the Ombudsman recommended that the local council should, upon production of the relative fiscal receipts, reimburse the complainant on an *ex gratia* basis for the expenses which he had incurred to repair his vehicle. On the advice of its legal counsel, however, the local council resisted the Ombudsman's recommendation and, *inter alia*, claimed that the Ombudsman's action went beyond the terms of his remit because his investigation had not focused on an administrative action. The local council held that the complainant should instead have made a claim for damages in court. The Ombudsman replied that the failure to maintain roads in proper condition and free from hazards to motorists is an administrative omission that in fact falls within his remit.

A similar experience occurred in *Case No. C 353* where an individual lodged a complaint that his car had been damaged by a traffic sign that was sheared by a strong gust of wind. Following his investigation, the Ombudsman concluded that the bad state of repair of this sign was the sole contributor to the accident and held that the government department involved in the maintenance and upkeep of traffic signs was responsible for the accident. This department in turn offered an *ex gratia* payment to cover the expenses involved. In his final report on this case the Ombudsman commented that the complainant could have sued the Government in court for damages but dismissed this suggestion as a more expensive and time-consuming alternative.

Yet another similar case was lodged by an individual whose car was damaged after it got stuck in an area where road-paving works were under way.[100] The complainant stated that the hazard was not visible and claimed compensation for the damages that had been sustained. Even in this case the Ombudsman maintained that the complaint was justified and recommended financial compensation upon production of the repair bills.

Cases very similar to the ones described, instituted in court, include *Michael Balzan v. Enemalta Corporation.*[101] The *Michael Balzan* case concerned a plaintiff who sued for damages incurred after being involved in a traffic accident caused by poorly marked road works. *Martin Bonello Cole v. Commissioner of Police*[102] also concerned a traffic accident that happened as a result of road works that were not adequately indicated. Another case which appeared in court was *Elvira Abela v. Prime Minister*[103] which was instituted by the widow of an individual who drowned after he drove over an unmarked pier. The Government was found responsible for the accident for not having taken adequate measures to prevent the accident from occurring.[104]

The Maltese legislators foresaw the possibility of overlap between the two institutions under discussion. In fact, section 13(5) of the *Ombudsman Act* states clearly that:

> The Ombudsman shall not proceed to investigate any complaint on the subject-matter of which proceedings are pending in court or other tribunal, and shall suspend the investigation if any interested person shall file a demand before any court or other tribunal on the subject-matter of
>
> the investigation; provided that an investigation may be proceeded with in respect of problems of general interest contained in the complaint.

The law, therefore, clearly requires an aggrieved person to reach a decision as to whether to go to the Ombudsman or to institute proceedings in court.

On the other hand, section 13(3) of the *Ombudsman Act* allows the Ombudsman the option to decline to investigate a case where adequate means of redress are available or have been available to the complainant under any other law. This provision serves to reduce overlap because, as a general rule, the Ombudsman advises complainants to seek other means of redress whenever these exist and to consider the ombudsman institution only as a means of last resort for the resolution of grievances caused by public bodies. In these circumstances, where a right to appeal from a decision exists and is readily available, complainants are advised to exercise this right. In doing so, however, the aggrieved person often loses his or her right to resort to the Ombudsman because such appeals are lodged with tribunals and the Ombudsman has no right to review decisions that are taken by *ad hoc* or other administrative review mechanisms.

By contrast, whereas the Ombudsman is precluded from investigating matters dealt with by the courts, the courts are not precluded from going into matters that are dealt with by the Ombudsman.[105]

In this regard, it must be stated that the overlap that exists in the functions of the Ombudsman and of the courts is limited merely to the Ombudsman's functions in the field of review of maladministration. The role of the Ombudsman is wider and covers a broader spread of functions, responsibilities, and activities that are in no way associated with the role of courts and tribunals. These other functions of the Ombudsman are the following:

- The Ombudsman as a promoter of good administration by means of a sustained and determined drive to eradicate maladministration by public officials. In the Maltese context this has meant a regular flow of publications that provide assistance, guidance, and advice to those holding public office regarding their obligations towards citizens and towards the right of the community at large to good public administration. This has taken the form of the regular release of documents, leaflets, and other promotional material including *A Guide to Standards of Best Practice*, advice on customer care, a model forefficient complaint handling and management, *The Ombudsman's Guide to Standards of Best Practice for Good Public Administration,* and *Redress: The Introduction of a New Culture in Maltese Public Administration*.

- The Ombudsman as an adviser on administrative matters. In his reports on cases that are brought to his attention, both those which are sustained and those which are not upheld, the Ombudsman generally pinpoints administrative shortcomings and other weaknesses that lie at the root of the cases under investigation and suggests how these problems are to be tackled with a view to ensuring that maladministration in the public service that causes frustration, grievance, and undue worry to citizens will be eliminated.

- The Ombudsman as an adviser to the public at large seeking assistance in their day-to-day contacts with the intricate machinery of public administration. Since it is widely recognized that approaching the public administration may prove a daunting experience especially to those who, as a result of their educational or social background, are not familiar with the way in which the public sector operates, the ombudsman institution is meant to serve as a means of assistance to those who need to approach a government department or a public body on government-related issues or who feel that their entitlements are not being given to them in a proper way. At the same time, persons who need advice on matters that cannot be considered by the Ombudsman are guided on the way in which these issues can best be tackled and provided with assistance so that these difficulties may be overcome while being directed on the most appropriate course of action. This facility is generally provided by the Public Relations Officer of the Office of the Ombudsman who maintains close liaison with all government departments and public bodies falling under the Ombudsman's jurisdiction and is able to provide proper guidance on the strength of direct and personal level of communication with representatives of these public authorities.

- The Ombudsman as a guardian of the underprivileged. During the years that the institution has been in existence in Malta, the Ombudsman has built a reputation among the Maltese as a protector who looks after the needs of the vulnerable sections of society and who promotes administrative justice towards people who are otherwise likely to find themselves at a disadvantage in their contacts with government institutions. This role is given due recognition by the *Ombudsman Act* itself which lays down special procedures intended to ensure that persons who are held in custody or who are patients in mental institutions are able to approach the Ombudsman by means of letters that are sent directly to the Ombudsman without any form of censure.[106] The Ombudsman has also in recent years built further on this role by a number of own initiative investigations into such issues as conditions in prison for female inmates, the treatment of mental patients, and the treatment of detained immigrants.

- The Ombudsman as a support to Parliament. Under section 13(4) of the *Ombudsman Act*, any committee of the House of Representatives may at any time refer a petition to the Ombudsman for his consideration so that he may make any such report to the committee as he thinks fit. Section 13(6) of the *Ombudsman Act* also enables the Prime Minister at any time to refer to the Ombudsman for investigation and report any matter, other than a matter which is subject to judicial proceedings, which the Prime Minister considers should be investigated by the Ombudsman.

> When any such matter is investigated, the Ombudsman shall report on the matter to the Prime Minister and make such report to Parliament on the matter as he thinks fit.

There is little overlap, if any at all, between the Ombudsman and the *ad hoc* tribunals set up by law.[107] As stated earlier, the reason for this is that the Ombudsman as a general rule advises complainants to resort to these bodies where a case falls within their competence. The possibility of overlap lies between the Ombudsman and the courts and, at least under certain circumstances, it is up to the aggrieved individual to decide whether to submit his grievance to the Ombudsman or go to court.

The choice is clear. A person may prefer to go to court because he is in a position to do so and is prepared to pay the fees that are involved, he may be prepared to wait for a relatively long period before a court decision is taken, and, perhaps more significantly, he may want to win an executive title in the form of a court judgement in his favor in contrast with a recommendation by the Ombudsman that is likely to be respected and implemented but which, in the case of default, cannot be enforced. On the other hand, another individual might prefer to go to the Ombudsman because his services are free of charge, matters are resolved expeditiously, and, at the end of the day, an unfavorable outcome usually allows the individual to institute court proceedings on the issue at stake.[108] The Ombudsman may also be the choice of persons daunted by the formalities involved in instituting court proceedings. In this scenario, it is possible that in the absence of the ombudsman institution there might be citizens who would refrain from seeking to assert their rights and who would be unable to find a platform. Grievances with public administration bodies would be dropped, with the result that administrative injustices go unchecked, precisely because the formalities serve as a deterrent, obviously in the administration's favour.

Alternatively, there might be others who might feel that their grievance is not sufficiently serious as to be worth the bother of going to a lawyer to open a case in court and seek redress. How many people, for instance, would be prepared to take a local council to court to recoup moneys paid replacing a car tire damaged by a pothole in a street for which the local council is responsible? On the other hand, it is not unlikely to envisage a situation where a person who finds himself in similar circumstances will not find it so difficult to send a letter of complaint with his grievance to the Ombudsman for his consideration.

Another consideration in this regard is the fact that an individual might win a case before the Ombudsman which would otherwise be lost in court. Indeed, one such instance is Case No. B 670 where the Ombudsman held that, although the executive government had acted according to law, it had still acted in an unjust manner. The case concerned acceptance by the complainant of a refund "in full and final settlement". While acknowledging that legally the complainant had given up the right to contest any further the matter under dispute, the Ombudsman recommended that the department in question should resolve the matter with the complainant because, among other things, the circumstances under which the refund was accepted were not fair. The refund was sent over and over again until the complainant finally stopped sending it back and instead wrote to the department that he was accepting it but not in full and final settlement. At law this cannot be done and the proper procedure for the complainant was to continue to return the cheque, uncashed, as many times as necessary, in order to reserve his rights at law.

This episode clearly demonstrates the different circumstances under which the two institutions operate. The Ombudsman is not as constrained in his outlook as the courts are and is able to go beyond the wording of the law. The various *ad hoc* tribunals tend to be in the same position as the courts.

This overlap in functions could be considered as an advantage to the authorities in the sense that resort to the ombudsman institution serves to cut litigation-related costs, reduce the caseload in courts, and lightens their workload. This is of course a vital consideration, especially in a country such as Malta where an adversarial culture is known to be somewhat deeply ingrained among the community and where the backlog in courts is a perennial problem that successive administrations have so far been incapable of resolving. Indeed, it is a well-known fact that delays in Maltese courts have tended to erode the people's confidence in this institution and in the country's legal system.

Reflections on the Situation in France

People might tend to think that, because of the functional differences between the two institutions, the *Médiateur* could develop doctrines that are different from the case law of administrative courts. People might also envisage a situation of rivalry in the fact that both institutions have equal jurisdiction in relation to a large number of cases. This rivalry might increase as a result of the fact that citizens may prefer to lodge a complaint with the *Médiateur* because of the simplicity and the lack of formalities in the procedures of this institution.

It is our view, however, that this rivalry is mainly theoretical since practice has shown that the two institutions are rarely in a situation of rivalry. On the contrary, the differences between them have enabled the *Médiateur* to collaborate with administrative courts to the benefit of citizens in the defence of their rights and individual freedoms when challenged by the administration. As past *Médiateur* M. Bernard Stasi has stated: "there is no competition between the administrative court and my Office but rather complementarities in those cases where the main thing is not to pronounce the law but to arrive at an equitable settlement of a dispute; a coupling of our respective action for the benefit of the citizen and the rule of law."[109]

Citizens have found in the *Médiateur* an institution that is more accessible than administrative courts and often better suited to solve their conflicts with the administration. In various instances, the *Médiateur* can solve a conflict more easily than administrative courts because of the flexibility granted to the institution to deal with complaints. The legislator has also taken care to ensure that the Ombudsman exists as a pragmatic and evolutionary institution by giving the *Médiateur* the necessary flexibility in respect of procedures and powers to execute his or her functions. Firstly, the rules of procedure governing the institution of the *Médiateur* are free of particularly stringent formalities. The lack of representation by a lawyer, the absence of a preclusive time limit, and the absence of stringent formal rules that may cause concern to or even deter the average citizen are factors known to have contributed towards the success of the institution.

The lack of formal procedures has also been considered as favorable to the dialogue that is necessary to resolve a conflict. The *Médiateur* is careful not to put the administration in a position of accusation but to seek to understand the motives behind its actions. If they seem right to the *Médiateur*, they are explained to the complainant. This pedagogical and psychological functions exercised by the *Médiateur* towards both the administration and the citizen are a key means whereby conflicts are resolved, the *Médiateur's* action "...will have some value if it operates a change in the mentalities of each of the parties...."[110] This dialogue is facilitated in various ways. For instance, the correspondents of the *Médiateur* in each ministry play a decisive role in the ongoing dialogue with the administration to ensure an efficient application of the *Médiateur's* recommendations.

The creation of the *délégués départementaux* has also allowed the *Médiateur* to come closer to citizens while decreasing the workload of the central *Médiateur* institution. The educational role of these *délégués départementaux* is enhanced by the fact that they are better aware of specific local characteristics. In addition, they can help to establish a network with local public services and local elected representatives and assist them in their work. As a result, the number of cases dealt with by *délégués départementaux* has increased.

There is also a wide margin of flexibility in the exercise of the powers of the *Médiateur*. In particular, contrary to administrative courts, the *Médiateur* can rule *ultra petita* and the fact that his or her action is not limited by the pleas raised by complainants broadens the *Médiateur's* margin of action. As a result, in a case where the complainant has not put forward any valid legal arguments, the *Médiateur* can intervene by raising the relevant legal arguments. For instance, the *Médiateur* was approached by a complainant whose request to receive his French pension in a foreign country had been rejected by the administration since one of the legal conditions to receive a French pension is to have a residence in France. The complainant lodged a grievance with the *Médiateur* to protest against the administration's refusal to pay his pension. In this case, the *Médiateur* intervened *ultra petita* and considered that the issue arose because of the fact that the complainant could not have his residence permit renewed. The *Médiateur* intervened with the administration in connection with this renewal and finally obtained a positive reply.[111]

Another example of the flexible powers granted to the *Médiateur* is the ability to submit a recommendation and propose legislative and regulatory reforms on the basis of the principle of equity provided that the conditions for the *Médiateur* to rely on the principle of equity are met. As a result, in cases where a citizen would not otherwise find before a court a solution to an unfair situation arising, for instance, from the application of a regulation, he may find in the *Médiateur* an appropriate defence. For instance, the *Médiateur* alerted the legislators to the difficulty experienced by homeless people in receiving a national identity card.[112] Reliance on the principle of equity therefore gives the *Médiateur* the necessary flexibility to play a key role in society.

Experience has shown that lodging a complaint with the *Médiateur* generally leads to fast results. On average it takes two years for *tribunaux administratifs* to give their judgements and two and one-half years for the administrative courts of appeal, whereas the majority of cases lodged with the *Médiateur* can be dealt with in a few months.[113] As a result, in some instances administrative courts themselves have advised citizens to lodge a complaint with the *Médiateur*.[114]

Administrative courts have seen in the *Médiateur* a collaborator in many other aspects. For instance, the *Médiateur* can help the courts to ensure enforcement of their judgements. Besides this intervention in the context of the non-execution of a judgement, the *Médiateur* can also clarify for the complainant or for the administration concerned the meaning of a judgement as can be seen from the following instance where the *Médiateur* had to deal with a case where an administrative court of appeal gave a judgement in favour of a citizen regarding the expulsion of an inhabitant from a flat. The citizen could not obtain the execution of the judgement and asked for the intervention of the police who in turn refused to intervene on the grounds that the judgement of the court of appeal did not foresee their intervention. Although the court of appeal was of the view that its decision stated plainly that the police could intervene to ensure its execution, it was only the intervention of the *Médiateur* which served to explain to the Ministry of Internal Affairs the error of interpretation made by the police and helped to ensure that the error was subsequently corrected.[115]

The complementary function of the *Médiateur* in relation to administrative courts has proved successful. Figures in the last annual reports of the *Médiateur* confirm this success and show that the institution in fact responds to the real needs of citizens. In 2003, the *Médiateur* received 55,635 cases:[116] of these, 26,175 were complaints and 29,460 were requests for information. Out of the 26,175 complaints, 21,159 were lodged with *délégués départementaux* and 5,016 were lodged with the central services of the *Médiateur*.[117] While 57% of complaints lodged with the *Médiateur* fell within jurisdiction, 25% of these complaints led to a mediation that was successful in the large majority of cases (81%).[118] At the same time, 71.3% of complaints lodged with *délégués départementaux* were admissible, while 76.3% of admissible cases which they investigated were successfully solved.[119]

These figures can be compared with the workload of administrative courts. In 2003, the *Conseil d'État* received about 10,000 cases and still had to deal with another 10,000 cases; the administrative courts of appeal received about 15,700 cases and had to deal with another 40,000 cases; while *tribunaux administratifs* received 127,000 cases and had to deal with another 200,000 cases.[120]

In addition, the number of requests for reforms has increased dramatically: eighty-four new requests were introduced before the *Médiateur* in 2003 compared with fifty-two in 2002 while requests led to twenty new proposals of reform and twenty-one proposals became law. For instance, the *Médiateur* proposed to include the financing of the medical cover and nursing care of citizens who are remanded in police custody in the list of judicial expenses established by Article R. 92 of the *Code of Criminal Proceedings.*[121] The legislators intervened by adopting *Law No. 2002-73* of January 17, 2002 that integrated the proposed reform in the *Code of Social Action and Families.*

It should be pointed out that the success of the institution of the *Médiateur* in France prompted the creation of *médiateurs* specializing in various sectors. Thus *Decree No. 98-1082* of December 1, 1998[122] created a *médiateur* in charge of national education who receives and deals with complaints lodged against the educational and teaching public service.

Experience has shown that the institution of the *Médiateur* is useful and necessary and that it complements the action of administrative courts for the benefit of citizens. Differences and similarities in terms of procedures and powers are such that the *Médiateur* rarely appears as a rival of the administrative courts but rather acts as a successful collaborator. However, some procedural requirements introduced by legislators may be preventing a broader development of the institution of the *Médiateur* and of the institution's collaborative function with administrative courts. The authors of this paper propose the following preliminary ideas to tackle some of these issues.

First, the actions of the *Médiateur* and his or her collaboration with the courts could be improved by making it possible for the lodging of a complaint to the *Médiateur* to suspend the preclusive time limit in administrative courts. Currently, by lodging a complaint to the *Médiateur* and waiting for the submission of his or her recommendation(s), the citizen's right to make an application to an administrative court may fall outside the preclusive time limit. As a result, citizens tend to lodge their complaints with both the *Médiateur* and administrative courts when the sole intervention of the *Médiateur* may be adequate.

Second, as stated earlier, in rejecting an application on the grounds of inadmissibility or lack of jurisdiction, some courts have advised citizens to lodge their complaints with the *Médiateur*. At present, administrative courts do not have the power to forward a case to the *Médiateur* or to the *délégués départementaux*. Allowing administrative courts this possibility could serve to increase collaboration between both institutions to the benefit of citizens, especially in cases of conflict that might find a positive outcome on the basis of equity.

Third, it also appears that the filtering of complaints by Members of Parliament has slowed down the success of the *Médiateur*. It has been reported, for instance, that many complaints are considered inadmissible because they are not filed by a Member of Parliament.[123] While the authors of this paper are in favor of retaining this procedure, they propose a system whereby the *Médiateur*, upon receiving an "unfiltered" complaint, instead of informing the complainant of this requirement, devise a system whereby the *Médiateur* sends the complaint to the relevant Member of Parliament for "filtering".

Finally, the institution of the *Médiateur* may prove even more efficient if citizens have a wider knowledge of the institution's work. It is of course recognized that the publication of reports is indeed one of the main means of pressure at the *Médiateur's* disposal to ensure the implementation of his or her recommendations by the administration. It would therefore be a desirable step if the most noteworthy cases that are solved by the *Médiateur* are given greater coverage in the print media and in other means of communication so that a wider audience may be aware of the potential of this institution for the defence of the citizens' right to good public administration.

Conclusion: Further Reflections on the Roles of the Courts and Ombudsman Institutions in Society

The French system of administrative courts, whereby the executive government reviews its own actions, is regarded as a success, as authors Neville Brown and John Bell explain:

> Confidence in the administrative courts is shared by the administration and public alike. Members of the *Conseil d'État* are not only judges, they are fully trained in the expertise of administration.... In its relations with the public, the *Conseil d'État* attracts extensive press reporting of its activities—and enjoys considerable respect, at least comparable to that shown to the senior judiciary of the United Kingdom....
>
> In 1979, President Giscard d'Estaing complimented the *Conseil d'État* on its achievement: "The essential contribution of the *Conseil d'État* is to have succeeded, without any intervention of the legislature, simply by virtue of a slow and judicious development of case-law to impose a spirit of legality on the French administration...." [124]

As already stated elsewhere in this paper, in Malta there are no administrative courts in the French sense, i.e., the executive arm of Maltese government does not have its own particular institution responsible for adjudicating causes lodged by individuals who have been adversely affected by administrative action. It provides instead a number of *ad hoc* tribunals set up under particular laws to deal with specific matters and, where no *ad hoc* tribunal exists, the aggrieved individual may take the matter to the judicial arm of government.

Another difference between the Maltese and the French systems is that the French have a three-tier system dealing with all administrative matters, instead of the odd hundred tribunals in Malta and the courts of justice. However, we submit that if one were to set aside this difference and the one mentioned in the previous paragraph, it would seem that the Maltese and the French systems are two different approaches—to setting up one institution in France's case and a collection of institutions in Malta's case—that play a broadly similar role in their respective countries, in strikingly similar ways. In both countries, this role is to adjudicate over causes lodged by individuals who have been adversely affected by administrative action. In both countries, individuals affected by a particular administrative action apply to the court or tribunal. The process is an adversarial one, with the applicant putting forward the best case possible with a view to convincing the adjudicator to decide the matter in the applicant's favor. This occurs in the presence of the defendant, who is always the "administration".[125] The defendant seeks to rebut the case and convince the adjudicator to turn down the applicant's requests. The procedures are also strikingly similar. For example, in both countries the institutions under discussion are restricted in their judgements to the causes brought before them and cannot go beyond the subject matter in issue.[126] In both countries, the procedures are formal.

The Maltese system suffers from drawbacks which are not commonly found in the French system. For instance, whereas the tribunals are composed of people with expertise in particular fields,[127] the courts are disadvantaged because judges do not normally possess experience in public administration and might therefore find themselves somewhat at a disadvantage when it comes to the evaluation of administrative procedures in the public sector. Second, *ad hoc* tribunals do not share common procedures and principles, and consequently lack uniformity and consistency. There is also the risk, as has actually happened on occasion, that certain tribunals remain unconstituted even for years at a stretch, perhaps because the costs involved are considered too high to justify the small workload; in the meantime persons are left with nowhere to turn to in their search for an effective remedy for their concerns.

We have discussed these issues with representatives of the Maltese Government and Opposition, who seem to agree that the Maltese system is in need of an overhaul. Both representatives were in favor of the present system being replaced with one more akin to that on the European Continent. The Opposition Member of Parliament in particular was keen to use the French system as a model. More recently, the Maltese Government has publicized its plans to set up a single institution to replace the *ad hoc* tribunals currently in existence.[128] Therefore, it appears that the Maltese system is due for an overhaul in the near future, which should lead to a more efficient and generally better system.

Turning now to the Maltese Ombudsman and the French *Médiateur*, both are based on the Scandinavian ombudsman model and, consequently, have a lot in common. They are both independent, impartial institutions conferred with the task of receiving complaints against the administration. If a complaint is admissible and is investigated, this is done free of charge and expeditiously. Investigations, and procedures in general, are as informal and flexible as possible. Both institutions also operate in a non-adversarial manner. When it comes to upholding a complaint and remedying a wrongdoing, both the Maltese Ombudsman and the French *Médiateur*'s powers are restricted to recommending remedial action.

However, whereas the French administrative courts and their Maltese equivalent have a lot of differences, but ultimately play a broadly similar role in their respective societies, the situation is the opposite in the case of the Maltese Ombudsman and the French *Médiateur*. As stated earlier, the French administrative courts and their nearest Maltese equivalent represent two different approaches to performing the same function. The two ombudsmen, on the other hand, are a case of the same approach being adopted to carry out different functions.

The roles of the two ombudsmen are different based on their founding legislation. The first difference is that the French *Médiateur,* as the name implies, is a mediator, a resolver of disputes[129] between the complainants and the administration who makes recommendations aimed at finding a solution to the dispute.[130] The Maltese counterpart, as "Commissioner for Administrative Investigations"[131] is not a mediator, but an administrative controller. The Ombudsman does not assist in the resolution of disputes, but enquires into complaints received by aggrieved parties.[132] The Ombudsman does not collaborate in the work of another, but is a person with an independent mission. In the process, the Ombudsman reviews administrative action and decides whether it is contrary to law, or unreasonable, unjust, improperly discriminatory, based on a mistake of law or fact, or wrong.[133] This is a different function from that of the French *Médiateur*. Also different are the criteria the Ombudsman uses when considering complaints received against the administration. The Maltese Ombudsman's function is similar to that of the Maltese courts, without the limitations imposed on them by section 469A of the *Code of Organisation and Civil Procedure*.[134] The Ombudsman's function is perhaps also not too unlike the French administrative courts, as reflected for example by the fact that the Maltese Ombudsman, like the French judge, can force witnesses to come forward, while the French *Médiateur* cannot.

There are three particular indications that the legislators had the Maltese courts in sight when drafting the *Ombudsman Act*. The first is the fact that the law specifically endows the Ombudsman with the status of a judge of the superior courts.[135] The second is the criteria laid down in section 22 of the law,[136] against which the Ombudsman is to measure complaints received. The third is the fact that the Ombudsman is specifically precluded from intervening when matters are dealt with in court or before other tribunals.[137] These three indications are not mere coincidence, but were built into the law by design. The legislators did not link the Ombudsman's salary to that of a judge for want of another benchmark, but because they envisaged an individual passing judgement on causes brought to his or her attention. The criteria laid down in section 22, as opposed to dispute resolution and suggesting modifications to "inequitable situations",[138] highlights the difference in roles and serves to approximate the role of the Maltese Ombudsman to that of the court. The third indication may be contrasted with article 11 of the French law, according to which the *Médiateur* can neither intervene in a procedure already before a court nor question the validity of a court ruling, but does have the capacity to make recommendations to the organization in question.

The function of both ombudsmen in their respective societies is linked with the courts in very different ways. Both in France and Malta the courts are the key players. In France, the administrative court is such a key player that back in the early 1970s, when the government set about creating a French Ombudsman, the debate focused on whether a mediator was necessary "in a country where, for the last century, a prestigious and independent administrative jurisdiction brought to bear an efficient and original check on the administration."[139] As explained earlier in this paper, the intention of the French legislator was to create an additional collaborator in the system whereby an aggrieved individual could resolve problems that occur with the administration. The French *Médiateur* is almost secondary in the system, not in the sense of "inferior" to the administrative courts, but in the sense of being an addition to the system. The role of the Maltese Ombudsman is neither an addition to nor a collaborator with the courts. The Ombudsman decides grievances that could go to court but end up before the Ombudsman instead, and others that neither the court nor any tribunal would go into such as issues involving discretionary matters.

The French *Médiateur* performs functions not undertaken by the Maltese Ombudsman. One of them is the resolution of conflicts before the courts. This no doubt serves to hasten proceedings. At least *prima facie*, it might not be a bad thing for the legislators to create an institution that can perform a quasi-surgical intervention on the courts' back-log.

A second function not carried out by the Maltese Ombudsman is that of suggesting modifications deemed necessary, even to laws.[140] It is not that the Maltese Ombudsman is precluded from doing so. In fact, section 22(3)(e) of the Maltese *Ombudsman Act* allows the Ombudsman to recommend the reconsideration of any law. In practice, however, the Ombudsman has refrained from making such recommendations.

Earlier in this paper on we referred to the French *Médiateur*'s power of injunction in case a *res judicata* judgement has not been implemented by the administration. Once again we find the French *Médiateur* attempting to resolve a fresh grievance between the already aggrieved individual who has suffered yet another setback and the administrative court, on the one hand, and the administration on the other. Although the Maltese Ombudsman has in fact received and considered the odd complaint against the administration, for failing to implement a court judgement, the Ombudsman does not have a specific power to consider such cases. Nor is there a specific procedure to be followed where such cases are brought to the Ombudsman's attention.

As for the *Médiateur*'s powers to initiate disciplinary proceedings where the administration fails to sanction a public official who has been found at fault, the Maltese Ombudsman has no such powers and has not been known to attempt anything of the sort.

One function that the two ombudsmen have in common is that petitions can be sent to them. The Maltese Ombudsman may be sent petitions by any Committee of the House of Representatives.[141] The French *Médiateur* may receive petitions from the President of the Senate or from the President of the National Assembly.[142]

The Irish Ombudsman states on her website that "[d]ue to differences in culture, history and approach, each National Ombudsman is in a sense unique."[143] This most certainly applies to the roles of the Maltese and French ombudsmen in their respective societies. France and Malta have different histories, different cultures, and different needs. The *Conseil d'État* and administrative courts are the fruit of the French Revolution and might have made it to Malta, had the French occupied Malta for a longer period of time. Now it seems that a system more akin to that of continental Europe is to be introduced in Malta. In the long run, if an administrative court akin to that in place in France were to be introduced in Malta, and were to work as well in Malta as it works in France, the next step might very well be for the Ombudsman's role to change to one more akin to that of the French *Médiateur*. This remains to be seen.

Endnotes

1. *Arrêté du 25 Prairial, an VI* (June 13, 1978), arts. 4 and 6.

2. *Code of Organisation and Civil Procedure*, ch. 12, *Laws of Malta*.

3. Unless the parties agree, for example, to resort to arbitration.

4. L. Neville Brown & John S. Bell, *French Administrative Law* (Oxford: Clarendon Press, 1998) at 44.

5. It is interesting to note, for example, that the Public Contracts Regulations, set up under Legal Notice 299 of 2003, refers to appeals as *"complaints"* and their consideration by the Public Contracts Appeals Board as *"determining complaints"*. In the process of determining complaints, the Public Contracts Appeals Board will review the award of the contract.

6. As described in B. L. Jones, ed., *Garner's Administrative Law*, 7th ed. (London: Butterworth, 1989) at 276-277.

7. Ch. 359, *Laws of Malta*.

8. *Ibid.*, s. 14(1).

9. Hereinafter referred to as the "Authority".

10. Ch. 435, *Laws of Malta*.

11. *Ibid.*, s. 16.

12. *Constitution of Malta Act 1964*, ss. 95 and 99, *Laws of Malta*.

13. Hereinafter referred to as the "First Hall Civil Court" or the "First Hall".

14. About €12,000.

15. *Supra* note 2, s. 47.

16. *Development Planning Act*, *supra* note 7, s. 15, Third Schedule (*Proceedings before the Planning Appeals Board and Appeals Therefrom).*

17. The same of course applies to the *ad hoc* tribunals, as emerges from general law including the *Civil Code*. For example, although the *Development Planning Act* does not state that appeals must be lodged by persons possessing the requisite legal capacity, this is a foregone conclusion, because persons not possessing such legal capacity cannot apply for development planning permission. Nor can they be subjected to enforcement action.

18. The notion of "juridical interest" has featured in a number of court judgements including *Alexander Eminyan v. Joseph Mousu pro et noe* (Court of Appeal, February 28, 1997). The plaintiff must have a "real... actual...(and)...personal" interest, i.e. his own rights must be violated or under threat of violation because otherwise he would lack the "juridical interest" to institute court proceedings.

19. *Supra* note 2.

20. *Ibid.*, ss. 125 and 161, respectively.

21. *Ibid.*, s. 195 (1).

22. *Ibid.*, s. 213.

23. *Ibid.*, s. 255 lists the type of judgements enforceable after the lapse of twenty-four hours from delivery. The law also allows for a shorter time for the enforcement of judgements on grounds of urgency (s. 257) and for provisional enforcement (s. 266).

24. *Ibid.*, s. 197(2).

25. *Ibid.*, s. 637(3) states that: "It shall not be lawful to demand the production of any exempt document which forms part of any correspondence of any civil, military, naval or air force department or of any report belonging to any such department." Section 637(4) is a list of exempt documents. Such documents include those that would cause damage to the security of Malta or to the international relations of Malta and documents classified as "Cabinet Documents".

26. *Ibid.*, s. 469A(1).

27. *Ibid.*, s. 469A(4).

28. Mr. Justice Magri (October 23, 1998), First Hall Civil Court.

29. *Supra* note 2, s. 469A(6): "For the purposes of this section, and of any other provision of this and any other law, service with the government is a special relationship regulated by the legal provisions specifically applicable to it and the terms and conditions from time to time established by the Government, and no law or provision thereof relating to conditions of employment or to contracts of service or of employment applies, or ever heretofore applied, to service with the government except to the extent that such law provides otherwise."

30. *Ombudsman Act 1995*, ch. 385, *Laws of Malta*.

31. Under the *Education Act,* ch. 327, *Laws of Malta,* s. 30(15).

32. Under the *Commissioner for Children Act,* ch. 462, *Laws of Malta*.

33. *Supra* note 30 at s. 13(1).

34. Whereas the Ombudsman has undertaken a number of own motion investigations in the last years, the House of Representatives and the Prime Minister have not so far availed themselves of this facility to ask the Ombudsman to undertake investigations on their behalf.

35. Complaints may therefore also be lodged by non-citizens and legal persons.

36. *Supra* note 30, s.13(5).

37. There is no appeal from the Ombudsman's decision.

38. Hereinafter referred to as the *Médiateur*.

39. Although in some circumstances administrative courts may rely on the *Civil Code*.

40. In order to distinguish the French administrative tribunals from the administrative tribunals in Malta, their French nomenclature (i.e. *tribunaux administratifs*) will be maintained throughout this article.

41. In particular, in cases where a single judge gives judgement.

42. Bordeaux, Douai, Lyon, Marseille, Nancy, Nantes, Paris, and Versailles.

43. E.g., in *tribunaux administratifs*, a single judge gives judgement in relation to matters such as pensions, communication of administrative documents, and audiovisual royalties.

44. These are acts that deal with relations between the Government and Parliament and foreign institutions.

45. Subject to various exceptions.

46. The absence of a reply from the administration within two months is considered to be an implicit refusal and the applicant can then lodge an action before the administrative court within the following two months.

47. Illegality proceedings.

48. E.g., incompetence, errors in the scope of the law, principle of non-retroactivity, and lack of legal existence of an act.

49. E.g., in respect of the content of the act; the reasons of the act, i.e. error in law, error in the legal qualification of facts, error of facts; or the purpose of the act, i.e. misappropriation of power.

50. E.g., irregularity in competence or procedural irregularity.

51. Except for documents of national defence and security.

52. Full jurisdiction proceedings.

53. As of May 4, 2000 this *Code* was replaced by the *Code of Administrative Justice* which has integrated other legal texts.

54. (January 4, 1973), *Official Journal* (1973) at 164.

55. (December 28, 1976), *Official Journal* (1976) at 7493.

56. (January 14, 1989), *Official Journal* (1989), art. 69, 542.

57. (February 8, 1992), *Official Journal* (1992), art. 9, 2064.

58. (April 13, 2000), *Official Journal* (2000), art. 26, 5650.

59. (Ass. July 10, 1981), *Conseil d'Etat* (Retail) at Recueil Lebon 303.

60. *Law on the Médiateur*, art. 1.

61. *Ibid.*, art. 3.

62. The decision to remove the *Médiateur* from office must be adopted unanimously by a college composed of a Vice-President of the *Conseil d'État*, the President of the Court of Auditors, and the First President of the *Cour de Cassation*.

63. Translated as "district delegates".

64. (March 27, 2004), *Official Journal* (2004), art. 30.

65. Translation by authors.

66. *Supra* note 60, art. 6, al. 2.

67. The *Annual Report* of the *Médiateur de la République* for 2003 at 58 stated that during the year under review the declaration of admissibility at this stage covered only 24% of the claims.

68. *Supra* note 60, art. 1.

69. *Ibid.*, art. 6.

70. Except when the latter have left their post.

71. *Supra* note 60, arts. 12-13.

72. *Ibid.*, art. 9.

73. The *Médiateur* must take due account of the public interest involved as well as the financial means of the administration.

74. *Supra* note 60, art. 9, al. 2.

75. *Ibid.*, art. 9 stipulates that the power of the *Médiateur* to propose reforms can be exercised in two situations: (1) to remedy an ongoing dysfunction of a public service or (2) to end an inequitable situation brought about by the application of a law or by the absence of adequate legislation.

76. *Ibid.*, art. 11.

77. *Ibid.*

78. *Ibid.*, art. 10.

79. Generally speaking, the same applies to the *ad hoc* tribunals.

80. A case in point concerns complaints dealt with recently by the Ombudsman concerning a number of households which are being denied a water supply because the local council of the locality is in disagreement with the Water Services Corporation as to whether re-surfaced roads are to be dug up for the laying of a new piped water system or whether the old pipe network is to be retained so as to avoid having to dig up the roads. Obviously, complainants have to be provided with a water supply service although in this case they are caught in the crossfire between two sides that consider themselves as adversaries. The Ombudsman's role in this situation is to recommend a workable solution and to reconcile the two opposing sides with a view to ensuring that in the end the aggrieved citizens will be provided with a reliable water supply service.

81. *Supra* note 2, s. 170.

82. *Ibid.*, s. 199.

83. *Ibid.*, s. 201.

84. In an interview with a local newspaper *The Times* on June 23, 2004 the Parliamentary Secretary at the Ministry for Justice and Home Affairs referred to cases that are "trapped" in court for anywhere between four to fifteen years and warned that "...if we let things stay as they are, the chances are that the courts will come to a standstill."

85. *Supra* note 12, ss. 97 and 100, respectively.

86. *Supra* note 2, ss. 733-740.

87. The *audi alteram partem* rule.

88. *Supra* note 2, s. 811(b).

89. *Development Planning Legislation—the Maltese Experience* (Mireva Publications) at 142; *Code of Organisation and Civil Procedure*, *supra* note 2.

90. The *Planning Appeals (Fees) Regulations* established by means of *Legal Notice No. 7* of 1993 as amended by subsequent notices lays down that appeals that are lodged against decisions of the Malta Environment and Planning Authority are to be accompanied by a fee corresponding to 5% of the development permit fee subject to a minimum of Lm80 (circa €185).

91. Case PAB 131/98 SMS took approximately three years to be concluded while case PAB 306/01 KA took some seven months.

92. This time limit is mainly justified by legal security reasons since it is necessary to ensure that an administrative act cannot be annulled at any time after it has been adopted. Moreover, it should be noted that the time limit could be suspended, for instance, by making a non-contentious application to the administrative authority which is responsible for the contested decision.

93. It should be noted here that representation by a lawyer is not systematic when it is not required by the law. Moreover, administrative courts have, as a practice, to interpret with leniency applications made by non-

represented applicants.

94. Except for conflicts arising between serving public officials and the department of the administration employing them and which fall under the jurisdiction of administrative courts.

95. The principle of equity is at the origin of major judicial evolutions such as the recognition of general principles of law and the no-fault liability rules.

96. *Supra* note 60, art. 11.

97. File number 02-1147, *Annual Report 2003* at 19.

98. *Supra* note 30, s. 22(2).

99. *Supra* note 2, s. 469A.

100. *Case No. B 604.*

101. First Hall Civil Court (December 6, 2002).

102. First Hall Civil Court (October 3, 2003).

103. Court of Appeal (December 30, 1994).

104. This court case bears a striking resemblance to Case No. C 275 not just because both cases involved a falling vehicle but also because complainant informed the Ombudsman that had the accident in which he was involved taken place after a heavy downpour, the ditch into which he had fallen would have been filled with rainwater and he might have drowned, trapped inside his car.

105. All other things being equal, e.g., provided that the time limit within which a case should have been instituted has not already lapsed.

106. *Supra* note 30, s. 16(2).

107. Many also ask the Maltese Ombudsman to spare them the trouble of resorting to one of the *ad hoc* tribunals, but he usually declines.

108. *Case No. C 515* was actually one such instance where a case that was lost before the Ombudsman was eventually won in court.

109. Author's translation of statement made by M. Stasi in the 7th Round Table of the Council of Europe with the European Ombudsmen (Zurich, November 21-24, 2001) on the topic "Ombudsmen and Administrative Justice".

110. Antoine Pinay quoting from M. Legrand in "Quelques réflexions sur l'institution du Médiateur" (1973) 26 La Revue Administrative 618 at 618.

111. File number 00-2004, *Annual Report 2003* at 19.

112. Reform proposal INT 93-01, *Annual Report 1993*.

113. It should be noted, however, that *Law No. 2000-597* of June 30, 2000 on summary applications to administrative courts led to a substantial decrease in the average time necessary for administrative courts to give their judgements. In cases of summary proceedings, the courts can give their judgements in a few hours, even in judicial decisions requiring deportation.

114. Administrative courts do not have the power to forward a file to the *Médiateur*.

115. Claim No. 02-4478, *Annual Report 2003* at 46.

116. An increase of 16.8% over 2002.

117. *Annual Report 2003* at 130.

118. *Ibid.*, at 58.

119. *Ibid.*, at 121.

120. René Chapus, *Droit du contentieux administratif*, 11th ed. (Paris: édition Montchrestien 2004) at 62.

121. Reform Proposal No. 00-R17, *Annual Report 2003*, at 84.

122. *Official Journal*, (December 2, 2004).

124. The *Médiateur* reported that in 2003 this constituted the leading reason for the inadmissibility of complaints that were lodged with his institution, *Annual Report 2003* at 57.

125. *Supra* note 4 at 290-291.

125. In France's case, the "administration" could, under certain circumstances, be a private organization.

126. In Malta's case, given the large number of *ad hoc* tribunals, the odd exception to this is not excluded.

127. A case in point is the "person versed in planning matters" who sits on the Planning Appeals Board.

128. *In-Nazzjon Taghna* (December 1, 2004).

129. *Supra* note 60, art. 9.

130. The American Bar Association in *Model Standards of Conduct for Mediators* (1995) describes a mediator as an impartial third party who facilitates the resolution of a dispute by promoting voluntary agreement or "self-determination". The mediator facilitates communications, promotes understanding, focuses the parties on their interests, and seeks creative problem solving to enable the parties to reach their own agreement.

131. *Supra* note 30, s. 3.

132. The Ombudsman in Malta was promoted by the government as the direct successor of the Commission for the Investigation of Injustices established in 1987 by means of *Act XV of 1987.* This Commission was always intended to be a temporary measure, to be replaced by a permanent institution. Dr. Paula Mifsud Bonnici, a Maltese lawyer, in *The Ombudsman Under the Ombudsman Act 1995: A Comparative Study* (Msida, Malta: University of Malta, 1997) describes him at 20-21 as "a weapon which has been given to the individual to use not only against an oppressive government but also...against a government that fails to administer properly." It may be stated, furthermore, that so strong is the need in Malta for such an institution that in 1997 another institution was set up, called the Tribunal for the Investigation of Injustices. This was created by means of *Act VIII of 1997* to deal with pre-1995 cases, which are all outside the Ombudsman's jurisdiction. Applicants had six months from when the Act came into force to lodge a complaint. The Ombudsman, however, enjoys an advantage over both the Commission and the Tribunal, at least in the eyes of the Maltese public: whereas both the Commission and the Tribunal were appointed soon after changes in government (the Commission by the Nationalist Government and the Tribunal by the Labour Government) and therefore were suspected of having political agendas, the fact that the Ombudsman institution was not

set up after a change in government and is appointed by approval of both the Government and the Opposition in the House of Parliament relieves the Ombudsman of such political connotations.

133. *Supra* note 30, s. 22.

134. Discussed *supra* text accompanying note 29.

135. *Supra* note 30, s. 10(5).

137. Contrary to law, unreasonable, unjust, oppressive, etc.

137. *Supra* note 30, s.13(5).

138. *Supra* note 60, art. 9.

139. *Supra* note 108 at 9.

140. In 2000 the *Médiateur* submitted twenty new reform proposals, eleven in 2001 and seventeen in 2002. In 2000, twelve reform proposals were accepted, fourteen in 2001 and twenty-two in 2002, *ibid*.

141. *Supra* note 30, s. 13(4).

142. *Supra* note 60, art. 6.

143. "The Evolving Role of the Ombudsman", online: Irish Ombudsman <http://ombudsman.gov.ie>.

BIBLIOGRAPHY

Aquilina, Kevin, *Development Planning Legislation—The Maltese Experience* (Msida, Malta: Mireva Publications, 1999).

Aubry, Jean-Marie & Drago, Roland, *Traité des Recours en Matière Adminisrative* (Paris: Litec, 1992).

Brown, L. Neville & Bell, John S., *French Administrative Law* (Oxford: Clarendon Press, 1998).

Chapus, René, *Droit du Contentieux Administratif* (Paris: Montchrestien, 2004).

Conseil d'Etat homepage, online: <http://www.conseil-etat.fr>.

Delaunay, Bénédicte, "Le Médiateur de la République, 3422 Que sais-je 126 (Presses Universitaires de France, 1999).

Ducarouge, Françoise, "Le juge administratif et les modes alternatifs de règlement des conflits: transaction, médiation, conciliation et arbitrage en droit public français" (1996) 12:1 Revue Française de Droit Administratif 86.

Jones, B.L., ed., *Garner's Administrative Law*, 7th ed. (London: Butterworth & Co. Publishers Limited, 1989).

Le Gars, Jean-Marc, "Conciliation et médiation en matière administrative" (juin 20, 2000) 56:6 L'Actualité Juridique, Droit Administratif 507.

Legrand, André, "Répertoire du contentieux administratif" (Juin 2001) Dalloz 1.

Mifsud Bonnici, Paula, *The Ombudsman Under the Ombudsman Act 1995: A Comparative Study* (Msida, Malta: University of Malta, 1997).

Pierot, Robert, "Le Médiateur: Rival ou allié du juge administratif?" Mélanges offerts à Marcel Waline, II 683 (Paris: La Mémoire du Droit, 1974).

Pinay, Antoine, "Quelques réflexions sur l'institution du médiateur de la république" (1973) 156 Revue Administrative 615.

Stasi, Bernard, "The Médiateur de la République (Ombudsman) and Administrative Justice" *7th Round Table with European Ombudsman*, Zurich (November 21-23, 2001).

Valette, Bernard, “Quelles perspectives pour la médiation administrative?” (Juillet 13, 1999) 138 Petites Affiches 12.

ADMINISTRATIVE MEDIATION AND OMBUDSMEN: AN ENCOUNTER WITH INTERNORMATIVITY

Marie-José Chidiac*

Le travail des ombudsmans repose sur la notion d'internormativité, c'est-à-dire la mise en pratique de standards et d'exigences divers. La médiation, en particulier celle de type administratif, fait respecter l'application des lois nationales en y ajoutant une liste d'indicateurs et de paramètres: par exemple, les principes de bonne gouvernance et de gestion consciencieuse, qui sont des outils importants de régulation sociale pour les administrés. Dans le traitement des plaintes, les ombudsmans doivent également tenir compte des règles d'équité, de moralité et d'éthique. Leur travail aide à faire prendre conscience de l'utilité des divers standards, et du besoin de les harmoniser. La médiation, en tant que forme alternative de résolution des conflits, fait appel à toutes ces procédures pour créer une nouvelle forme de justice, qui soit, en fin de compte, plus sociale et plus humaine.

****

La internormatividad, definida como la teoría que crea relaciones entre estándares, constituye la esencia del trabajo de los ombudsmen. La mediación, en particular la mediación administrativa, aplica la ley del estado y agrega una serie de indicadores y parámetros de la buena administración y las normas de gestión responsable, los cuales también constituyen instrumentos de regulación efectiva en la vida social. Asimismo, los ombudsmen estudian la disputa desde la perspectiva de las reglas de igualdad, moralidad y ética. Los ombudsmen crean

* Marie-José Chidiac, Doctor of Law, Senior Lecturer at the Faculty of Law in Namur. This article is dedicated to the memory of Margarita Retuerto Buades, my friend, my guide, and my mentor.

conciencia de que existe una diversidad de estándares útiles, de la necesidad de aunar disciplinas y de armonizarlas. La mediación, como forma alternativa para resolver disputas, está formada por una conjunción de normativas que promueven una nueva justicia, cuya aplicación puede ser a la larga sólo más social y humana.

Internormativity, defined as the theory that constructs relationships between standards, is continually gaining ground in our contemporary world, and in my opinion constitutes the very essence of the work of mediators and ombudsmen. Professor Jean Carbonnier developed the concept of internormativity in his book *Sociologie du Droit* (*Legal Sociology*),[1] but it was Senti Romano[2] who developed the idea at length prior to the creation of the term itself.

According to Professor Guy Rocher,[3] the concept of internormativity postulates "the coexistence of complementary or antagonistic parallel differentiated normative orders or systems."

He attributes two meanings to this, stating that:

> The first refers to the transfer or passage of a standard or rule from one normative system to another. Internormativity is then seen as a rule produced or formulated within one given normative system that is found as such or in a very similar form in another normative order.
>
> This is the case when the law, through the intervention of the legislature or a judge, introduces a technical rule into the body of legal rules and thus gives it the "force of law". The technical rule is then incorporated into two normative orders: the normative order that governs a technique or a profession from where it was born, and the legal order that has adopted it.
>
> In the second sense, the concept of internormativity refers to the dynamism of contacts between normative systems, in the relationships of power and the forms of interinfluence or interaction that can be observed between two or more normative systems.
>
> Seen in this other sense, internormativity does not necessarily presume the passage of a rule from one normative order to another. In this second sense,

> internormativity can take on the form of resistance to such a passage, just as much as that of borrowing from a foreign standard.[4]

Internormativity would thus be a bridge built between the law and social sciences, between lawyers and social scientists and other scientists. It is a kind of mutual harmonization of legal systems, but above all harmonization between legal systems and other normative systems.

State law is in fact an instrument of social regulation. However, it is not the only one, "even if it has a pre-eminent position in the state."[5] Mediation, in particular administrative mediation, applies state law while adding to the legal considerations a list of indicators and rules that are also instruments of social regulation that play a considerable and effective role in the lives of people. In fact, administrative mediators or ombudsmen will certainly ensure that administrative action is:

- Legal (principle of legality);
- Justified in reality and in law (act on the formal justification of administrative actions);
- Accessible (principle of access by the people to administrative documents and even the act on the active and passive public nature of administrative actions);
- Adopted within the legally required deadlines; and,
- Respectful of the rights of defense.

However, ombudsmen will enhance their analysis of the problem presented, the dispute and the administrative action, with a list of parameters relating to the "principles of good administration" and the rules of "conscientious management" such as observance of:

- The proper treatment of the people and courtesy towards them;
- The use of clear, comprehensible, and explicit language towards the people;
- Good information for them;
- The principle of impartiality;
- The principle of reasonableness and proportionality;
- The principle of common sense;
- The Public Services User Charter or the Code of Good Conduct for Civil Servants; and
- The principle of reasonable time.

Ombudsmen or mediators will also study the dispute from the

perspective of the rules of equity, morality, and ethics—for example observance of the right to be believed and good faith (these two criteria are in fact rules of good conduct in social groups that the law itself has "accepted" and incorporated). The principle of equity in particular characterizes mediation, in comparison to other forms of regulating disputes.

An ombudsman is not a judge who settles a dispute and who imposes his decision. This institution exerts a "magistrature of influence", suggesting solutions or guiding the parties concerned to find the solutions themselves. In the jargon of ombudsmen, it is called a form of "gentle justice". The power of the ombudsman is thus based more on persuasion than on coercion. It assumes on the part of the parties concerned an openness, an attitude, an aptitude to negotiate, and a subjective desire to negotiate. The ombudsman, always neutral and impartial, will encourage them to negotiate, and contrary to a judge, his basis is not one of precedents or "the authority of final judgements": it is the unforeseeability that pushes the parties to negotiate. As Fathis Ben Mrad asserts "mediators must not use legal rationale as a basis to foster balanced relationships. It is their human capacity to listen and their ability to enable communication on which their powers are based."[6]

The ombudsman will lead the administration and the citizen to find the solution themselves in agreement, one that will better suit them. He will favor a kind of self-regulation between the parties concerned, and there will be two winners, or at least a winner and less of a loser, at the end of the dispute. The work of ombudsmen and mediators thus fits in with the order of "negotiated law".

The belief in the almost hegemonic effectiveness of positive law, in order to propose or prompt solutions, will thus be tempered or in any case modified—in the work of administrative mediators—by recourse to principles, rules, and standards other than just law: for example, sociological and psychological standards, professional rules, codes of ethics, morality, and equity.

As Carole Younes asserts, "the process of mediation sheds light on the facets of law that until then were in a certain obscurity. Mediation, on a social level, highlights the pluralism of normative orders."[7] The process of administrative mediation is thus no different to "social mediation". While staying within the framework of the constitutional state, it goes beyond statutes and case law. Administrative mediation crosses boundaries and opens up new horizons by creating awareness of the dynamism of the interfaces between normative systems and the interactions between law, sociology, and philosophy. Ombudsmen become "people who cross borders."[8]

The examination of claims by ombudsmen is thus more open to other fields of internormativity than is positive state law. According to Louise Lalonde, Professor at the University of Sherbrooke, in order to prevent and regulate disputes:

> The dispute being dealt with by mediation does not boil down to the dispute itself between the parties and legal

normativity alone as a reference framework for the decision of the parties. It embraces or can embrace a set of social, moral, technical and even legal normativities, that the rules of evidence would not allow to be accepted. The power of mediation resides in the normative pluralism that can be integrated into its management of the dispute, and its compulsory nature decided by the parties through a decision-making process that builds up the consensus.[9]

Ombudsmen create awareness of the usefulness of the diversity of standards, the need to bring disciplines together, and to coordinate and harmonize them. The internormativity applied by ombudsmen thus encourages the practice of interdisciplinarity.

The assertion of Professor Jean Carbonnier, that "to argue for the absence of law would not mean the absence of standards,"[10] takes on its full meaning in mediation and with ombudsmen.

Henceforth, thanks to ombudsmen and mediators, a science other than that of law, even the hegemony of law, is not only possible but desirable in the regulation and settlement of disputes between the authorities and the people who believe they have been wronged by the authorities. As this "negotiated law", this mutual consent brought on by the ombudsman will foster social bonds and bring about a new equilibrium in the relations between the authorities and the people, thus reconciling the people with the state.

Mediation as an alternative form of settling disputes is ultimately formed by a conjunction of normativities conveying a new justice, a "living law."[11] In fact, the standards of sociology, psychology, morals, ethics, mores, decorum, philosophy, professions, and science modify the standards of law in the most realistic and enriched sense, the application of which can ultimately only be more social and human. The demand of our contemporaries for "broader justice" that is accessible, flexible, and human seems to have been met by the ombudsman and this concept.

Endnotes

1. Jean Carbonnier, *Legal Sociology*, 2nd ed. (Paris: University Press of France, 2004).

2. L. Francois & P. Gothot, *The Legal Order*, trans. by Senti Romano (Paris: Dalloz, 1975).

3. Guy Rocher, "The Phenomena of Internormativity: Facts and Obstacles" in Jean-Guy Belley, ed., *Soluble Law, Quebec Contributions to the Study of Internormativity* (Paris, LGDJ, 1996) vol. 16 at 26.

4. *Ibid*. at 27.

5. See Michel Coipel, "Some Considerations on the Law and its Relationship With Other Regulations of Social Life" (2002) 22 J. of the Centre for Law & Info. Tech. Research at 31.

6. Fathi Ben Mrad, "For a Discussion on the Fundamental Principles of Mediation" [forthcoming in 2006].

7. Carole Younes, "Mediation, Subjectivisation of the Standard and Decentring of the Subject" in Carole Younes & Etienne Le Roy, eds., *Mediation and Cultural Diversity: For What Society?* (Paris: Karthala, 2002) at 53.

8. The expression comes from Marcel Jollivet, *Sciences of Nature. Sciences of Society. The People Who Cross Borders* (Paris: CNRS Editions, 1992.)

9. Louise Lalonde, "Mediation and Law: Opposition, Integration or Conversion? The Continuum in the Civil and Commercial Practice of Mediation" (2001) 162 Recent Developments in Mediation 73.

10. Jean Carbonnier, "Preface" in Jean-Guy Belley, ed., *Soluble Law, Quebec Contributions to the Study of Internormativity* (Paris, LGDJ, 1996) vol. 16 at 2.

11. The expression comes from Eugène Ehrlich, considered to be the founder of sociology of law, cited by Louise Lalonde, in an excellent study entitled "The Forms of Prevention and Settlement of Disputes: A New Concept of Justice? Some Considerations", Journal of the Prevention and Settlement of Disputes (Montréal: Carswell, 2001) at 15, note 17.

GOOD GOVERNANCE AND DEVELOPMENT CHALLENGES IN THE SOUTH PACIFIC: THE PROMISE OF OMBUDSMANSHIP

'Dejo Olowu*

Cet article soutient que l'institution de l'ombudsman mérite davantage d'attention dans les études qui s'intéressent aux diverses facettes du développement, car elle y est largement négligée. Bien que cette institution ne soit pas nouvelle dans le Pacifique-Sud, la plupart des discours en limitent la portée aux contextes nationaux et thématiques. En effet, jusqu'à une date récente, l'institution de l'ombudsman ne représentait pas une véritable plate-forme de protection des droits de l'Homme dans cette région. Qui plus est, comme on n'en voyait pas l'utilité pour la bonne gouvernance et le développement national, son application dans ces domaines ne faisait pas souvent l'objet de discussions. Devant les défis de plus en plus grands auxquels les petits pays du Pacifique-Sud doivent faire face–construction nationale, démocratisation des institutions, imputabilité publique et bonne gouvernance–,

* LL.B. (Hons.), LL.M., Obafemi Awolowo University, Ile-Ife, Nigeria; LL.M. Human Rights & Democratization, University of Pretoria, Pretoria, South Africa; PG Dip. Int'l Hum. Rts., Abo Akademi University, Turku, Finland; J.S.D. *Cum Laude*, University of Notre Dame, Indiana, USA; Barrister & Solicitor (Nigeria); Lecturer, School of Law, University of the South Pacific, Emalus Campus, Port Vila, Vanuatu; Articles Editor, *Journal of South Pacific Law*. Email: <djolowu1@yahoo.co.uk>. I appreciate the comments of Mr. Hannington Alatoa, former Ombudsman of Vanuatu, and to the Library Staff of the University of the South Pacific Library at the Emalus Campus in Vanuatu for their helpful assistance in assembling research materials. I also acknowledge the encouragement of Professor Linda Reif when I suggested the idea of contributing this piece. The responsibility for the views in this paper is entirely mine.

l'institution de l'ombudsman ne pourrait-elle pas avoir une grande fonction d'intégration? Jusqu'à quel point le travail déjà effectué par les ombudsmans leur permettra-t-il d'assumer ces nouvelles responsabilités? Comment repenser l'institution de l'ombudsman afin qu'elle joue un rôle véritable dans la bonne gouvernance et le développement national de la région entière? En étudiant ces questions essentielles, cet article tente de définir une praxis intégrative pour les ombudsmans du Pacifique-Sud.

****

Esta comunicación señala que la institución del ombudsman no ha recibido mayor atención en estudios de desarrollo y postula que merece ser atendida adecuadamente en el proceso de desarrollo. Aunque la institución del ombudsman no es reciente en la región del Pacífico Sur, los discursos se han limitado a temas y contextos nacionales restringidos. En efecto, hasta recientemente, la función del ombudsman no ha constituido una plataforma para lograr un compromiso riguroso con los derechos humanos en esta subregión. Aun más, dicha función no ha sido explorada todavía como un instrumento potencial para la buena gobernabilidad y el desarrollo nacional. En resumen, las discusiones sobre el trabajo del ombudsman como vehículo para promover buena gobernabilidad y desarrollo nacional en el Pacífico Sur son incipientes y escasas. En el marco de los desafíos crecientes de la construcción nacional, la democratización institucional, la responsabilidad ante el público y la buena gobernabilidad en los países más pequeños del Pacífico Sur, ¿puede tener el ombudsman un rol conector?¿Hasta qué punto sirven las experiencias pasadas de los ombudsmen para asumir este papel creador?¿Cómo se puede reconceptualizar la función del ombdusman de manera que tenga un verdadero rol en la buena gobernabilidad y el desarrollo nacional en el Pacífico Sur? En esta comunicación se discuten estas preguntas críticas y se trata de definir una praxis para una agenda integral en términos concretos para dicha región.

> Leaders believe the Pacific region can, should and will be a region of peace, harmony, security and economic prosperity, so that all of its people can live free and worthwhile lives...We seek a Pacific region that is respected for the quality of its governance, the sustainable management of its resources, the full observance of democratic values and for its defence of human rights.[1]

Background Discussion

The formulation of goals and policies towards development is a recurring item on the agenda of developing countries. However, the two aspirations of "development" and "democracy" which are the key items in this mix have not been fully reconciled either in theory or practice. Rather, "modernization" is commonly used as a generic concept to cover these aspirations of developing countries.[2] With David Apter's contention that the process of modernization is one of moral choice,[3] one cannot afford to ignore the underpinning value-premises in development and democratic aspirations. The first suggests the maximization of the condition of freedom which leads to equity, and the other emphasizes the fulfilment of potentiality.[4] Apter's conceptualization, though not necessarily his entire argument, provides a point of agreement:

> The explicit rationale of a modernising society is development, it is ordinarily expressed in terms of realising potentialities, human and social...The political nexus between equity and liberty, on the other hand, and equity and potentiality, on the other, has been historically, the ideal of equality. In modernising societies, it (i.e. the ideal of equality) remains a powerful moral force.[5]

However, while democracy and development are conceptually linked, scholars are totally unclear on the possibility of developing countries achieving both together especially at early modernization stages.[6] Practical experience confirms the uncertainty of scholars on this issue.

One remarkable aspect of this concern is the role of social institutions in the modernization process. In fact, it has long been contended that modernization is a process of institutionalizing.[7] The roles of political parties, the bureaucracy, and the military have been key areas of institutional studies. These institutional studies have been mainly directed at the older and more generally recognized social institutions. If social institutions are "the sum total of the patterns, relations, processes, and material instruments built up around any major social interest...and dealing with some of the basic universal problems of ordered social life,"[8] then it is possible to identify newer and less generally recognized institutions that have been unfortunately neglected in modernization studies.

The focus of this paper is one of these institutions largely neglected in development studies—the ombudsman—and it posits that ombudsmanship is an institution that appropriately deserves attention in the process of development. While the idea of ombudsmanship is itself not new in human experience,[9] in the last four decades it is the Swedish version of the institution that has gained large popularity and has been adopted in various shapes in many developing countries around the world.[10] Today, ombudsmanship is recognized as a critical institution for the establishment of genuine democracy and participatory governance.[11]

The close connection of ombudsmanship with the development process underpins the first task of this paper. Conceptually, ombudsmanship has been closely associated with democratic values, but its relationship with development is mostly seen as ambiguous or downright incompatible. This paper contends that the ombudsman institution is not incompatible with development aspirations. Rather, the current conceptual picture is the result of the neglect and unimportance attached to the subject. In this paper, I shall attempt to demonstrate how ombudsmanship is a modernizing instrument for good governance and development and make a case for its repositioning in the smaller states of the South Pacific.

Introduction

From its humble Scandinavian beginnings, the modernized concept of ombudsmanship has gained such phenomenonal recognition and acceptance among modern nations that it can safely be regarded as a significant cornerstone of law-ordered societies. By one recent and reliable survey, there are some 120 ombudsman offices in six regions around the world.[12] While the nomenclatures, mandates, and statutory functions of ombudspersons are not the same in all the countries and territories where they exist, a common denominator in the activities expected of them is to serve as protectors of the general well-being of all citizens and promoters of fairness in the polity. Underpinning the increasing discourses on the role of the ombudsman has been the popularity of the concept among democratic nations and nations that are formally committed to the democratic process.[13]

The global trend in this field has rubbed off on the states of the South Pacific and, today, seven smaller states and self-governing territories in the South Pacific have established one form of ombudsmanship or other. These states and territories are: Cook Islands, Fiji Islands, Papua New Guinea, Samoa, Solomon Islands, Tonga, and Vanuatu.[14] There are ongoing diplomatic efforts by Leaders of the Pacific Island Forum towards establishing ombudsman institutions in the South Pacific states of Kiribati, Nauru, Palau, and Tuvalu.[15]

It is gratifying to note that since 1962 when New Zealand emerged as the first English-speaking country to set up an ombudsman institution,[16] writers across the world have increasingly explored the manifold capabilities of this dynamic concept to respond to diverse issues that arise in modern states. From the question of public service efficiency to the subject of leadership,[17] from the idea of administrative justice to the general promotion of human rights,[18] from the subject of children's rights to gender equality,[19] from the question of accountability to the subject of transparency,[20] the ombudsman concept has continued to find relevance and wholesome linkage to the day-to-day challenges of modern states.

In more recent times, there have been some notable efforts towards exploring the significance and role of the ombudsman institution in the newer fields of good governance[21] and transitional conflict resolution.[22] In her groundbreaking essay published in 2000, Linda Reif had strongly contended that within conducive human rights contexts, ombudspersons can be vital channels for the promotion of good governance.[23] In subsequent years, the advocacy of ombudsmanship as a platform for the promotion of good governance has continued to garner more attention in diverse circles.[24]

While scholarly discourse about the ombudsman institution is not a recent development in the South Pacific, the discourse has practically been limited to narrower national and thematic contexts.[25] Indeed, until recently, ombudsmanship had not been considered a platform for rigorous human rights engagement in the sub-region.[26] And more importantly, ombudsmanship is yet to be explored as a potential instrumentality for good governance and national development. Discussions on ombudsmanship as a vehicle for promoting good governance and national development in the South Pacific are thus incipient and scanty.

Against the backdrop of the mounting challenges of nation-building, institutional democratization, public accountability, and good governance in the smaller states of the South Pacific, is the ombudsman such an institution for which a direct or connective role can be identified? To what extent have the existing ombudsmen in these states evinced the will to be purveyors of addressing these mounting challenges? How can the institution of ombudsmanship be reconceptualized such that it would become a veritable actor in good governance, nation-building, and national development in the South Pacific?

This paper addresses these critical questions and attempts to define praxis for an integrative agenda for ombudsmanship in the South Pacific in concrete terms.

Good Governance and Development: The South Pacific Challenge

Although one must concede that the term "good governance" has acquired checkered interpretations as an abstract concept,[27] it is hard to deny its characteristic indicators including "a professional civil service, elimination of corruption in government, a predictable, transparent and accountable administration, democratic decision-making, the supremacy of the rule of law, effective protection of human rights, an independent judiciary, a fair economic system, appropriate devolution and decentralization of government, appropriate levels of military spending, and so on."[28] Among these enumerated essentials, the question of corruption has emerged as perhaps the most volatile albatross against the ideal of good governance in many countries. This is quite understandable as corruption (including its attendant variants) naturally engenders lack of accountability, shields a culture of ineptitude, stifles genuine democratization, and retards development goals.[29]

Over the course of the past decade, perceptions about the tremendous challenges militating against the establishment of a good governance ethos have been the subject of numerous thinkers in the South Pacific. In a region where customs and traditional values occupy a place of preeminence, scholars have often identified these values and customs as the very basis for the weakness of the state, for the lack of genuine democratization, for endemic corruption, and also for the stunted pace of development.[30] Just as potent as the critical views on this subject have been, so too has been the wealth of well-reasoned approaches proffered towards strengthening the values of good governance, democratization, transparency, and development in the South Pacific.[31] Apart from individual intellectual efforts, there have also been remarkable institutional inputs towards these challenges. Since the 1990s, the World Bank, the International Monetary Fund, the Asian Development Bank, and the Pacific Islands Forum have promoted the ethics of transparency and good governance as channels of development in the South Pacific, in different capacities and to different degrees.[32] Furthermore, several governments have evolved initiatives that seek to address these concerns, at least at the level of formal commitment. These initiatives are in consonance with the vision of the Leaders of the Pacific Islands Forum as expressed in the *Pacific Plan for Strengthening Regional Cooperation and Integration* (the "Pacific Plan").[33]

In another commendable dimension, the Pacific Institute of Advanced Studies in Development and Governance of the University of the South Pacific (PIAS-DG) has assumed a frontline role in enlarging the think-tank on these challenges and deepening multifaceted discussions on the themes of good governance and development in the sub-region.[34]

While all these approaches and initiatives are indeed plausible and far-reaching, they fail to recognize the capacity of ombudsmanship as a viable mechanism for achieving the institutional reforms that they all identify as prerequisites for good governance and development.

Although a subject of reticent investigation, a cursory survey of the normative frameworks establishing the ombudsman institutions in the seven states of the South Pacific present a viable conceptual basis for the recognition of ombudspersons as agents of promoting good governance and national development.

Overview of the Normative Frameworks of Ombudsman Institutions in the South Pacific

Over a period of time, the preoccupation of the intellectual and political classes in the South Pacific had been with ministerial responsibility, that is, the relationship between government and the legislature as the central pillars of constitutional arrangements. Although the constitutional models adopted in the South Pacific encapsulated the basic tenets of the rule of law, separation of powers, checks and balances, and an independent judiciary, they did not address the problem of corruption or accountability. However, since 1975 when Papua New Guinea introduced the idea of a Leadership Code for senior government officials and politicians, the idea has been emulated in Solomon Islands (1980) and Vanuatu (1998).[35]

Numerous factors, including shortcomings of ministerial responsibility to the legislature and the limitations on what members of the legislature can achieve in imposing responsibility on ministers, led to the creation of the offices of the ombudsman in the different countries of the Pacific region where they exist.[36] While Fiji, Cook Islands, Papua New Guinea, Solomon Islands, and Vanuatu retained the nomenclature "Ombudsman", Samoa uses the title "Komesina o Sulufaiga" while Tonga calls the holder "Commissioner for Public Relations".[37] For the purposes of this paper, I will refer to the officer as Ombudsman and to the institution as ombudsmanship.

Creation

The classical concept of ombudsman has taken constitutional or statutory root with modifications in seven South Pacific countries. Each of these countries operates with the "Westminster Model" style constitutions.[38] All of the countries which are sovereign and independent states are founded on the rule of law and governed by written constitutions, the supreme law of the state which guarantees fundamental human rights and freedoms, and creates, on the principle of the separation of powers, a Legislature, a Cabinet of Ministers, the Executive, and an independent Judiciary. This model also applies in the territory that is not independent—the Cook Islands.[39]

In the South Pacific, two methods of creating the office of an ombudsman have emerged. One approach is constitutional, the other is through statute. Fiji Islands was the first country among Pacific Island countries to create an ombudsman institution. The office was originally created by the *Constitution of Fiji, 1970*, and elaborated in the *Ombudsman Act* of the same year. The first holder of the office was appointed in 1972.[40] Despite the political turmoil in Fiji Islands, its successive constitutions have ever since retained the office, with corresponding statutory elaboration on the procedure to be observed, the manner in which complaints and requests for investigation are made, and the powers, duties, and privileges of the Ombudsman regarding the disclosure of information.[41] Likewise, in Papua New Guinea, Solomon Islands, and Vanuatu, the Ombudsman is a creature of both the states' respective constitutions and at least one statute.[42] In the Cook Islands, Samoa, and Tonga, the Ombudsman is a creation of statute only.[43]

Appointment

In the Cook Islands, the Ombudsman is appointed by the Queen's Representative on the advice of the Prime Minister.[44] In Fiji Islands, the Ombudsman is appointed by the Constitutional Offices Commission following consultation with the Prime Minister.[45] In Papua New Guinea, members of the Ombudsman Commission are appointed by the Head of State, acting with, and in accordance with, the advice of an Ombudsman Appointments Committee.[46] In

Samoa, the Ombudsman is appointed by the Head of State on the recommendation of the Legislative Assembly.[47] In Solomon Islands, the Ombudsman is appointed by the Governor-General, acting in accordance with the advice of a committee consisting of the Speaker, the Chairman of the Public Service Commission and the Chairman of the Judicial and Legal Service Commission.[48] In Tonga, the Commissioner is appointed by His Majesty in Council,[49] while in Vanuatu, the Ombudsman is appointed by the President of the Republic after consultation with the Prime Minister, the Speaker of Parliament, the leaders of the political parties represented in Parliament, the Chairman of the National Council of Chiefs, the Chairmen of the Local Government Councils, and the Chairmen of the Public Service Commission and the Judicial Service Commission.[50]

Tenure

In the Cook Islands, the Ombudsman holds office for a period of three years.[51] In Fiji Islands, the Ombudsman is appointed for a term of four years.[52] In Papua New Guinea, members of the Ombudsman Commission have staggered terms of office allowing first appointments to the Commission to be arranged so that the terms of each member expires at a different time.[53] In Samoa, the Ombudsman holds office for a period of three years.[54] In Solomon Islands, the Ombudsman "shall vacate his office at the expiration of five years from the date of his appointment."[55] In Tonga, the Ombudsman holds the office for a term of five years,[56] and in Vanuatu, the office is also held for a term of five years.[57]

It is worthwhile to note that, to a large extent, all the existing ombudsmen in the South Pacific enjoy adequate guarantee of tenure and their establishing instruments all stipulate the circumstances and procedures for their suspension or removal.[58] What has become discernible, going by experience in the region, is that where the ombudsman is a creature of a constitution, to some extent the official is afforded stronger protection from any legislative erosion but not so where the ombudsman is a statutory creature since his/her mandate could be amended just like any other statute.[59]

Mandate

All the laws pertaining to ombudsmanship in the South Pacific confer on the ombudsman the power of investigation—either pursuant to a formal complaint or on the office holder's own initiative.[60] However, the same laws equally confer on the ombudsman the discretionary power to decline an investigation.[61] In such instances where the ombudsman declines an investigation, an order of *mandamus* will not avail.[62]

For the purposes of this article, it is critical to observe that the powers conferred on the ombudsmen in the seven South Pacific states where they exist relate to matters of governance and the administration of governmental functions.

In the Cook Islands, the relevant language is:

> [I]nvestigate any decision or recommendation made, or any act done or omitted, whether before or after the passing of this Act, relating to a matter of administration and affecting any person or body of persons in his or its personal capacity, in or by any of the Departments or organisations specified in the Schedule to this Act, or by any officer, employee, or member of any such Department or organisation in his capacity as such officer, employee, or member.[63]

Obviously, the investigation only comes into play in respect of circumstances where detriment in consequence of a fault in administration has or may have been sustained.

In Fiji Islands, the jurisdictional words are "investigate action, being action that relates to a matter of administration, taken either before or after the commencement of this Constitution by a department or by a prescribed authority, and in respect of which a complaint has been made to the Ombudsman";[64] meaning that investigation is not contingent upon the occurrence of injustice or detriment.

More comprehensive than the foregoing are the jurisdictional words of Papua New Guinea's *Organic Law*, namely:

> [I]nvestigate, on its own initiative or on complaint by a person affected, any conduct on the part of—
> (a) any State Service or a member of any State Service; or
> (b) any governmental body, or an officer or employee of a governmental body; or
> (c) any other service or body referred to in Section 219(a) (*functions of the Commission*) of the *Constitution* that the Head of State, acting with, and in accordance with, the advice of the National Executive Council, by notice in the National Gazette, declares to be a service or body for the purposes of this section.[65]

Equally extensive are the Samoan operative words:

> [I]nvestigate any decision or recommendation made (including any recommendation made to a Minister of Cabinet), or any act done or omitted, relating to a matter of administration and affecting any person or body of persons
>
> in his or its personal capacity, in or by any of the Departments or organisations named in the Schedule to this

> Act, or by any officer, employee or member thereof in the exercise of any power or function conferred on him by any enactment.[66]

The Solomon Islands provides another comprehensive investigative mandate where the relevant words are "investigate any action taken by any officer or authority to which this section applies in the exercise of the administrative functions of that officer or authority in any case"[67]

The Tongan Ombudsman is empowered to

> investigate any decision or recommendation made, or any act done or omitted, whether before or after the passing of this Act, relating to a matter of administration and affecting any person or body of persons in his or its personal capacity, in or by any department or organisation to which this Act applies or by any officer (including the Minister or Governor), employee, or member of any such Department or organisation in his capacity as such officer, employee, or member.[68]

In Vanuatu, the operative words assume a broader dimension as the *Ombudsman Act* provides:

> The Ombudsman has the following functions:
> (a) to enquire into any conduct on the part of any government agency;
> (b) to enquire into any defects in any law or administrative practice appearing from any matter being enquired into;
> (c) to enquire into any case of an alleged or suspected discriminatory practice by a government agency;
> (d) in respect of conduct of a leader occurring on or before the 1st day of July 1998, to enquire into any case of alleged or suspected breach of Chapter 10 (Leadership Code) of the Constitution;
> (e) in respect of conduct of a leader occurring after 1st July 1998, to conduct an investigation in accordance with Part 5 of the Leadership Code Act No. 2 of 1998;
> (f) to undertake mediation in accordance with section 13.[69]

The implications of the normative framework of the Vanuatu Ombudsman are thus very extensive and far-reaching particularly when taken in conjunction with the *Leadership Code Act.*[70]

It is instructive to note that although not all the existing ombudsman institutions in South Pacific countries have *direct and explicit* mandates for human rights promotion and protection, all their statutory mandates are broad enough to lend themselves to strategic responses to human rights concerns through innovative means. The extent to which this ominous lacuna in the establishing instruments of some of these ombudsman outfits has negatively affected the activities and perceptions of ombudsmen in this regard need not becloud the immediate focus of this paper but is nonetheless worthy of future scholarly enquiry.

Interface with Governmental Agencies

Although in all the countries under examination, the laws make explicit references to governmental departments, agencies, or authorities over which the ombudsman will exercise investigative powers, these laws nevertheless do not seek to create a super-watchdog whose singular pursuit will be fault-finding. From the tone of the language employed in the relevant laws, the ombudsman is in a position to resolve conflicts in positive and constructive ways through conciliatory skills as opposed to adversarial processes. To this end, elaborate provisions have been made for consultations, mediation, and privacy of investigations.[71]

In the relevant laws of all the countries under discussion, the ombudsman must inform the appropriate head of the affected government department of the intention to investigate, and every such investigation must be conducted in private.[72]

Extrapolating from the above statutory provisions, it becomes conceivable that rather than being an antagonistic agent of change, the South Pacific ombudsperson occupies the position of a "tranquil" but effective seeker of progress.

From the totality of the expressive language employed in the relevant ombudsman statutes in the South Pacific, five crucial hypotheses emerge:

1. All ombudspersons in the South Pacific are empowered to commence investigations on their own initiative, meaning that the efficacy of the office is more dependent on the personal skills and dynamism of each office holder.

2. For a complaint to fall within the mandate of an ombudsman in all the South Pacific territories considered, it must be with respect to action taken in the exercise of administrative functions of any course of conduct or anything done or omitted by any person in the exercise of administrative functions or any decision or recommendation made or act done or omitted to be done as a result of the administrative function.

3. Matters to which the constitutional and/or statutory mandates of ombudspersons relate in the South Pacific are exclusively governmental.

4. The central philosophy behind ombudsmanship in the South Pacific is the elimination of maladministration and, conversely, the promotion of accountable government, purposeful administration, and good and effective governance.

5. While South Pacific ombudsmen do not have identical mandates, the general mandates of these officials/bodies for *investigating* maladministration and abuse of power are broad enough to accommodate their crucial involvement in promoting good governance and development where they exist.

Flowing from the foregoing, the question that confronts us is: How effectively have the ombudsman institutions in the South Pacific utilized these empowering means and modalities for the purposes of rooting out maladministration and promoting good governance towards the goal of national development? This is where the ombudsman concept makes its entry point in the thematic context of this paper.

Since the 1980s and 1990s, accusations and counter-accusations of corruption, maladministration, and other acts which impeach the integrity of governments have become common phenomena in the South Pacific sub-region. Larmour has argued that "[t]he greater visibility of corruption is partly a reflection of the effectiveness of anti-corruption agencies, such as Ombudsmen enforcing leadership codes in Melanesia, the courts in Kiribati, *ad hoc* Commissions of Inquiry in Solomon Islands, or the Auditor General in Western Samoa."[73]

From shady timber licensing to irregular privatization of public enterprises, from inflated disbursement of foreign aid to the commercialization of sovereignty, the prominent roles played by ombudsmen in many South Pacific territories in exposing unfair dealings in governmental administration have received considerable attention and need not detain us here.[74]

Apart from the celebrated revelations of corrupt practices and "sharp deals" in governmental administration, there can be no gainsaying the fact that the increasing transfer of ombudsmanship (and its significance) as an institutional mechanism for good governance across the states of the South Pacific emerges as one of the strongest policy indicators that the modernization process is alive and evolving in the sub-region.[75]

Where then lies the linkage between the normative framework of ombudsmanship in the South Pacific and the agenda for good governance and development in the countries of the sub-region? To this we now turn.

Ombudsmanship, Good Governance, and Development: Conceptual Dynamics and Linkages

Going by the "classical" definition that has now almost assumed universality,[76] the ombudsman is

> an office provided for by the constitution or by action of the legislature or parliament and headed by an independent, high-level public official who is responsible to the legislature or parliament, who receives complaints from aggrieved persons against government agencies, officials, and employees or who acts on his own motion, and who has the power to investigate, recommend corrective action, and issue reports.[77]

The only snag in the foregoing definition is that it excludes all non-governmental ombudsman initiatives. Notwithstanding this limitation, it yet remains a feasible working definition for the purposes of this paper.

The popularity of the institution and its adoption in different cultures and contexts has, not surprisingly, caused modifications in this definition. But certain key features endure as essential. The ombudsman is generally expected to be a person of prestige and influence. To operate effectively, the office holder must be assured permanence, continuity, independence, and resources. The ombudsman must operate with objectivity, competence, efficiency, and fairness and should use fast, inexpensive, and informal procedures and be easily accessible. The office holder's main weapon to secure action should be the use of reasoned persuasion and publicity. The ombudsman is thus a national counsellor, a custodian of public conscience, who might indeed be called a guardian of public conscience.[78]

It is apt to note that the basic underlying value of the Swedish ombudsman idea is democracy. This was an institution that emerged as part of the attempt to strengthen the control of the people through their representative institution over the executive. It is also noteworthy that the Swedish *justitie-ombudsman*, as it was called, developed under a constitutional monarchy.[79] Both the design of the institution and the initial delay in its worldwide popularity is understandable by virtue of its origin. The early nineteenth century, when the Swedish ombudsman emerged, was a period when the position of the bureaucracy was generally still regarded as obscure and merely instrumental. And, at least in Scandinavia, bureaucracy had not clearly emerged as an issue in democracy discourses. Besides this, the absence of immediate worldwide appeal could be linked to the linguistic and other socio-cultural difficulties that limited its spread beyond Sweden.[80]

However, by the twentieth century, bureaucracy had been clearly identified as a problem in democratic societies. The works of Lord Hewart,[81] Mosca,[82] Michels,[83] and Weber[84] had considerably contributed to the increased intellectual discussions on the subject in the twentieth century. Bureaucracy became more and more dominant in the twentieth century with the expansion in the role of government.[85] The instrumental conception of bureaucracy was also now seriously questioned, and received the final blow with the works of Paul Appleby and Herbert Simon.[86] Attention shifted to how the bureaucracy could be sufficiently made accountable in democratic society. Consequently, the focus of the ombudsman also shifted squarely to the bureaucracy. The spread of the ombudsman idea followed. More impetus to the spread of the institution came after the idea was adopted in Denmark. The ability of the first Danish ombudsman to read and write in English helped greatly to publicize the ombudsman idea to the English-speaking world. And with the adoption of the idea in New Zealand, the first non-European country, the spread progressed earnestly.[87]

It is significant to note the ideological consensus in the initial spread of the ombudsman which was concentrated in Western liberal democratic countries. The emergence of the "Newer States" in the aftermath of the Second World War (WWII) brought with it renewed complexities especially in the role of the bureaucracy in modern society. For these newer states, the social ideology became modernization. To pursue the goal of rapid national development which is the central attention, the bureaucratic machinery assumed an unprecedented dominance because of the obvious potentials it possessed.[88] The power position of the bureaucracy has been even further strengthened by political instability, and various administrative reforms and management development—to name a few.[89]

On the other hand, the weakness of other social institutions left the dominant power of the bureaucracy virtually unchecked. In fact, some of these countries, including those in the South Pacific, initially took for granted that their bureaucratic institutions were premature, at least in the Weberian sense, and would sooner or later suffer from "overload".[90] Anyway, "bureaucratism" in the shape of various pathologies such as corruption, nepotism, aloofness, red-tape, and inefficiency became a serious problem for the newer states.[91] These countries had become caught in a dilemma which had seen them in frantic search for suitable relief. They wanted to develop their bureaucracies in order to reap all the potentialities for the development process and, at the same time, they were compelled to find various means to curtail bureaucratic power.[92] It was in this frantic search that the idea of the Swedish ombudsman reached many developing countries.[93]

If we follow Vickers' discussion on appreciative judgement,[94] the dilemma in which developing nations found themselves in regard to the bureaucracy necessarily becomes an integral part of these countries' appreciation and subsequent adoption of the ombudsman. The popularity of the ombudsman institution in developing countries reasonably suggests that the institution is ideologically compatible with the modernization goals of the newer states.

Since the 1960s, there has been a reconceptualization of public accountability and its relationship to effective performance of the bureaucracy.[95] Increased public disenchantment with public policies, for example in the United States, led to increased public demand for control over public policies. Accompanying this demand was the belief that public accountability and responsiveness of government programs is also cardinal to the efficiency and effectiveness of public administration.[96] It is not enough to stimulate the managerial capabilities of public bureaucracies to implement public programs. Implied in the whole activities of public management is service to the public.

These developments greatly influenced public administrative reforms in the developing countries. The rethinking on the public accountability of bureaucratic organizations provided a kind of philosophical support for developing countries to strengthen their public accountability instruments. Four other reasons strengthen the attraction towards the ombudsman idea in particular. First, the design and operations of the institution. All other attractions arose out of this. Second, the ombudsman's major dependence on the report of grievances by members of the public provides a constant means of monitoring and gauging the implementation of government development programs. Indeed, this is germane for national development as a process of distributing public benefits and services. Third, the spread of the ombudsman concept across different societies has seen the idea proved and reconciled with the interests of the bureaucracy itself. In Britain particularly, the adoption of the ombudsman initially met strong opposition from the civil service.[97] The belief was that its introduction would erode morale and consequently reduce performance. As it turned out, the ombudsman rather improved these virtues of the civil service. The ombudsman is not anti-bureaucracy; rather, the ombudsman vindicates the bureaucrat when wrongly accused and might sometimes become the spokesperson for the bureaucrat and source of succour as well. Simply put, the experience from the older ombudsman institution relieves the dilemma of developing countries since it does not discourage potentials for control. And fourth, the ombudsman institution proves quite flexible and can be easily involved in some other related activities. A number of developing countries that have adopted the idea have taken advantage of its flexibility and reconceptualized it to fit their ideological and practical needs.[98]

As already mentioned, the main preoccupation of the ombudsman with the problem of a democratic society, *per se*, has remained the central theme in the adoption of the idea in developing countries. Since the aspiration for a democratic society is integrally identified with modernization ideals, the idea of the ombudsman has not been out of place. It is argued, though controversial, that without democracy and active participation of the people in the political process, violence and instability tend to result and these invariably obstruct the development process.[99] As illustration, the committee set up to midwife the support of Tongans to sustain the stranglehold of the monarchy on the country's democratic process in the late 1990s assumed this premise in recommending the creation of an ombudsman institution.[100] Although the monarchy did not accept all the terms of recommendation, this was the launchpad for the establishment of the Commissioner for Public Relations pursuant to the *Commissioner for Public Relations Act*.[101] The point here is that the ombudsman is, in this sense, identified as a potential instrument for political participation and even social mobilization for development.

In the twenty-first century world, it would be erroneous to suggest that the objective of the classical ombudsman has remained intact in the numerous countries where it has found acceptance. As the abounding wealth of literature on the subject shows, the ombudsman now pursues various novel objectives including: righting wrongs done to individuals, making bureaucracies more humane, lessening popular alienation from government, preventing abuses by acting as a bureaucratic watchdog, vindicating civil servants when unjustly accused, introducing administrative reforms, and reforming and developing social morality.[102]

No doubt, modernization is a complex process involving various social changes. It is "a process of increasing complexity in human affairs within which the polity must act. This is why it creates severe political problems."[103] Concentrating on political development, Finkle and Gable agree that it is "a process closely related to other dimensions of social change but occupying a uniquely central position in it....Political development, then, depends upon, is associated with, and most important, may regulate, control, and order other kinds of social change when a society chooses to modernize."[104] It is specifically in this central political development sector that the ombudsman's contributions are most marked.

Within the context of this paper, the broad contributions of the ombudsman to national growth and development may be classified as: the development of the bureaucracy, political participation, and development of social values and attitudes. I conjecture that there are four problem areas which impair the effectiveness of bureaucracies in the developing countries of the South Pacific, namely: structural problems, problems relating to administrative attitudes and behavior, problems of client attitudes and behavior, and problems relating to political input into the administrative system. A fifth problem that may be added is the dearth of technical expertise.

Certainly, it is not in all these problem areas that the ombudsman is capable of contributing effectively. But there is no doubt that the ombudsman's familiarity with bureaucratic activities is a valuable resource which a government would do well to tap, especially for its development programs. This paper therefore proceeds to appraise the ombudsman as an institutional imperative in the South Pacific agenda for good governance and development, identifying some of the key characteristics that should be considered in galvanizing the relevance of the office holder toward these goals.

Ombudsmanship, Good Governance, and Development in the South Pacific: Pointing to the Future

Without doubt, "development", whose ultimate goals are material improvement in the peoples' condition of life and political stability including the atmosphere for people-oriented governance, constitutes a reasonable agenda to be pursued in South Pacific countries. After all, at the core of the rapid growth in the spread of the ombudsman concept is the belief that creating and strengthening democratic institutions is a precursor to good governance at the national level.[105] However, the strategy by which these goals should be achieved enjoys no easy consensus.

Since ombudsmanship facilitates a broad overview of administration which is not usually available from within any individual agency, the ombudspersons in the South Pacific can over the course of time remould bureaucratic culture towards the goal of development, if only they will deepen their interest in the more intricate details of governance. The development of public bureaucratic ethics, for which example the Israeli Ombudsman has been recognized, is instructive here.[106] The ombudsman strives to identify unsavory values and attitudes, encourages those involved to desist, and informs others who learn from his/her findings.

As a public control mechanism, South Pacific ombudsman institutions can foster the effective operations of the bureaucracy through efforts at monitoring and uncovering deviations from broad social ideals as well as indicate corrections. The bureaucracy's really strong point is that it can reconcile its control effort with the need for initiative and relative independence for the bureaucracy. The ombudsman should be tactful, knowledgeable, and understanding in his/her operations. The office holder should therefore respect bureaucratic expertise and should not frustrate it even though he/she raises some questions about the social use of this expertise.

Furthermore, the ombudsman can be a link between the people and the administration. To this end, the office holder should provide cheap and easy access for all, especially those who otherwise feel alienated from and helpless towards government. The ombudsman should provide redress for the helpless when such persons are aggrieved by governmental action. The ombudsman should also increase the bargaining position of the helpless citizens, their sense of worth, and reduce their distance from government. The demands of good governance and development make it non-negotiable for the office holder to establish effective partnership with civil society.[107]

The development process also calls for socio-psychological changes in the societies constituting the South Pacific. The efforts of the ombudsman to improve bureaucratic values and attitudes should normally extend into the entire society. Because the ombudsman is not purposely biased against the bureaucracy, he/she should try to encourage the larger society to cultivate positive attitudes towards the bureaucracy. The ombudsman should thus endeavor to promote social values and attitudes most appropriate for development. The demonstrated ability of the ombudsman to check unacceptable behavior can provide a strong force against "the folklore of corruption". In this regard, the ombudsman idea may provide an answer to the problem of leadership which apparently is one of the enduring issues in the conflict between modernization and traditionalism in the South Pacific.

The ombudsman can make tangible contributions to the development process without impairing efforts by other institutions even though the ombudsman's impact may be stunted due to funding and staffing difficulties. This is why the effective contribution of the ombudsman is greatly dependent on its institutionalization. An ombudsman institution contributes effectively to the modernization process if it sufficiently asserts its legitimacy, builds itself into an authority figure, and aggressively demonstrates its capacity and worth. Such an ombudsperson is best found in the "ombudsman motherland"—Scandinavia.

The prescribed consultative and conciliatory methods of investigations make the ombudsman a veritable agent for the promotion of overall national development as the office holder can identify and suggest resolutions to systemic problems, improve the overall quality of public administration, and perhaps prevent future complaints relating to the same matter.

With respect to those Pacific Island countries without ombudsmen, establishing an ombudsman for each would strengthen the sincerity of those territories to openness, transparency, and accountability as essentials of good and democratic governance. But these countries themselves must express the willingness to have ombudsman institutions as this would be a sign that their governments are prepared to have independent scrutiny of their actions.

However, in formulating the framework of future ombudsman institutions in the South Pacific and learning from current experiences, it will be important to bear in mind that both the authority and the effectiveness of the ombudsman will depend to a large extent on the vision, charisma, and skills of the person holding the office regarding the critical issues of good governance and the goal of national development.

Conclusion

It will be a befitting way of concluding this paper to echo the recent admonition by Peter Masi, the Ombudsman of Papua New Guinea:

> Every one in our own way and in our personalised and/or official settings can do one little good and one lawful act to make a little difference but imagine that one little ripple can generate a wave of change on self, another individual, the community and the nation. It is all about the re-examination of the present attitude we have toward others, community and public offices and the lack in contributing to social order that we must recognise and [become] resolute to make

> transformation and change...the tone of good governance for a new Pacific has been set. Our captains in the region—I am now going back to the Pacific Plan—have decided to pursue efforts that would have economical, security and sustainable impact in the region. And the significant and readily available tool to realise all that is the application of good governing practices by every government official.[108]

This paper is one modest attempt at reconceptualizing the framework of that desired change in the South Pacific milieu.

The thrust of this paper has been the interconnectedness of democratic governance and national development as values which modern nations pursue and ombudsmanship as an institutional channel for promoting those values. The unmistakable argument in the paper is that as an institution whose origin lies in the promotion of democratic governance, the ombudsman institution is not only capable of promoting democracy and good governance but also capable of being a veritable vehicle of national development ethos in the South Pacific region.

Furthermore, a case has been made for the deeper recognition of the mandates of the ombudsmen in the region as catalysts for attitudinal changes within governmental circles and the broader society at large. However, the success or effectiveness of an ombudsman will to some extent be influenced by, if not dependent on, the level of rapport the office holder has struck with civil society.

Far from being an *ex cathedra* pronouncement on all the dynamics that should inform the future of ombudsmanship in the smaller states of the South Pacific, this paper will have served its purpose if it stimulates further intellectual discussions in this regard.

Endnotes

1. Pacific Islands Forum Special Leaders' Retreat, *Leaders' Decisions*, Auckland, New Zealand (April 6, 2004), online: <www.dfat.gov.au/geo/spacific/regional_orgs/spf_leaders_decisions.html>.

2. See *e.g.* Olusegun Oladipo, "Modernisation and the Search for Community in Africa: Crisis and Conditions for Change" in Olusegun Oladipo, ed., *Remaking Africa: Challenges of the Twenty-First Century* (Ibadan: Hope Publications, 1998) 106; Vijay Naidu, "Modernisation and Development in the South Pacific" in Anita Jowitt & Tess Newton Cain, eds., *Passage of Change: Law, Society and Governance in the South Pacific* (Canberra: Pandanus Books, 2003) 7 at 10-11; Graham Hassall, "Governance, Legitimacy and the Rule of Law in the South Pacific" in Anita Jowitt & Tess Newton Cain, eds., *Passage of Change: Law, Society and Governance in the South Pacific* (Canberra: Pandanus Books, 2003) 51 at 53-54.

3. David E. Apter, *The Politics of Modernisation* (Chicago: University of Chicago Press, 1965) 1 [Apter].

4. Apter, *ibid.* at 5-7. For a contemporary elucidation on this point, see Amartya Sen, *Development as Freedom* (Oxford: Oxford University Press, 1999) at 75-77.

5. Apter, *ibid.* at 13.

6. See Jason L. Finkle & Richard W. Gable, *Political Development and Social Change*, 2d ed. (New York: John Wiley & Sons, 1971) c. 12 & 15 [Finkle & Gable]; Ron Duncan, "Governance and Growth: Theory and Empirics? Where do we Stand?" (Paper presented to the Development Research Symposium, Governance in Pacific States: Reassessing Roles and Remedies, held at the University of the South Pacific, Suva, Fiji Islands, September 30-October 2, 2003), online: <www.usp.ac.fj/fileadmin/files/Institutes/piasdg/governance_papers/Duncan_Governance_Growth.pdf>.

7. Samuel Huntington, "Political Development and Political Decay" *World Politics*, April 17, 1965; Asesela Ravuvu, "Culture and Traditions: Implications for Modern Nation-Building" in Ron Crocombe et al., eds., *Culture and Democracy in the South Pacific* (Suva: Institute of Pacific Studies, University of the South Pacific, 1992) 57 at 59.

8. Donald A. Hobbs & Stuart J. Blank, *Sociology of the Human Experience*, 3d ed. (New York: John Wiley & Sons, 1982) at 238-239.

9. Donald C. Rowat, *The Ombudsman Plan: The Worldwide Spread of An Idea,* 2d rev. ed. (Lanham, Md: University Press of America, 1985) at 7-10.

10. See International Ombudsman Institute, *The History and Development of the Public Sector Ombudsman Office*, online: <www.law.ualberta.ca/centres/ioi/eng/history.html> (observing that by 2004, there were 120 ombudsman offices around the world).

11. For general readings on the role of the ombudsman in democratization, see L.B. Hills, *The Model Ombudsman: Institutionalising New Zealand's Democratic Experience* (New York: Princeton University, 1976); Linda C. Reif, *The Ombudsman, Good Governance and the International Human Rights System* (Leiden: Martinus Nijhoff Publishers, 2004) at 59-62 [Reif]; Peter Masi, "The Realities Facing the Pacific Forum Countries' Governments and the Public Service on the Issues of Governance: The

Leadership Code of Papua New Guinea—A Law Designed to Improve Governance" (Paper presented at Second Annual Savenaca Siwatibau Memorial Lecture on Good Governance, held at the University of the South Pacific, Suva, Fiji Islands, April 27, 2005) at 9, online: <www.usp.ac.fj/fileadmin/files/Institutes/piasdg/governance_papers/masi_png_speech.pdf> [Masi].

12. See International Ombudsman Institute, *Ombudsman Worldwide Offices*, online: <www.law.ualberta.ca/centres/ioi/eng/worldwide.html>.

13. See Reif, *supra* note 11 at 7. The conspicuous absence of ombudsmanship in the Arab world, at least as it is known in contemporary times, lends credence to this suggestion.

14. This paper elaborates more on the concept and mandate of the ombudsman institutions in each of these countries in a short while. I am aware that the phrase "South Pacific" has been used by various writers and institutions in different contexts and with varying meanings. For the purposes of this paper, however, I am employing the term to refer to the sixteen independent states and self-governing territories in the Pacific Ocean region that make up the "Pacific Islands Forum", excluding Australia and New Zealand. See Australian Government, Department of Foreign Affairs and Trade, online: <www.dfat.gov.au/geo/spacific/regional_orgs/spf.html>. The territories covered are, therefore, those of the Cook Islands, Federated States of Micronesia, Fiji Islands, Kiribati, Marshall Islands, Nauru, Niue, Palau, Papua New Guinea, Samoa, Solomon Islands, Tonga, Tuvalu, and Vanuatu.

15. See Masi, *supra* note 11 at 4.

16. See J.F. Northey, "New Zealand's Parliamentary Commissioner" in Donald C. Rowat, ed., *The Ombudsman: Citizen's Defender,* 2d ed. (Toronto, Ont.: University of Toronto Press, 1968) 127.

17. See *e.g.* Mary A. Marshall & Linda C. Reif, "The Ombudsman: Maladministration and Alternative Dispute Resolution" (1995) 34 Alta. L. Rev. 215.

18. See *e.g.* Anand Satyanand, "The Ombudsman Concept and Human Rights Protection" (1999) 29 V.U.W.L.R. 19; Jeremy Sarkin, "The Role of National Human Rights Institutions in Post-Apartheid South Africa" in Jeremy Sarkin et al., eds., *Human Rights, The Citizen and the State: South African and Irish Approaches* (Dublin: Round Hall Sweet & Maxwell, 2001) 13 at 35-38; Victor O. Ayeni, "The Ombudsman in the

Achievement of Administrative Justice and Human Rights" (2001) 5 Int'l Omb. Yrbk. 32 at 43 [Ayeni]; C. Raj Kumar, "National Human Rights Institutions: Good Governance Perspectives on Institutionalization of Human Rights" (2003)19 Am. U. Int'l L. Rev. 259.

19. See *e.g.* M.G. Flekkoy, *A Voice for Children: Speaking Out as Their Ombudsman* (London: UNICEF & Jessica Kingsley Publishers, 1991) at 197-205; Ian Hassall, "The Commissioner for Children in New Zealand: Constituencies and Their Expectations" in Paul Hunt, ed., *Human Rights—How Are They Best Protected?* (Auckland: Human Rights Commission, 1998) 40.

20. See *e.g.* John Hatchard, "Developing Governmental Accountability: The Role of the Ombudsman" (1992) Third World Legal Studies 215.

21. For an exposition on the intercourse between ombudsmanship and the concept of "good governance", see Reif, *supra* note 11 at 62-80.

22. Mehmet Semih Gemalmaz, "Constitution, Ombudsperson and Human Rights Chamber in 'Bosnia and Herzegovina'" (1999) 17 Neth. Q. Hum. Rts. 277; Council of Europe, *Opinion on Human Rights in Kosovo, adopted by the Venice Commission*, 60th Plenary Session, Venice, Italy, (October 8-9, 2004) at 32.

23. Linda C. Reif, "Building Democratic Institutions: The Role of National Human Rights Institutions in Good Governance and Human Rights Protection" (2000) 13 Harv. Hum. Rts. J. 1 at 26-27.

24. See *e.g.* Ayeni, *supra* note 18 at 34; G.H. Addink, "Good Governance and the Ombudsman from a Comparative Perspective", online: <www.knaw.nl/indonesia/pdf/osm2003/ssh10.pdf>; Caribbean Regional Seminar on the Role of the Ombudsman in the Fostering of Good Governance and Democracy, Basseterre, St. Kitts (January 12-15, 2004)—Communiqué, online: <www.thecommonwealth.org /Templates/Internal.asp?NodeID=36744>; United Nations Development Programme (UNDP), "UNDP calls on the government to set good governance targets, in a meeting with Azerbaijan's Ombudsperson" (April 11, 2005), online: <ww.reliefweb.int/rw/RWB.NSF/ db900SID/VBOL-6BDJ97?OpenDocument>; "Accra, Ghana—Background Paper for Participants" Conference on the Role of National Human Rights Institutions and the Ombudsman in the Fight against Corruption, (November 14-16, 2005) [on file with author].

25. See *e.g.* Greg Toop, "The Ombudsman Commission of Papua New Guinea: An Overview of the First 17 Years" in Graham Hassall & Cheryl Saunders, eds., *The Powers and Functions of Executive Government: Studies from the Asia Pacific Region* (Melbourne: University of Melbourne Centre for Comparative Constitutional Studies, 1994) 131 [Toop]; Renee Lal, "The Diversified or Strict Role of an Ombudsman: A Comparison in the Roles of the Ombudsman in Vanuatu and Fiji"(1997) 1 J.S. Pac. L., online: <www.vanuatu.usp.ac.fj/journal_splaw /Working_ Papers/Lal1.htm> [Lal]; Mareva Betham-Annandale, "A Comparison and Contrast of the Roles of the Ombudsman in Vanuatu and Samoa: Who, What and How Can They Investigate?" (1997) 1 J.S. Pac. L., online: <www.vanuatu.usp.ac.fj/journal_splaw/Working_Papers /Annandale1.html>; Alice de Jonge, "The Pacific Ombudsman's Complaints Function: Comparative Perspectives on Fiji, Papua New Guinea and Vanuatu" (Paper presented at the Corruption and Accountability in the Pacific Workshop, Australian National University, Canberra November 6-7, 9-10, 1998), online: <rspas.anu.edu.au /papers/melanesia/ conference_ papers/1998/dejonge.html> [de Jonge]; Edward R. Hill, "The Vanuatu Ombudsman" in Anita Jowitt & Tess Newton Cain, eds., *Passage of Change: Law, Society and Governance in the South Pacific* (Canberra: Pandanus Books, 2003) 81 [Hill, *The Vanuatu Ombudsman*]; Edward R. Hill, *A Structural Analysis of the Ombudsman of Vanuatu*, Unpublished LL.M. Thesis (Port Vila: University of the South Pacific, 2004).

26. Some of the significant works in this area are H.A. Amankwa & K.I. Omar, "Buttressing Constitutional Protection of Fundamental Rights in Developing Nations: The Ombudsman Commission of Papua New Guinea—A New Hybrid" (1990) 18 Melanesian L.J. 74; de Jonge, *ibid.*

27. Francis N. Botchway, "Good Governance: The Old, the New, the Principle, and the Elements" (2001) 13 Fla. J. Int'l L. 159.

28. *Supra* note 23 at 16-17. See also the World Bank's definition of "good governance" in World Bank, *Governance: The World Bank's Experience* (Washington, D.C.: World Bank, 1993) vii.

29. See Yash Ghai, "The Rule of Law, Legitimacy and Governance" (1986) Int'l J. Soc. 179; Saladin Al-Jurf, "Citizens, National Governments, and International Financial Institutions: Changing Conceptions of Development in the 1990s" (1999) 9 Transnat'l L. & Contemp. Probs. 193 [Al-Jurf]; Robert Hughes, "Corruption" in Anita Jowitt & Tess Newton Cain, eds., *Passage of Change: Law, Society and Governance in the South Pacific* (Canberra: Pandanus Books, 2003) 32 at 42-44 [Hughes].

30. See *e.g.* Ron Crocombe, "The Future of Democracy in the Pacific Islands" in Ron Crocombe, Uentabo Neemia, Asesela Ravuvu & Werner Vom Busch, eds., *Culture and Democracy in the South Pacific* (Suva: Institute of Pacific Studies, University of the South Pacific, 1992) 9 at 11-14; Fana'afi Le Tagaloa, "The Samoan Culture and Government" in Ron Crocombe et al., eds., *Culture and Democracy in the South Pacific* (Suva: Institute of Pacific Studies, University of the South Pacific, 1992) 117; Peter Larmour, "Corruption and Governance in the South Pacific", State, Society and Governance in Melanesia, Discussion Paper No. 5 (The Australian National University, 1997) 2-4 [Larmour]; Hughes, *ibid.* at 45-47.

31. See *e.g.* Asesela Ravuvu, "Culture and Traditions: Implications for Modern Nation-Building" in Ron Crocombe et al., eds., *Culture and Democracy in the South Pacific* (Suva: Institute of Pacific Studies, University of the South Pacific, 1992) 57; Ron Duncan, Teuea Toatu & Azmat Gani, "A Conceptual Framework for the Development of Composite Governance Indices for the Pacific Island Countries", Pacific Institute of Advanced Studies in Development and Governance, Governance Programme Working Paper (Suva: University of the South Pacific, 2004) 13-17; Ruth Nicholls, "Corruption in the South Pacific: The Potential Impact of the UN Convention Against Corruption on Pacific Island States" (2005) 2 N.Z. Yrbk. Int'l L. 207-266.

32. See Peter Larmour, "Corruption and Accountability in the Pacific Islands", Policy and Governance, Discussion Paper 05-10 (Canberra: The Australian National University, 2005) 8.

33. The core "goals and objectives" of the Pacific Plan are "economic growth", "sustainable development", "good governance", and "security". See Pacific Islands Forum Secretariat, "The Pacific Plan for Strengthening Regional Cooperation and Integration, adopted by Leaders of the Pacific Islands Forum" (October 2005), online: <www.pacificplan.org/tiki-page.php?pageName=The+Pacific+Plan>. For a scholarly appraisal of the Pacific Plan, see Robbie Robertson, "The Pacific Plan is the Pacific's Plan", *Fiji Times* (August 23, 2005), online: <www.usp.ac.fj/fileadmin/files/Institutes/piasdg/dev_studies/papers/robertson_pacific_plan.pdf>.

34. See the broad array of intellectual works on the themes of development and governance produced under the auspices of the PIAS-DG, online: <www.usp.ac.fj/index.php?id=piasdg_downloads>. It is also remarkable to note that in furtherance of these regional initiatives, the School of Law of the University of the South Pacific has very recently introduced a core course on "Corruption" within its LL.B. and LL.M. curricula. See

University of the South Pacific, *2006 Calendar* (Suva: University of the South Pacific, 2006) 160, 267.

35. For scholarly analysis of the importance of the Leadership Code idea in these three Melanesian states, see Ted Hill, "The Ombudsman Act and the Leadership Code Review Committee" (Paper presented at the Vanuatu Governance Update 2002, University of the South Pacific, August 9, 2002); Greg Toop, "The Leadership Code" in Anthony J. Regan, Owen Jessep & Eric L. Kwa, eds., *Twenty Years of the Papua New Guinea Constitution* (Sydney: Lawbook Co., 2001) 213; Peter Larmour, *Foreign Flowers: Institutional Transfer and Good Governance in the Pacific Islands* (Honolulu: University of Hawaii Press, 2005) 30.

36. See *supra* note 16 at 140-143; Toop, *supra* note 25 at 132, 147.

37. See *Ombudsman Act*, No. 40, 1988, s. 2 (Samoa) and *Commissioner for Public Relations Act*, No. 10, 2001, s.3(1) (Tonga), respectively.

38. By "Westminster Model" style constitution, I mean the constitution which Viscount Dilhorne and Lord Fraser of Tullybelton spoke of in *Hinds v. R.* [1976] 1 All E.R. 353 at 376 as follows: "Though they differ in some respects, in the main they follow what our noble and learned friend Lord Diplock has felicitously called "The Westminster Model". They are more sophisticated than many written constitutions of greater antiquity and none of them, which are not federal constitutions, we believe, limit the legislative capacity of the Parliament of the territory to which they apply."

39. The Cook Islands remains a self-governing territory with "Her Majesty the Queen in Right of New Zealand" being the Head of State. See *Constitution of the Cook Islands,* s. 2, 1964 (New Zealand). See also Don Paterson, *Selected Constitutions of the South Pacific* (Suva: Institute of Justice and Applied Legal Studies, 2000) 1; Isaacus Adzoxornu, "The Cook Islands" in Michael A. Ntumy ed., *South Pacific Legal Systems* (Honolulu: University of Hawaii Press, 1993) 3 at 6-7; Guy Powles, "Changing Pacific Island Constitutions: Methods and Philosophies" (1982) 22 V.U.W.L.R. 63-83.

40. Lal, *supra* note 25.

41. See the *Constitution of the Sovereign Democratic Republic of Fiji, 1990*; *Constitution (Amendment) Act, 1997*; *Ombudsman Act*, Cap. 3, *Laws of Fiji, 1985*; *Ombudsman Decree 1987*. The most current law on ombudsmanship in Fiji is contained in the *Constitution (Amendment) Act, 1997* and the *Ombudsman Act*, Act No. 11, 1998.

42. See *Constitution of the Independent State of Papua New Guinea, 1975*, s. 217, and the *Organic Law on the Ombudsman Commission*, 1975 and Part III of the *Organic Law on the Duties and Responsibilities of Leadership*, 1975, *Organic Law on the Guarantee of the Rights and Independence of Constitutional Office-Holders*, 1975 (as amended up to February 1, 2001), *Revised Legislation of Papua New Guinea, 2001*; *Constitution of Solomon Islands, 1978,* ss. 96-99 and *Ombudsman (Further Provisions) Act* [Cap 88], *Laws of Solomon Islands, 1996*; *Constitution of Vanuatu, 1980,* ss. 61-65, the *Ombudsman Act* No. 14, 1995 (replaced by the *Ombudsman Act* No. 27, 1998) and the *Leadership Code Act* No. 2 (1998) (Vanuatu), respectively.

43. See *Ombudsman Act*, Cap. 8, 1984 (as amended by the *Ombudsman Amendment Act*, Cap. 24, 1991 (Cook Islands)); *Ombudsman Act*, No. 40, 1988 (Samoa); *Commissioner for Public Relations Act*, No. 10, 2001 (Tonga), respectively.

44. *Ombudsman Act* (Cook Islands), *ibid*., s. 3(2).

45. *Constitution (Amendment) Act, 1997* (Fiji Islands), s. 163(1).

46. *Constitution of the Independent State of Papua New Guinea,* 1975, s. 217(2).

47. *Ombudsman Act* (Samoa), *supra* note 43, s. 2(2).

48. *Constitution of Solomon Islands, 1978*, s. 96(2).

49. *Commissioner for Public Relations Act (Tonga), supra* note 43, s. 3(1).

50. *Constitution of Vanuatu, 1980*, s. 61(1).

51. *Ombudsman Act* (Cook Islands), *supra* note 43, s. 5.

52. *Supra* note 45.

53. *Organic Law on the Ombudsman Commission*, *1975* (Papua New Guinea), s. 5.

54. *Ombudsman Act* (Samoa), *supra* note 43, s. 4(1).

55. *Supra* note 48 at s. 96(5).

56. *Commissioner for Public Relations Act* (Tonga), *supra* note 43, s. 5(1).

57. *Ombudsman Act* No. 27 (Vanuatu), 1998, s. 3(1).

58. See *Ombudsman Act* (Cook Islands), *supra* note 43, s. 6; supra note 45, s. 163 (1); Organic *Law on the Guarantee of the Rights and Independence of Constitutional Office-Holders*, 1975 (Papua New Guinea), s. 7; *Ombudsman Act* (Samoa) *supra* note 43 s. 5 *supra* note 48, ; s. 96(6); Commissioner for Public Relations Act (Tonga), *supra* note 43, s. 6; supra note 50, s. 61(3).

59. See David Cannings, "The Ombudsman Commission: Jurisdiction, Functions and Performance" in Anthony J. Regan, Owen Jessep & Eric L. Kwa, eds., *Twenty Years of the Papua New Guinea Constitution* (Sydney: Lawbook Co., 2001) 197 at 200.

60. See *Ombudsman Act* (Cook Islands), *supra* note 43, s. 11; *supra* note 45, s. 158; *supra* note 46, s. 219; *supra* note 53 s. 13; *Ombudsman Act* (Samoa), *supra* note 43, s. 11; *supra* note 48, s. 97(1); *Commissioner for Public Relations Act* (Tonga), *supra* note 43, s. 11; *supra* note 50, s. 62; *supra note 57,* s. 11.

61. *Ombudsman Act* (Cook Islands), *supra* note 43, s. 14; supra note 45, s. 159(1); supra note 53, s. 16(3); *Ombudsman Act* (Samoa), *supra* note 43, s. 14; *Ombudsman (Further Provisions) Act, 1996* (Solomon Islands), s. 21; *Commissioner for Public Relations Act* (Tonga), *supra* note 43, s. 13; supra note 50, s. 18.

62. See generally *Re Fletcher's Application* [1970] 2 All ER 527.

63. *Ombudsman Act* (Cook Islands), *supra* note 43, s. 11(1).

64. *Supra* note 45, s. 158(1)(a).

65. *Supra* note 53, s. 13.

66. *Ombudsman Act* (Samoa) *supra* note 43, s. 11(1).

67. *Ombudsman (Further Provisions) Act, 1996* (Solomon Islands), s. 5(1).

68. *Commissioner for Public Relations Act* (Tonga), *supra* note 43, s. 11(1).

69. *Supra* note 57, s. 11(1).

70. For a scholarly analysis of the interrelationship between the *Ombudsman Act* and the *Leadership Code Act vis-à-vis* the powers of the Vanuatu Ombudsman, see Ted Hill, "The Ombudsman Act and the Leadership Code Review Committee" (Paper presented at the Vanuatu Governance Update 2002, University of the South Pacific, August 9, 2002).

71. Apart from the general provisions on these points as found in the laws of the other six countries, the law in Vanuatu expressly provides a mediatory mandate for the Ombudsman. See *supra* note 57, s. 13.

72. *Ombudsman Act* (Cook Islands) *supra* note 57, s. 15(1) & (2); supra note 45, s. 4(1) & and (2); supra note 53, s. 17(1)(a); *Ombudsman Act* (Samoa), *supra* note 43, s. 15(1) & (2); *supra* note 67, ss. 9(1)(a) & 10(2); *Commissioner for Public Relations Act* (Tonga), *supra* note 43, s. 14(1) & (2); supra note 57, s. 21(1). On the nature of the obligation to inform a "leader" of an intention to investigate, see *John Nilkare v. The Ombudsman Commission of Papua New Guinea* [1996] P.N.G.L.R. 413.

73. Larmour, *supra* note 30 at 1.

74. For diverse experiences emanating from the South Pacific, see Toop, *supra* note 25 at 132-56; Larmour, *ibid.* at 4-8; Hill, *The Vanuatu Ombudsman*, *supra* note 25 at 80-83.

75. For the view that the reproduction of the Papua New Guinea anti-corruption model in Solomon Islands and Vanuatu is an indication of successful South-South institutional transfer, see Manuhuia Barcham, "South-South Policy Transfer: The Case of the Vanuatu Ombudsman Office" (2003) Pac. Econ. Bull. 108 at 113.

76. Reif, *supra* note 11 at 2-3.

77. Ombudsman Committee, International Bar Association Resolution (Vancouver: International Bar Association, 1974), quoted in Reif, *ibid.* at 3.

78. See Canadian Ombudsman Association, "A Federal Ombudsman for Canada—A Discussion Paper" (May 20, 1999), online: <www.ombudsman.on.ca/pdf/EN-Discussion-Paper.pdf>.

79. Walter Gellhorn, *Ombudsmen and Others: Citizens' Protectors in Nine Countries* (Cambridge, Mass.: Harvard University Press, 1967) 3.

80. See Paavo Kastrai, "The Chancellor of Justice and the Ombudsman" in Donald C. Rowat, ed., *The Ombudsman: Citizen's Defender,* 2d ed. (Toronto, Ont.: University of Toronto Press, 1968) 58 at 59. See also Anand Satyanand, "Growth of the Ombudsman Concept" (1999) 1:3 J.S. Pac. L., online: <www.vanuatu.usp.ac.fj/journal_splaw/articles/Satyanand1.htm>.

81. Lord Hewart of Bury, *The New Despotism* (London: Ernest Benn, 1929).

82. Gaetano Mosca, *The Ruling Class* (New York: McGraw-Hill, 1939).

83. Robert Michels, *Political Parties* (New York: The Free Press, 1962).

84. Max Weber, *The Theory of Social and Economic Organisation* (New York: The Free Press, 1964).

85. Peter M. Blau & Marshall W. Meyer, *Bureaucracy in Modern Society* (New York: Random House, 1971).

86. See Dwight Waldo, "The Study of Public Administration" in Richard J. Stillman, *Public Administration* (Boston, Mass.: Houghton Mifflin, 1980) 4.

87. Kenneth J. Keith, "Development of the Role of the Ombudsman with Reference to the Pacific" (Paper presented at the 22nd Australasian and Pacific Ombudsman Regional Conference, Wellington, New Zealand, February 9-11, 2005) 1.

88. See K. Younger, *Public Service in New States* (New York: Oxford University Press, 1960).

89. *Supra* note 87.

90. Graham Hassall, "Governance for Human Development" (Paper presented at the Pacific Islands Political Studies Association Conference, Noumea, New Caledonia, December 3-5, 2004) 2.

91. *Ibid.* See also James S. Wunsch, "Foundations of Centralization: The Colonial Experience and the African Context" in James S. Wunsch & Dele Olowu, eds., *The Failure of the Centralized State: Institutions and Self-Governance in Africa* (Boulder, Colo.: Westview Press, 1990) 23.

92. *Supra* note 90. See also Anand Satyanand, "Human Rights in the Commonwealth: The Ombudsman Role" (2002) 28:1 Commonwealth L. Bull. 547 [Satyanand]; Nina Karpachova, "First Annual Report of the Ukrainian Parliament Commissioner for Human Rights," online: <www.ombudsman.kiev.ua/de_01_2.htm>.

93. Satyanand, *ibid.*

94. Geoffrey Vickers, *Value Systems and Social Process* (London: Penguin, 1970) at 42-43.

95. See *e.g.* Scott Greer, Ronald D. Hedlund & James L. Gibson, eds., *Accountability in Urban Society* (Beverly Hills: Sage Publications, 1978).

96. See *e.g.* Burton D. Friedman, *The Quest for Accountability* (Chicago: Public Administration Office, 1973) at 45-50.

97. Roy Gregory & Peter Hutchesson, *The Parliamentary Ombudsman* (London: Allen & Urwin, 1975) c. 8.

98. Isaac Scott, "The Ombudsman, the Executive and Collective Rights in Underdeveloped Countries" (1979) 13:2 Q.J. Admin. 101 at 102.

99. See Jon Frankel, "Do Pacific Electoral Systems Matter or is Political Culture Everything?" (Paper presented at the Conference on Political Culture, Representation and Electoral Systems in the Pacific, Port Vila, Vanuatu, July 10-12, 2004); Finkle & Gable, *supra* note 6 at c. 12.

100. *Commissioner for Public Relations Act* (Tonga), *supra* note 43. See Kerry James, "Tonga" (2003) 15:1 Contemporary Pac. 187; Transparency International, *Transparency International Country Study Report – Tonga 2004* (Blackburn, Australia: Transparency International) 19.

101. *Commissioner for Public Relations Act* (Tonga), *ibid.*

102. See generally Dennis Pearce, "Who Needs an Ombudsman?", online: <www.ombudsman.act.gov.au/news_current_issues/essay/who_needs_an_ombudsman_pearce.doc>; Anand Satyanand, "Reflections—10 Years As An Ombudsman" (Address to 22nd Australasian & Pacific Regional Ombudsman Conference, Wellington, New Zealand), online: <www.ombudsmen.govt.nz/APOR%20docs/Anand%20Satyanand.pdf.>.

103. Monte Palmer, *Dilemmas of Political Development: Dilemmas and Challenges* (Itasca, Ill.: Peacock Publishers, 1997) 64.

104. Finkle & Gable, *supra* note 6 at 65.

105. See *supra* note 23 at 18-19; Al-Jurf, *supra* note 29 at 195-97.

106. By virtue of the *Basic Law: The State Comptroller, 1971* (as amended in 1988), the ombudsman in Israel combines the functions of State Comptroller and Public Complaints Commissioner. See Gerald E. Caiden, "New Directions in State Audit" in Benjamin Geist, ed., *State Audit: Developments in Public Accountability* (London: Macmillan, 1981) 136.

107. See generally Ralph Nader, "Ombudsmen for State Governments" in Donald C. Rowat, ed., *The Ombudsman: Citizen's Defender*, 2d ed. (Toronto: University of Toronto Press, 1968) 240 at 245; Henry J. Abraham, "The Need for Ombudsmen in the United States" in Donald C. Rowat, ed., *The Ombudsman: Citizen's Defender,* 2d ed. (Toronto: University of Toronto Press, 1968) 234 at 237.

108. Masi, *supra* note 11 at 8-9.

A SPECIALIST OMBUDSMAN FOR PRISONERS

Stephen Shaw*

Cet article dresse l'histoire du Bureau de l'ombudsman chargé des prisons et des libertés conditionnelles en Angleterre et au Pays de Galles. Il examine aussi la double fonction de ce bureau: enquêter sur des plaintes et sur des décès survenus lors de détention provisoire. Il fournit des détails sur le travail de ce bureau et soutient qu'une approche réparatrice est particulièrement adaptée à la résolution de plaintes soumises par des détenus.

Cet article rappelle la souveraineté des nations en ce qui concerne la définition des responsabilités de leurs ombudsmans et des moyens à mettre en œuvre pour gérer leurs prisons. Il souligne néanmoins le fait que les enquêtes sur les plaintes émanant de détenus ressemblent plus souvent qu'on pourrait le croire à celles traitées par les ombudsmans non spécialisés.

Cet article donne aussi des renseignements sur les services fournis par les autres ombudsmans du Royaume-Uni.

****

Esta comunicación describe la historia de la oficina del ombudsman dedicada a las prisiones y las libertades condicionales en Inglaterra y Gales, así como también su función doble de investigar quejas y muertes bajo detención provisional. El autor ofrece detalles de su trabajo sobre las quejas y sostiene que un enfoque reparador en la resolución de problemas es muy adecuado para las quejas presentadas por los prisioneros.

El autor señala que cada nación crea sus propios acuerdos con el ombudsman y su propio enfoque para monitorear las prisiones. Sin embargo, dice que la investigación de las quejas de los prisioneros tiene más en común con los casos

* Prisons and Probation Ombudsman for England and Wales.

habituales de los ombudsmen que lo que pueda creerse.

Esta comunicación da detalles de otros servicios del ombudsman en le Reino Unido.

As the ombudsman concept has spread globally, so the range of responsibilities and ways of working have likewise mushroomed. It is widely accepted that human rights issues and anti-corruption now sit alongside the traditional complaints-handling role, especially in the newer democracies. As a former Parliamentary Ombudsman for England and Wales wisely commented, such is the degree of differentiation that ombudsmen are best thought of as a genus not a species.

Indeed, given that powers and remit differ so much from one jurisdiction to another, I think it may fairly be speculated that each and every ombudsman is actually unique. Certainly, I am unaware of any ombudsman's office with an identical mix of responsibilities to those I enjoy as Prisons and Probation Ombudsman for England and Wales. That said, there are well-established correctional ombudsman organizations in Canada, Argentina, and parts of the United States, and the newly established office of the Prisoner Ombudsman for Northern Ireland is closely based on my own, although its remit does not extend to probation supervision or immigration detention as mine does.

I would like to use this contribution to explain how and why my office was established, our twin roles in respect of complaints and deaths in custody, and the connections between my office's work and that of other ombudsmen. But first I should offer some context on ombudsmen services within the United Kingdom.

After a slow start—the office of the Parliamentary Ombudsman was not established until the late 1960s—the U.K. now has a highly developed structure of ombudsmen and complaints investigators. Three features of that structure are important to explain. The first, but least important in terms of this article, is that different arrangements apply in England, Wales, Scotland, and Northern Ireland. In terms of prisoners' complaints, I cover both England and Wales, the analogous office of Prisoner Ombudsman, established in 2005, covers Northern Ireland, and the (I think it may be fairly said) rather weaker office of the Scottish Prison Complaints Commissioner covers Scotland.

The second feature is that, while the Parliamentary Ombudsman has a wide remit, citizens do not have a right of direct access to her services. Cases may only be drawn to the Parliamentary Ombudsman's attention by a Member of Parliament, and this so-called "MP filter" has limited the number and type of cases investigated. Before my office was established, very few prisoner cases had been referred to the Parliamentary Ombudsman. This contrasts with the position in many administrations where generalist public sector ombudsmen are often fearful of being swamped by prison cases to the detriment of other work.

The third feature of the British system is that there has developed a wide range of specialist ombudsmen within both the public and private sectors. The largest of these—the Financial Services Ombudsman—employs no fewer than 1,000 staff and covers such matters as banking, insurance, and personal investments. Other important ombudsmen in the private sector oversee telecommunications, estate agents, and the removals industry. Within the public sector, there are specialist agencies for complaints against the tax authorities, social welfare agencies, and the police, amongst others.

The benefits of specialist ombudsmen versus a single "one stop shop" have been frequently debated. The Financial Services Ombudsman was the result of the merger of half a dozen smaller schemes. But given the size of the public sector in Britain, my own view is that any single public sector ombudsman risks becoming an unwieldy bureaucracy. I also place a high value on specialist expertise. However, I acknowledge the counter-arguments that a single point of call is easier for potential clients and that a single office can better handle complaints that involve more than one agency.

Moves to encourage greater integration of the public sector ombudsmen in England and Wales (the Parliamentary Ombudsman and the Local Government Ombudsmen) have made some progress, but my own office has always been excluded from this process on the grounds that we occupy a "niche" position. The balance of argument might be different in countries where the state is less pervasive, or where the prison system is much smaller.

A word here about nomenclature. I am proud to enjoy the title Ombudsman but its application to my office proved controversial in the past, and my predecessor was treated with some discourtesy. The British and Irish Ombudsman Association (BIOA) still distinguishes its membership between "Ombudsmen" and "other Complaints Handling Bodies" based on what BIOA regards as essential, but I see as arcane and arbitrary, rules governing independence.[1] On BIOA's website, you will find my office in the second category.[2] Yet everyone accepts that I am utterly independent of the Prison and Probation Services. While my office's constitutional position could and should be improved (there is a Government commitment to legislate to do so), far too much emphasis has been placed on this one aspect of our affairs. How you actually do the job should count for at least as much as the status of your governing instrument.

As I have noted, ever since the establishment of the office of the Parliamentary Ombudsman, prisoners have enjoyed a right of access. However, this was rarely invoked—in large part because of the existence of the MP filter. The relatively mundane nature of many prisoner complaints—food, visits, minor infractions of prison rules—may also have been unappealing to the Parliamentary Ombudsman's office itself. It was certainly not the case in Britain, as I know has been the case in some countries, that the generalist Ombudsman has felt itself overwhelmed by prisoner cases and in danger of seeing its whole workload skewed as a consequence.

Although there had been some pressure group lobbying in favor of a separate Ombudsman for prisoners,[3] the origins of my office can be traced directly to a series of prison riots that took place in some twenty or so prisons across England, most notably in Strangeways prison in Manchester, over the Easter of 1990. These were the most destructive and widespread prison disturbances in our history and came after two decades of increasing instability in the prisons. As so often in public administration, long-standing structural weaknesses in the system were only addressed after a catastrophic failure. The subsequent enquiry into the riots, conducted by a senior judge, Lord Justice Woolf, in association with the then Chief Inspector of Prisons, Sir Stephen Tumim, concluded that one of the central causes was a belief on the part of prisoners that their grievances were not being properly addressed:

> A recurring theme in the evidence from prisoners who may have instigated, and who were involved in, the riots was that their actions were a response to the manner in which they were treated by the prison system. Although they did not always use these terms, they felt a lack of justice.[4]

They continued:

> A proper system of justice within prisons is important for every prisoner and everyone who has to work in prisons. If a prisoner does not feel that he is being treated with justice, he will legitimately feel debased, he will bear a grievance, and he will be a difficult prisoner to control. The absence of justice can poison relations between prisoners and staff and ultimately play a part in bringing about the explosive situation which existed in some prisons in April 1990.[5]

Woolf and Tumim proposed a fundamental reform to the prison complaints process:

> Proper structures are necessary in order to achieve justice. Within a prison in particular, it is an important requirement of justice that justice should not only actually be done but should be seen to be done. It will not be seen to be done if there is no proper procedure, if there are no established rules, if the prisoner is not made aware of those rules, and if there is not, at least at the final stage of the process, recourse to an independent element.[6]

Accordingly, the report recommended the appointment of what was termed an Independent Complaints Adjudicator for Prisons (ICAP) to investigate individual grievances and act as the final avenue on appeal against findings at disciplinary hearings. Not only would this appointment help to resolve individual complaints, it would also have wider advantages:

> The influence of an independent element would permeate down to the lowest level of the grievance system. It would give the whole system a validity which it does not otherwise have. It would act as a spur to the Prison Service to maintain proper standards. It would encourage the resolution of difficulties in advance of an appeal.[7]

This recommendation was accepted in principle by the Government in its 1991 White Paper *Custody, Care and Justice*.[8] The White Paper proposed that:

> There should be an independent avenue of appeal against a disciplinary finding once avenues within the Prison Service have been exhausted.... Appeals against decisions made in response to complaints should also be considered by the same independent body.[9]

Following a process of consultation carried out in 1992, the name of the office was changed to Prisons Ombudsman.[10] The first Prisons Ombudsman was appointed in May 1994 and began receiving his first complaints on October 24 that year.

Working initially with thirteen staff, the new office encountered something of a rough ride in its early years. To some extent this may have been unavoidable—any new "watchdog" body is likely to be regarded with some suspicion, especially by what was then a rather conservative, secretive, and inward-looking Prison Service. But it was also a reflection of the political climate. The Home Secretary at the time, Michael Howard, had little sympathy for the notion of prisoners' rights or for the office of Prisons Ombudsman that he had inherited. Howard vetoed the appointment of the first three candidates put forward by an independent interview panel for the post of Ombudsman (the present writer was one of the three). He then oversaw what was believed at the time to be a significant limitation to the terms of reference granted to the Ombudsman—following a clash between the Ombudsman and the Home Office over a complaint brought by a life sentence prisoner.[11]

In retrospect, the implications of this clash were far less significant than either side acknowledged at the time. The change (or clarification) to the terms of reference affected very few cases indeed. In the very different political climate since 1997, I have found no impediments to my taking up any case I choose.

That more favorable climate has been demonstrated by two major extensions of remit. In 2001, complaints by those subject to probation supervision (either as an order of the court or as part of their post-release license) were brought within my purview and the office was re-badged as Prisons and Probation Ombudsman. In principle, this quadrupled the number of people eligible to use my office as, for every one person in prison, there are around three supervised by probation (75,000 as against 210,000 in broad figures in early 2006). In practice, the workload increased much more modestly as those on probation complain much less frequently (and, it must be said, the Probation Service's complaints procedure is less well publicized and more intricate and time consuming than that of the Prison Service).

The second major extension of remit took place on April 1, 2004 when I became responsible for the investigation of all deaths (self-inflicted, natural cases, accidental, homicide) of prisoners, of the residents of probation hostels, and of those in immigration detention. In total, I conduct between 200-250 such investigations each year, and the new responsibilities have enhanced both the authority and public visibility of the office—as well as requiring a doubling of the number of staff. My independent reports into the deaths of those in the care of the state are published (in anonymized form) on my website following the Coroner's inquest. Relatively few reports are currently available, but in time they will build into a unique archive of international significance.[12]

Compared with the investigation of complaints—even complaints going to the heart of human rights in prisons such as allegations of assault or racism—investigations following a death in custody are of a different order of gravity. The investigations too tend to be on a different scale. (Even our investigations into deaths from natural causes can raise major issues about the quality of healthcare in prisons and about the moral dilemmas surrounding the early release of prisoners who are terminally ill.) But both types of investigation are ultimately about confidence in the penal system: the confidence of prisoners that they are being treated fairly and legitimately, and the confidence of the public (including that special sub-set of the public who are the bereaved relatives of prisoners who have died) that closed institutions are properly accountable for the care and decent treatment of those in their charge.

Just as mainstream ombudsmen take up the complaints of citizens, I am unashamed in saying that I take up the grievances of citizens who happen to be behind bars. Accessibility, the relevance and effectiveness of our recommendations, and working in an informal, restorative manner that best fits our purposes are as central to my work as to those of the wider ombudsman movement. Operating from a single base in London, with a small satellite in Manchester, the office has now grown to around ninety staff, divided more-or-less equally between complaints and fatal incident investigations with an administrative team in their support.[13]

During 2004-05, we received a total of 4,076 complaints about the Prison Service and 309 about probation, making a total of 4,385. In 1999-2000, the total number of complaints received was 1,937, so volumes have more than doubled in the last five years.

Our complaints investigation role encompasses most aspects of prison and probation work. The Ombudsman's office explores issues that range from allegations of physical abuse through to the state of the food and lost socks. Subjects include prison discipline, the content of reports, security categorization, decisions on early or temporary release, lost or damaged property, and visits. Some of these are matters of fundamental human rights. Others may at first sight seem petty or undeserving. But as I often point out, nothing in prison is really trivial. As those of us who have ever been inpatients in a hospital know, the minor inconveniences of life take on enormous significance in any closed institutions.

Not all prisoners make use of our services. We super-serve long-term, adult, high security male prisoners. Those serving short-term or held on remand are significantly under-represented, and women are also under-represented to a degree. However, the major correlate is not sentence length or gender, but age. Young prisoners (under twenty-one) are hugely under-represented in my caseload and juveniles (under eighteen) scarcely feature at all.

Indeed, even among adult prisoners, it is the age group thirty-five and over who are most likely to refer cases to me. I have been amused (but not surprised) to learn that the age profile of users of other ombudsmen matches my own. Complaining via hierarchical and bureaucratic complaints systems is a habit rarely learned before the onset of middle age.

Unlike some ombudsmen, I am not restricted to judging whether there has been maladministration, but may look at policy as well as practice. However, I try to assess if the professional expertise of prison and probation staff has been exercised reasonably—and do not readily substitute my opinion for that of a prison or probation officer if their decision has been reasoned and is proportionate. If a decision—say on determining a prisoner's security classification—is not unreasonable in the circumstances, I am most unlikely to overturn it notwithstanding that an alternative decision could reasonably have been made. I believe that reasonable people can reasonably disagree, and it is not my role to impose my judgement over that of someone else unless they have acted irrationally or in ignorance of relevant facts.

In common with most ombudsmen, I can only make recommendations rather than binding decisions. This has sometimes been criticized by prisoners as indicating my inferior status to that of the courts. Despite this, I have never sought the power to make enforceable decisions, believing that this would undermine the necessary accountability of Prison Service management. In any event, I prefer to work by persuasion. It may also be said that, where I do make recommendations following complaints investigation, something in the region of ninety-eight percent of them are accepted. (It is an interesting commentary on the way the authority of my office is now respected that in the early days as many as one-in-five recommendations was rejected by the Prison Service.)[14]

As what I have termed the default position, wherever possible our investigators are expected to resolve complaints informally. This has necessitated the development of new skills in negotiation and conciliation, and a shift away from paper-based decision making. As a consequence, we no longer talk a great deal about the percentage of cases that is "upheld" or "not upheld".

However, as a broad rule of thumb, about one-third of those matters we investigate are settled with a positive outcome for the prisoner.

Where a more formal investigation is required, our investigative methodologies are less determined by the penal context—and have more in common with other complaints bodies—than might first be anticipated. We ask both sides of the dispute for their account. We assess the rules and regulations. We think about what other evidence we can gather. And we try to find a solution acceptable to both parties if we can.

My judgement is that the restorative approach to problem-solving is particularly well suited to complaints in a prison context. This is partly because financial compensation is rarely appropriate unless there is direct evidence of material loss: loss of wages, loss or damage to property, etc. It is also because I am keen to break down the "them and us" mentality both between prisoners and prison staff, and between prisoners and wider authority. Settling problems by negotiation and mediation, and encouraging prisoners to see the other person's point of view, are exercises in active citizenship and chime with much other resettlement activity in the prison system.

Every nation develops its own ombudsmen arrangements—reflecting its own political, administrative, and cultural circumstances. Likewise, each nation develops its own prison monitoring system (in Latin countries, these tend to involve the judiciary to a degree unknown in Northern Europe and in countries to which Britain exported the common law tradition). My role—and that of colleagues in Northern Ireland—as a specialist ombudsman for citizens behind bars has evolved in a distinctive historical context. I certainly do not argue that it is a model that would apply willy-nilly elsewhere in the world.

That said, prisoners' utter dependence upon the state and their potential vulnerability to neglect or abuse does mean that they are a special case. It is not surprising that many generalist ombudsmen find that prisoner cases take up an increasing proportion of their time.

The types of complaints that prisoners bring may differ from the mainstream. However, the investigative methodologies that are required to assess these grievances are less specialist than might popularly be supposed. (I acknowledge, however, that my investigations are assisted by the fact that prisoners in England and Wales have access to telephones and my investigators are able to meet face to face with prisoner-complainants with a minimum of fuss.)

Temperamentally, I suspect ombudsmen are amongst the least ideological of people. But an attachment to reason, proportionality, and the rights of the citizen constitute a fundamental ideology of their own.

The ideology of my office can be summarized in two axioms. First, that decent, just, and purposeful prisons serve the interests of prisoners, the prison authorities, and society at large. And second, that the informal, restorative, non-confrontational, pro-social approach of a specialist ombudsman is peculiarly well-suited to the handling of prisoners' grievances.

Endnotes

1. For example, the Parliamentary Commissioner for Administration—to give the post of Parliamentary Ombudsman its correct title—can only accept complaints on paper, brought via a Member of Parliament, and may only assess if there has been maladministration. I can take complaints in whatever form, direct from complainants, and I am free to judge policy as well as practice. Nevertheless, BIOA categorizes only the Parliamentary Commissioner as a "true" Ombudsman.

2. British and Irish Ombudsman Association, online: <www.bioa.org.uk>.

3. A report from the organization JUSTICE in 1980 and one from the Prison Reform Trust in 1983.

4. Lord Justice Woolf & Stephen Tumim, *The Woolf Report: A Summary of the Main Findings and Recommendations of the Inquiry into Prison Disturbances* (Cm 1456) (London: HMSO, 1991) at para. 9.24.

5. *Ibid.* at para. 14.298.

6. *Ibid.* at para. 14.297.

7. *Ibid.* at para. 14.347.

8. *Custody, Care and Justice: The Way Ahead for the Prison Service England and Wales* (Cm 1647) (London: HMSO, 1991).

9. *Ibid.* at para. 8.8.

10. The present author was a pressure group activist at the time and played a significant personal role in encouraging the title Prisons Ombudsman in place of the unhappy acronym ICAP. Little did I know of the controversy that would result from the appropriation of the word "Ombudsman".

11. The Ombudsman offered an account of this episode in Chapter 1 of his Annual Report for 1996 (Prisons Ombudsman, *Annual Report 1996* (Cm 3687) (London: Prisons Ombudsman for England and Wales, 1996), online: Prisons and Probation Ombudsman <www.ppo.gov.uk /annureps.htm>). See also Stephen Livingstone & Tim Owen, *Prison Law*, 2d ed. (Oxford: Oxford University Press, 1999) at 42-47.

12. Prisons and Probation Ombudsman for England and Wales, online: <www.ppo.gov.uk>.

13. I aspire to a more regionalized operation. However, it is important to note that, unlike in many countries, the Prison Service in England and Wales is a national service operated by central government. Local government has no role.

14. Prisons Ombudsman, *Six Monthly Report* (London: Prisons Ombudsman for England and Wales, 1995).

THE ENGAGED OMBUDSMAN—MORALITY AND ACTIVISM IN ATTAINING ADMINISTRATIVE JUSTICE

Gregory J. Levine*

Généralement, on considère l'ombudsman parlementaire ou législatif comme une tierce personne qui mène des enquêtes de manière impartiale et qui tente d'apporter une solution aux plaintes émanant du public par rapport à l'administration publique. Dans cet article, nous proposons que cette perception est à la fois correcte et incomplète. Nous analysons la signification des notions de neutralité et d'impartialité à la lumière de celles de moralité et d'activisme qui sont inhérentes à la fonction d'ombudsman. Cet article soutient que l'implication intellectuelle et morale de l'ombudsman dans les débats, les enquêtes et les rapports qu'il effectue est un aspect essentiel de son rôle dans une démocratie parlementaire. Nous soutenons également que c'est grâce à ses prises de position intellectuelles et sociales dans le cadre de ses enquêtes que l'ombudsman peut agir, au nom du public, sur les structures administratives et y apporter des changements.

****

La concepción tradicional del ombudsman legislativo o parlamentario como un tercero neutral, que investiga en forma imparcial, trata de resolver e informa sobre quejas contra la administración pública, es en cierta medida una definición exacta pero no es completa. Este artículo analiza el significado de la neutralidad e imparcialidad del ombudsman sobre la base de la moralidad y el activismo inherentes en el papel del ombudsman. Propone que la participación

*Ph.D., Barrister and Solicitor, London, Ontario. A version of this paper was first presented in the Law and Society Series at Green College, University of British Columbia, February 2005. A version was also presented at the Conference of the Forum of Canadian Ombudsman in May 2005.

intelectual y moral del ombudsman, a través del debate, la investigación y la información, tiene una importancia crítica en una democracia parlamentaria. Este artículo postula que el ombudsman, con su accionar intelectual, investigador e interpretativo, logra los cambios necesarios al hacer participar al público y a las instituciones.

The parliamentary or legislative ombudsman is typically portrayed as a neutral third party who impartially investigates, attempts to resolve, and reports on complaints about public administration. This view, while undoubtedly correct, is neither simply apprehended nor complete. Neutrality in the form of non-partisanship and impartiality cannot and ought not to mean being amoral in the face of injustice. Ombudsmen are supposed to be people of good judgement and credibility—visible and accessible to the public and open to a range of possibilities and projects which will enhance their abilities to effect meaningful and just complaint resolution. There are individual and social wrongs which call out for systemic understanding and activist resolution. What follows is an exploration of the meaning of neutrality and impartiality in the context of ombudsman legislation which in its wording and structure requires moral, albeit rational, analysis and humane, yet pragmatic, action.

It is my thesis that intellectual and moral engagement through debate, investigation, and report are critical to the role of the ombudsman in a parliamentary democracy. Neutrality and impartiality must not be seen as indifference nor can they permit disregard for injustice. Justice is the ombudsman's calling and responsibility and the ombudsman in Canadian provincial legislation is given an awesome ambit to help administrative agencies see that justice is done.

The Role of the Ombudsman

The role of the ombudsmen in the parliamentary model established in nine Canadian provinces and one territory is to investigate complaints about public administration, to opine on any improper administrative actions, and to recommend changes where it is appropriate to do so. This is a truly profound responsibility, one which ought not to be approached either lightly or with timidity.

To appreciate the role it is useful to briefly consider the legislative expression of the role and its demands. Because they are clear examples of the classical model of ombudsman and because they are the guiding ombudsman legislation in two provinces of Canada which have had a profound and rich experience in the world of ombudsmanship,[1] it is instructive to consider the British Columbia and Ontario *Ombudsman Acts*.[2] Sections 10 and 23 of the *Ombudsman Act* of British Columbia and sections 14 and 21 of the *Ombudsman Act* of Ontario outline the investigative and reporting role of the ombudsman in the provinces. Sections 10 and 14 state the key investigative role. Section 10 of the *B.C. Act* indicates in part:

> 10 (1) The Ombudsman, with respect to a matter of administration, on a complaint or on the Ombudsman's own initiative, may investigate
> (a) a decision or recommendation made,
> (b) an act done or omitted, or
> (c) a procedure used
> by an authority that aggrieves or may aggrieve a person.

Section 14 of the Ontario *Act* states in part:

> (1) The function of the Ombudsman is to investigate any decision or recommendation made or any act done or omitted in the course of the administration of a governmental organization and affecting any person or body of persons in his, her or its personal capacity.
>
> (2) The Ombudsman may make any such investigation on a complaint made to him or her by any person affected or by any member of the Assembly to whom a complaint is made by any person affected, or of the Ombudsman's own motion.

While the Ontario statute is a bit more explicit about the role, both statutes convey that the core role of ombudsmen is to investigate complaints about administrative actions involving governmental entities or public bodies. The authorities or governmental organizations over which either Ombudsman has jurisdiction vary but the center, the heart, of their activity is to investigate administrative actions which may affect someone. Administrative actions of course are those actions which apply law and legally-derived policy and regulation to specific situations.[3]

Both Ombudsmen are empowered to investigate on their own motion or own initiative. This is a significant power, the empirical use of which is not always easy to chart. It is a clue, though, to the significance of the ombudsman role as a seeker of administrative justice. It implies that the ombudsman is to be a keen watcher of administrative action and that the ombudsman will have the ability and fortitude to proceed on his or her own when confronted with a situation which may be administratively inappropriate.

Section 23 of the B.C. *Act* and section 21 of the Ontario *Act* contain administrative justice codes of great intellectual and humane breadth. They guide the ombudsman investigative process, require the Ombudsman to state opinions where there is wrongdoing, and allow him or her to make recommendations.

Section 23 of the B.C. *Act* states:

23(1) If, after completing an investigation, the Ombudsman is of the opinion that
(a) a decision, recommendation, act or omission that was the subject matter of the investigation was
(i) contrary to law,
(ii) unjust, oppressive or improperly discriminatory,
(iii) made, done or omitted under a statutory provision or other rule of law or practice that is unjust, oppressive or improperly discriminatory,
(iv) based wholly or partly on a mistake of law or fact or on irrelevant grounds or consideration,
(v) related to the application of arbitrary, unreasonable or unfair procedures, or
(vi) otherwise wrong,
(b) in doing or omitting an act or in making or acting on a decision or recommendation, an authority
(i) did so for an improper purpose,
(ii) failed to give adequate and appropriate reasons in relation to the nature of the matter, or
(iii) was negligent or acted improperly, or
(c) there was unreasonable delay in dealing with the subject matter of the investigation,
the Ombudsman must report that opinion and the reasons for it to the authority and may make the ombudsman considers appropriate.

(2) Without restricting subsection (1), the Ombudsman may recommend that
(a) a matter be referred to the appropriate authority for further consideration,
(b) an act be remedied,
(c) an omission or delay be rectified,
(d) a decision or recommendation be cancelled or changed,
(e) reasons be given,
(f) a practice, procedure or course of conduct be altered,
(g) an enactment or other rule of law be reconsidered, or
(h) any other steps be taken.

Section 21 of the Ontario *Act* states:

21. (1) This section applies in every case where, after making an investigation under this Act, the Ombudsman is

of opinion that the decision, recommendation, act or omission which was the subject-matter of the investigation,
(a) appears to have been contrary to law;
(b) was unreasonable, unjust, oppressive, or improperly discriminatory, or was in accordance with a rule of law or a provision of any Act or a practice that is or may be unreasonable, unjust, oppressive, or improperly discriminatory;
(c) was based wholly or partly on a mistake of law or fact; or
(d) was wrong.

(2) This section also applies in any case where the Ombudsman is of opinion that in the making of the decision or recommendation, or in the doing or omission of the act, a discretionary power has been exercised for an improper purpose or on irrelevant grounds or on the taking into account of irrelevant considerations, or that, in the case of a decision made in the exercise of any discretionary power, reasons should have been given for the decision.

(3) If in any case to which this section applies the Ombudsman is of opinion,
(a) that the matter should be referred to the appropriate authority for further consideration;
(b) that the omission should be rectified;
(c) that the decision or recommendation should be cancelled or varied;
(d) that any practice on which the decision, recommendation, act or omission was based should be altered;
(e) that any law on which the decision, recommendation, act or omission was based should be reconsidered;
(f) that reasons should have been given for the decision or recommendation; or
(g) that any other steps should be taken,

the Ombudsman shall report his or her opinion, and the reasons therefor, to the appropriate governmental organization, and may make such recommendations as he or she thinks fit and the Ombudsman may request the governmental organization to notify him or her, within a specified time, of the steps, if any, that it proposes to take to give effect to his or her recommendations and the

> Ombudsman shall also send a copy of his or her report and recommendations to the minister concerned.

These are codes of immense moral magnitude. They are inspiring statements of administrative justice and they constitute challenges to any ombudsman to be creative and concerned. They require the issuance of opinions where an ombudsman sees wrongdoing. Here is not the place for an exegesis of each part and phrase[4] but it is critical to understand the generosity of spirit and moral expanse of these codes. They demand that ombudsmen opine on substantive and procedural wrongs and they use words and phrases of immense power such as "unjust", "oppressive", and "improperly discriminatory".

Clearly the Ombudsmen in both provinces are expected to bring good and moral judgement to bear and, where circumstances warrant, to act on their own initiative. Yet the conventional wisdom is that they are to be neutral, impartial, and reactive.

Impartiality, Neutrality, and Independence

That ombudsmen should be neutral, impartial, and independent comes from administrative law principles, statute, and ombudsman lore and literature.[5] The statutes provide a clue to these ideals, particularly respecting the appointment process, the term of office, and remuneration for the work.

Sections 2, 3, and 4 of the B.C. *Ombudsman Act*, for example, state:

> 2 (1) On the recommendation of the Legislative Assembly, the Lieutenant Governor must appoint as an officer of the Legislature an Ombudsman to exercise the powers and perform the duties assigned to the Ombudsman under this Act.
> (2) The Legislative Assembly must not recommend a person to be appointed Ombudsman unless a special committee of the Legislative Assembly has unanimously recommended to the Legislative Assembly that the person be appointed.
> 3 (1) The Ombudsman must be appointed for a term of 6 years and may be reappointed in the manner provided in section 2 for further 6 year terms.
> (2) The Ombudsman must not hold another office or engage in other employment.
> 4 (1) The Ombudsman is entitled to be paid, out of the consolidated revenue fund, a salary equal to the salary paid to the chief judge of the Provincial Court.

The appointment process is seen as significant because the Ombudsman must be unanimously recommended by a special committee of the Legislative

Assembly and, except in some extraordinary circumstance, such a committee will be comprised of representatives of all parties with members in the Assembly. This is said to ensure some sort of neutrality between parties and perspectives. Also, the person is actually appointed by the Lieutenant Governor, not the Lieutenant Governor in Council and so there is an appropriate distance from the government of the day.

The term of office is significant because six years is longer than any government can hold power by constitutional convention. Now, with B.C.'s fixed election dates, the term of office of a government is only four years.[6] Ostensibly, then, the Ombudsman is not beholden to the government which holds power at the time of appointment.

The condition of office that the Ombudsman must not be engaged in outside employment is also important for avoiding conflict of interest and bias. It reinforces notions of both neutrality and impartiality.

Setting the level of remuneration to a level of that of a judge is an indicator of importance and independence, that the Ombudsman is to be reckoned with, and to be respected as a senior public official. It is also a way to avoid salary-related pressure being brought to bear and to eliminate compromises and biases which could come from having negotiated salaries.

Ontario's system is somewhat different and one might argue that, at least theoretically, the Ombudsman of Ontario is in a weaker or less independent position. Sections 2 through 6 state in part:

> 2. There shall be appointed, as an officer of the Legislature, an Ombudsman to exercise the powers and perform the duties prescribed by this Act.
>
> 3. The Ombudsman shall be appointed by the Lieutenant Governor in Council on the address of the Assembly.
>
> 4. (1) Subject to subsection (2), the Ombudsman shall hold office for a term of five years and may be reappointed for a further term or terms, but is removable at any time for cause by the Lieutenant Governor in Council on the address of the Assembly.
>
> 5. (1) The Ombudsman shall devote himself or herself exclusively to the duties of the Ombudsman's office and shall not hold any other office under the Crown or engage in any other employment.
> (2) The *Public Service Act* does not apply to the Ombudsman.

6. (1) The Ombudsman shall be paid a salary to be fixed by the Lieutenant Governor in Council.
(2) The salary of the Ombudsman shall not be reduced except on address of the Assembly.

One might say that, because there is no all party recommendation system as in B.C., because the term of office is shorter, and because the salary is fixed by cabinet (although not reducible by cabinet), the Ontario Ombudsman's independence and neutrality may be seen to be somewhat compromised. Still, there are safeguards on salary and disentanglement of the Ombudsman which buttress the ideas of independence and impartiality.

Administrative law principles would also indicate that the ombudsman should not only be an advocate of fairness but be a model of it. Fairness has many meanings and there are substantive and procedural components. However, at a minimum, it incorporates the procedural ideals of natural justice which are that no one should be a judge in his or her own cause (the rule against bias) and that one should be able to know the case against him or herself.[7] The ombudsman is to be an impartial investigator and cannot carry into investigations of complaints preconceptions and prejudgements about specific cases. Nor can the ombudsman be a political advocate in the sense of favoring some political party in the legislature. The ombudsman must exude neutrality and impartiality in some sense.

But the justice codes coupled with the ability to investigate on one's own initiative appear to demand something else, something intensely engaged, something moral and activist. But what does it mean to speak of engagement, morality, and activism in a context of neutrality and impartiality and are they so antagonistic or contrary that they cannot be reconciled?

Engagement—Preliminary Thoughts

To be engaged is to be involved, to be bound up in something, or to be morally committed to it.[8] It is about being part of something and about contributing to it. Ombudsmen are in and of society writ large and are elements of democracy more narrowly.

There is a rich and growing literature on civic, civil, and citizen engagement. There are also growing organizations and movements within civil society which challenge and enhance people's ability to participate in their own governance and to help them hold government accountable for its actions and be responsive to citizen initiative. Engagement projects such as the Saguaro Seminar at Harvard attempt to "develop a handful of far-reaching, actionable ideas to significantly increase Americans' connectedness to one another and to community institutions."[9] Many universities and other public agencies are creating engagement initiatives to encourage citizen participation in all levels of government and governance.

The engagement effort throughout North America in general and in

Canada in particular is the result of an awareness that there has been a disconnect between government and those whom they govern.[10] For governments to function effectively and fairly, citizen involvement and citizen trust must be encouraged and recouped.

Citizen trust is ostensibly enhanced by accountability mechanisms particularly in democratic regimes where such instruments help bridge the gulf between government and citizen. Yet such so-called horizontal mechanisms as ombudsmen and comptrollers may share the distrust and alienation from which government generally suffers.[11] There have been calls to develop social accountability or vertical accountability mechanisms in which engaged citizens participate in decision-making processes at varying levels in those processes.[12]

It is submitted that engagement of ombudsmen is necessary partly to restore public access to and trust in governance processes but also to enhance ombudsman purposefulness and effectiveness. Engagement is, as argued above, inherent in the ombudsman calling.

Engagement in the ombudsman context encompasses morality (concern with right and wrong behavior and concern with others) and activism (visibility and credibility). The ombudsman is called on to consider great questions of right and wrong, albeit often in what seem like ordinary and even banal circumstances. The ombudsman must surely address such questions with integrity and thoroughness of purpose and method. Beyond that, however, to gain and enhance credibility as an investigator and resolver of problems, the ombudsman must be accessible and visible, that is, engaged. Engagement calls for moral commitment and for activism.

Morality and Ethics

To discuss morality and ethics is to encounter a very large topic, indeed one which is the quintessence of humanity. The purpose here is not to propose a theory of either ethics or morality or to create a meta-theory or meta-ethics although it is readily acknowledged that a theory of morality and ethics codes devised from such theory is useful for guiding action generally and public policy development specifically.[13] Nor is the purpose here to analyze the many theories of moral development such as command theories, natural law theory, utilitarianism, and the like.[14] Rather the purpose here is to outline some basic notions to help elucidate the ombudsman role which, after all, is about righting wrongs.

Morality is about judgement—the "judgment that provides critical control over present action."[15] Morality guides conduct. It entails judgements about value, virtue, and conduct.[16] Morality may be seen as necessary for social life because to be a member of a community is to have the obligations of fellowship, social responsibility, and justice in the form of fair treatment.[17]

Morality may be seen as reasoned or intuitive. It may be seen as reflexive but, more importantly and cogently, as reflected and refracted wisdom with which one encounters the world.[18] It may also be seen as rational, as a logical outcome of striving for right, and as a product of reason.[19]

Morality and ethical development may be seen as religious and spiritual.[20] Certainly the historical roots of moral consciousness are intimately bound with the religious impulse, the religious imagination, and the religious apprehension and awe of the other.

Morality is also contingent, contextual, cultural, and historical.[21] This is not to say that it is ephemeral or relative or totally subjective. Rather it is to say that understanding grows through encounter, through appraisal, and through activity. It has been said that "moral consideration is context sensitive" and that features or aspects of morality are only determined ultimately in particular instances or cases.[22] Moreover, morality and knowledge are intimately bound—knowledge of others and of situations requires moral capacities such as emotional intelligence, imagination, and sensitivity.[23] Each moment presents opportunities for, and indeed requires, appraisal and action.

The moral is often seen as the good or the right. It can be about right doing, as opposed to wrongdoing, although it is acknowledged that the pursuit of evil could be seen as a moral stance.

The ombudsman is about righting wrongs, about helping people to do so. It exudes the rational-based approach to moral growth and change. It is about the rational apprehension of the facts through investigation and reasoned discussion of those facts and circumstances.[24] Its justice code contains morally charged, often age old ideas and ideals which are subjected to circumstantial and factual interpretation.

The ombudsman plan is a rationally-based approach to moral evaluation. Yet it too contains an element of the reflexive. This is why early literature on the ombudsman plan called for people of good and sound judgement to be appointed ombudsman.[25] It is also why the justice codes contain the possibility of finding something to be simply "wrong".[26] Such a finding will depend on the disposition of the ombudsman, and the ombudsman's moral commitment and reflexivity. An ombudsman will not achieve moral perfection but a realistic and caring ombudsman will act through an integrity which exudes "[f]lexible, imaginative, and committed judgment."[27]

The ombudsman plan also creates a legal and moral obligation to act where he or she sees wrongdoing in public administration. The *Ombudsman Acts* of B.C. and Ontario, for instance, indicate that where he or she is of the opinion that a wrong has occurred he or she must report that to the authority or public body. Of course, an ombudsman may never find wrongdoing especially if his or her disposition is not to do so. Also, an ombudsman may constantly try to settle matters and so never get to the formal point of reporting especially if his or her proclivity is to avoid speaking out. It is submitted though that the morality of the ombudsman requires speaking out where there is wrong which cannot be readily rectified. Any ombudsman who chooses to turn a blind eye or who uses some of the tool kit of the ombudsman plan to persistently avoid reporting runs afoul of the law, purpose, and morality of the ombudsman plan. The ombudsman must act, it is a moral and legal duty.

There are essentially two moral duties of an ombudsman—to act with conscience and to act when wrongdoing is apparent.

Activism

Activism has many connotations, some of them negative. It is submitted that to be effective, to be credible, and, hence, to fulfill moral and legal obligations, the ombudsman must be active and activist. Effectiveness and credibility rely, of course, on skilled investigation, interpretive sensibility, integrity, sensitivity, and compassion. One may practice these things and have these characteristics but still not achieve full effectiveness. To be effective, it is submitted, ombudsmen must act from a reservoir of moral capital[28] which itself is fostered by activity and activism in the cause of fairness.

Activism in the judicial sphere has been the subject of much speculation and criticism.[29] The heart of the critique is that judges are making decisions pursuant to their own political positions, that is, that they are using the bench to forward the agendas of elites and those to whom they ostensibly owe allegiance. It is submitted that the critique is ill-founded in the Canadian legal arena.[30]

Activism in the sense of using one's office which is to be impartial and independent to further one's own agenda, be it financial, political, or other personal interest, would be clearly problematic. This is not the sense in which an ombudsman ought to be activist.

An activist in common parlance is one who pursues a policy or practice of direct, vigorous action in the pursuit of his or her goals.[31] An ombudsman is given legislated goals of investigating and reporting on complaints about public administration. As noted above, Ombudsmen in B.C. and Ontario are given the power to initiate investigations on their own. This is a call to watch and to pursue. At its most basic, activism in the ombudsman context means the vigorous pursuit of administrative justice. This, in turn, implies being keenly aware of the social fabric and societal situation in which the ombudsman operates. It implies a willingness to undertake investigation and to report when circumstances demand it. It also implies developing the credibility to be able to effect change and, as a corollary, this implies the public presence to command respect and to be able to serve the public.

Visibility, Reporting, Debating, and Outreach—Intellectual Action

The ombudsman plans in both B.C. and Ontario give the Ombudsmen of those provinces powerful tools to be constructively visible as well as to encourage change through publicity. The Ombudsman of B.C. may make special reports to the legislature and may make public reports at his or her own discretion and the Ombudsman of Ontario may report to the legislature when there has been no response to his or her investigatory reports.[32] Publicity may be used to mobilize shame such that administrative agencies will change practices or minimally resolve particular complaints.[33] Most ombudsman work is done in confidence and in private but there are these publicity possibilities which, used prudently but forthrightly, will enhance the credibility and visibility of the ombudsmen. To be seen to be thoughtfully appraising administrative problems will enhance the offices immeasurably. Conversely, to publicize trivialities will harm the offices in untold ways.

The ombudsmen statutes in these provinces do not have education or outreach sections. Yet it is well understood that education and outreach are important both to encourage administrators and the public to think about fairness and to prevent unfairness from occurring.

The ombudsmen statutes do not direct the Ombudsmen to discuss codes and checklists, yet they have done so. The Ombudsmen of both B.C. and Ontario have published their own interpretations of the justice codes within their respective statutes.[34] Such efforts are important for outreach and education but also for establishing standards by which the public may not only measure public administration but the efforts of the ombudsmen themselves.

To be effective, ombudsmen must be active in their communities. They must be promoters of ideals of administrative justice however they conceive of them. They have an office which allows them to contribute intellectually and pragmatically to the life of their communities.

Investigative Action

Forms of ombudsman investigation also permit an activist strand which may be both informative and transformative. Being able to investigate on their own initiative, the Ombudsmen of B.C. and Ontario have the capacity to enlarge their investigative scope. They need not be confined to the resolution of each particular complaint, they may see complaints together as parts of systems, and they may choose to look at complaints in a broad way.

A systems approach to ombudsman work allows for the identification of causes of complaints and allows for preventative and not only reactive work to be done.[35] Such an approach expands the role of the ombudsman while adhering to legislated tasks and jurisdiction.

A corollary of the systems approach is that it enhances individual complaints resolution by the encouragement of thinking and acting systemically and holistically.[36] A systemic approach to investigation sees individual complaints in larger contexts and is sensitive to the context in trying to effect change.

An enlarged appreciation of the role of the ombudsman is part of both a sense of the obligatory role of the ombudsman and the way an ombudsman may be more active in striving to ensure fair public administration.

Interpretive Action

The Ombudsmen in both provinces are called on to interpret circumstances in light of the justice codes within the ombudsman legislation in each province. As noted above, these Ombudsmen have created interpretive guides. These guides are suggestive, although not necessarily determinative, in each case. But ombudsmen must form their own opinions of circumstances and this in turn informs future interpretations which may be set down in documents such as interpretive guides and in reports.

Interpretation and investigation are in constant dialogue. New understandings emerge with new situations. New situations cry out for new solutions and imaginative renderings of established principles. This constant movement has the potential to inform ideas of administrative justice and to move social understandings of justice ideals in many ways. Ombudsman opinions have the potential to be an important source of law.[37]

In taking seriously the legal and moral obligation to opine when wrongdoing occurs, the ombudsman will help move the boundaries of administrative justice through interpretive activism.

Towards Ombudsman Engagement

If one conceptualizes the ombudsman plan as merely a receptacle of public complaints about which the ombudsman may respond when the urge moves him or her to do so, then one denies the potential of the ombudsman plan. Similarly when one sees the ombudsman as a siphon or safety valve for public distress and complaint, then one denies the value of the powers and obligations embedded in ombudsman legislation.

Seeing the ombudsman as encountering and imbuing moral consideration and commitment to the promotion and attainment of justice fulfills the intent of ombudsman legislation and provides the promise of a truly useful administrative justice mechanism. The ombudsman must make moral judgements and has the moral obligation not to shirk judgements. The ombudsman is called to consider and opine on matters of justice both great and small and through this calling there is great potential to contribute to society through intellectual, investigative, and interpretive activism.

Neutral and impartial in respect to complainants and authorities over whom he or she has jurisdiction, the ombudsman must be engaged, must understand the morality of justice, and must fulfill the moral obligation to act in the face of injustice. Independent in form, the ombudsman must be independent in spirit, guided by a sense of justice, compassion, and concern. So it is that the ombudsman should not shy away from engagement but rather should embrace it and encourage it.

Endnotes

1. The offices of the B.C. and Ontario Ombudsmen have long played an important role among such offices in Canada and indeed in the world. Case law involving both statutes has proven very important in the development of ombudsmanship in Canada and the Commonwealth (*e.g.* see *British Columbia Development Corporation v. British Columbia (Ombudsman)*, [1984] 2 S.C.R. 447; *Re Ombudsman of Ontario and Health Disciplines Board of Ontario et al.* (1979), 26 O.R. (2d) 105 (C.A.); *Re Ombudsman of Ontario and Ontario Labour Relations Board* (1986), 58 O.R. (2d) 225 (C.A.)).

2. R.S.B.C. 1996, c. 340 [B.C. *Ombudsman Act*]; R.S.O. 1990, c. O.6 [Ontario *Ombudsman Act*].

3. *Re Manitoba Language Rights Reference*, [1992] 1 S.C.R. 212.

4. For discussion and comparison of these codes, see G.J. Levine "Administrative Justice and the Ombudsman – Concepts and Codes in British Columbia and Ontario" (2004) 17 Can. J. Admin. L. & Prac. 239.

5. Neutrality in the form of nonpartisanship, impartiality in the sense of being unbiased or personally disinterested, independent in the sense of being empowered enough to act as one deems best, and, indeed, freedom to act nonpartisanly and in an unbiased fashion have long been acknowledged as core attributes of the classical, legislative ombudsman. For example, see Committee on the Concept of an Ombudsman, *Report of the Committee on the Concept of an Ombudsman* (Ottawa: Government of Canada, 1977) at 8 and, more recently, see American Bar Association, "Special Report: Ombuds Standards" (2002) 54 Admin. L. Rev. 535 at 560. With respect to the linking of the ideas of independence and impartiality see the clear and cogent discussion of Dean M. Gotterher and Michael Hostina, "Essential Characteristics of a Classical Ombudsman," online: United States Ombudsman Association <http://usombudsman.org/en/references/more_references/essential_characteristics.cfm> at A. For a discussion of the linking of independence to freedom of thought as well as to the exercise of moral authority, see M. Daniel Jacoby, *Le Protecteur du Citoyen* (Trois-Pistoles: Édition Trois-Pistoles, 1998) at 24-27.

6. *Constitution (Fixed Election Dates) Amendment Act*, S.B.C. 2001, c. 36.

7. David Phillip Jones & Anne S. de Villars, *Principles of Administrative Law*, 4th ed. (Toronto: Carswell, 2004).

8. *The Concise Oxford Dictionary*, 7th ed., *s.v.* “engagement”.

9. See online: The Saguaro Seminar: Civic Engagement in America <http://www.ksg.harvard.edu/saguaro/>.

10. Miriam Wyman, David Shulman & Laurie Ham, *Learning to Engage: Experiences with Civic Engagement in Canada* (Ottawa: Canadian Policy Research Networks, 1999) at 5-7.

11. William Reuben, “The Role of Civic Engagement and Social Accountability in the Governance Equation” (March 2003) Social Development Notes, Note No. 75, online: The World Bank <http://www.worldbank.org>.

12. *Ibid.* For a discussion of the idea of social accountability, see Carmen Malena, Reiner Forster & Janmejay Singh, “Social Accountability: An Introduction to the Concept and Emerging Practice” (December 2004) Social Development Papers: Participation and Civic Engagment, Paper No. 76, online: The World Bank <http://www.worldbank.org>.

13. Tom Sorell, *Moral Theory and Anomaly* (Malden, Mass.: Blackwell, 2000) at 3-5.

14. There is a huge literature on these ideas. Useful overviews are found in Mark Timmons, *Moral Theory: An Introduction* (Lanham, Md.: Rowman & Littlefield Publishers, 2002) and Anthony Weston, *A 21st Century Ethical Toolbox* (New York: Oxford University Press, 2001).

15. Jonathan Lieberson, “Why Should We Be Moral?” in Arthur L. Caplan & Daniel Callahan, eds., *Ethics in Hard Times* (New York: Plenum Press, 1981) 47 at 75.

16. Wilfrid J. Waluchow, *The Dimensions of Ethics: An Introduction to Ethical Theory* (Peterborough, Ont.: Broadview Press, 2003) at ch. 2.

17. See A.J.M. Milne, *Ethical Frontiers of the State: An Essay in Political Philosophy* (New York: St. Martin’s Press, 1998) at 41.

18. Francisco J. Varela, *Ethical Know-How: Action, Wisdom, and Cognition* (Stanford, Cal.: Stanford University Press, 1999) at Lecture 1.

19. For example, see *supra* note 15. See also, Timmons, *supra* note 14 at ch. 7 for a discussion of Kant’s moral theory.

20. Weston, *supra* note 14 at ch. 2.

21. For example, see Don E. Marietta, *Beyond Certainty: A Phenomenological Approach to Moral Reflection* (Lanham, Md.: Lexington Books, 2004) at ch. 4.

22. Daniel Patrone, *Leaving Morality Where It Is: Contingency and the Particularistic Approach to Morality* (New York: Lexington Books, 2005) at 136.

23. Terry Eagleton, *After Theory* (New York: Basic Books, 2003) at 132.

24. B.C. *Ombudsman Act, supra* note 2, ss. 14-15 (seen in relation to s. 23).

25. Donald C. Rowat, *The Ombudsman: Citizen's Defender* (London: George Allen & Unwin, 1968).

26. B.C. *Ombudsman Act, supra* note 2, s. 23; Ontario *Ombudsman Act, supra* note 2. The ombudsman must see wrong in a variety of manifestations, legal and otherwise. For a discussion of legal wrong in the context of wrongs seen more broadly which also sees law as reflective of morality, see A.D. Woozley, "Law and the Legislation of Morality" in Arthur L. Caplan & Daniel Callahan, eds., *Ethics in Hard Times* (New York: Plenum Press, 1981) 143.

27. See J. Patrick Dobel, *Public Integrity* (Baltimore, Md.: Johns Hopkins University Press, 1999) at 65.

28. For a discussion of this concept, see John Kane, *The Politics of Moral Capital* (New York: Cambridge University Press, 2001). Four factors help develop moral capital—cause, action, example, and symbolism. It is submitted that each of these is important in ombudsmanship.

29. For example, see Christopher P. Manfredi, *Judicial Power and the Charter: Canada and the Paradox of Liberal Constitutionalism*, 2d ed. (Toronto, Ont.: Oxford University Press, 2001). For a response to an empirical analysis of Manfredi and others' views on the role of the court, see also Christopher P. Manfredi & James B. Kelly, "Misrepresenting the Supreme Court's Record? A Comment on Sujit Choudhry and Claire E. Hunter, "Measuring Judicial Activism on the Supreme Court of Canada"" (2004) 49 McGill L.J. 741.

30. For example, see Kent Roach, *The Supreme Court on Trial: Judicial Activism or Democratic Dialogue* (Toronto: Irwin Law, 2001). For an empirical view of the activism question, see Sujit Choudhry & Claire E. Hunter, "Measuring Judicial Activism on the Supreme Court of Canada: A Comment on Newfoundland (Treasury Board) v. NAPE" (2003) 48 McGill L.J. 525 and their article "Continuing the Conversation: A Reply to Manfredi and Kelly" (2004) 49 McGill L.J. 765.

31. *Gage Canadian Dictionary* 1997, *s.v.* "activist".

32. B.C. *Ombudsman Act*, *supra* note 2, s. 31(3); Ontario *Ombudsman Act*, *supra* note 2, s. 21(4).

33. Philip Giddings, "The Future of the Ombudsman" in Roy Gregory & Philip Giddings, eds., *Righting Wrongs: The Ombudsman in Six Continents* (Amsterdam: IOS Press, 2000) 464.

34. Office of the Ombudsman (British Columbia), *Code of Administrative Justice 2003* (March 2003) Public Report No. 42; Ombudsman Ontario, *Opinions and Recommendations Statement* (1996).

35. Stephen Owen, "The Expanding Role of the Ombudsman in the Administrative State" (1990) 40 U.T.L.J. 670 at 675. An interesting example of a broad system assessment is provided by former Ombudsman Stephen Owen's investigation into the practices of the Workers' Compensation Board of British Columbia (see Office of the Ombudsman, *Workers' Compensation Board (No. 3)* (1987) Special Report 15). An interesting, current Ontario example of a broad investigation which traces problems and makes suggestions for change is that of Ombudsman André Marin into the municipal property assessment system and the provincial agency responsible for it (Office of the Ontario Ombudsman, *Getting It Right: Investigation into the Transparency of the Property Assessment Process and the Integrity and Efficiency of the Decision-Making of the Municipal Property Assessment Corporation*, Ombudsman Report (March 2006)).

36. For example, see D. Gotterher *et al.* "Advanced Ombudsman Investigative Skills Workshop" (June 2000) held in conjunction with Joint USOA/COA Meetings, San Francisco.

37. P. Bonnor, "Ombudsmen and the Development of Public Law" (2003) 9 Eur. Public L. 237. An interesting example in the B.C. context is provided by then Ombudsman Dulcie McCallum's report on the land use decision process respecting Clayoquot Sound which called for meaningful

consultation of the government with First Nations (Office of the Ombudsman, *Administrative Fairness of the Process Leading to the Clayoquot Sound Land Use Decision* (1993) Public Report No. 31). "Meaningful consultation" as a basic requirement in aboriginal title cases (and rights cases) has found its way into the courts and indeed has been used in a critical decision of the Supreme Court of Canada. Ombudsman reports may be seen to inform and develop concepts in law and administration. Even if one cannot draw a direct line between an early idea and a subsequent use elsewhere, it is unlikely that ombudsman interpretations will be part of and will have an effect on the milieu of administrative law ideas and ideals.

WHAT SHOULD BE THE PRIMARY FOCUS OF THE OMBUDSMAN INSTITUTION? PROTECTING HUMAN RIGHTS AND REDRESSING PUBLIC GRIEVANCES VERSUS FIGHTING CORRUPTION: EMPHASIS ON SOUTH ASIA AND THE COMMONWEALTH CARIBBEAN

Najmul Abedin*

L'objectif premier de l'institution de l'ombudsman au sens original/classique (suédois) du terme est de promouvoir et de défendre les droits et libertés des individus (c'est-à-dire les droits de la personne au sens large du terme, tel qu'on l'entend de nos jours) et, afin de garantir la transparence et la bonne gouvernance, de résoudre les plaintes que les citoyens soumettent à propos de procédures et d'abus administratifs. Récemment, on s'est toutefois rendu compte qu'il existait des perceptions et approches relativement différentes sur le sujet: par exemple, certaines voudraient donner plus de pouvoir à l'institution de l'ombudsman pour qu'elle puisse mieux lutter contre la corruption politique et bureaucratique. Cet article compare ces nouveaux points de vue à la définition traditionnelle de l'institution de l'ombudsman, et il suggère, pour nombre de raisons, que celle-ci devrait plus mettre de l'avant son rôle original/classique.

****

El papel principal de la institución clásica y original del ombudsman en Suecia es de proteger y defender los derechos y las libertades individuales; es decir, los derechos humanos en su sentido amplio y actual. Asimismo, su función consiste en resolver las quejas del público respecto a las acciones de la burocracia, los abusos y excesos; todo ello con el fin de asegurar el buen gobierno y la transparencia. Sin embargo, existen diferentes perspectivas que provienen de escuelas de pensamiento más recientes. Una de esas escuelas sostiene fervientemente que la institución del ombudsman debe tener el poder de luchar

*Professor, Department of Public Management, Austin Peay State University, Clarksville, Tennessee, U.S.A.

contra la corrupción política y burocrática. Este artículo analiza las perspectivas de dos escuelas de pensamiento y sostiene que, debido a muchas razones, la institución del ombudsman debería concentrarse en su papel original.

Over the years varying views and ideas of the role of the ombudsman institution have emerged. There are a number of schools of thought that are different, in varying degrees, from the original or classical school. One such school is strongly in favor of empowering this institution for fighting political and/or bureaucratic corruption—a radical departure from the classical approach. This paper examines and weighs, on a comparative basis, the arguments of these two schools of thought.

The Classical Ombudsman Institution

The salient features of the original/classical (Swedish) Ombudsman model are outlined below for a useful and meaningful comparison with those of another model that has been evolving lately. In democratic societies the ombudsman, who is not a member of the legislature or Parliament, usually acts as a legislative or "parliamentary agent to defend the law against official abuses affecting the interests of individuals."[1] He or she is "someone to whom any citizen may take complaints about actions of the people in government services. The Ombudsman will listen, examine and try to obtain redresses of an injustice or amends for a grievance."[2] He can also act on his own initiative. It has been pointed out by some authorities (notably by the International Bar Association), that the term "ombudsman" has been wrongly used in some parts of the world, particularly in the U.S.A., to mean any "complaint handling institution" whether government or non-government. The International Bar Association observes, from a strictly legalistic point of view, that the term ombudsman means:

> [1] An office provided for by the constitution or by the action of the legislature or parliament and headed by an independent high level public official who is responsible to the legislature or parliament, [2] who receives complaints from aggrieved persons against government agencies, officials and employees or who acts on his own motion and [3] who has the power to investigate, [only] recommend corrective actions and issues reports.[3]

However, long before the International Bar Association passed this resolution in 1972, a similar idea was expressed in 1965 by Donald C. Rowat, Professor Emeritus of Carleton University in Canada, a well known authority on the ombudsman system and one of the first few scholars who played a very significant role in spreading and popularizing the ombudsman idea outside Scandinavia, especially in those parts of the world where English is a primary language. His book *The Ombudsman: Citizen's Defender*[4] was the first serious book-length study of the ombudsman institution in the English language. He identified the following "three essential features" of the "original [*i.e.*, Swedish] Ombudsman system." First, "the Ombudsman is an independent and non-partisan officer of the legislature, usually provided for in the constitution, who supervises the administration." Second, "he deals with the specific complaints from the public against administrative injustice and maladministration." And, third, "he has the power to investigate, criticize and publicize, but not to reverse, administrative action." He strongly suggested that in order to avoid "public confusion," the use of the term ombudsman should remain confined only to those institutions, which have "this unique combination of characteristics."[5]

Another unique and notable feature of this process is that an ombudsman does not have the power to impose sanctions or to reverse or quash a decision or to order any official to that effect. "He relies upon criticism and publicity rather than the quashing of decisions."[6] He or she can even suggest overall changes or improvements in administrative procedures and legislation. By so doing he or she, in fact, "helps to keep the balance between the increasing encroachment of the government administration and the citizen's rights."[7]

The U.S. Ombudsman Association (USOA) also aptly points out that "since its creation the...[Swedish] ombudsman office has been the model for the public sector ombudsman," and provides the definition that is still accepted today: the ombudsman, "a public official, appointed by and responsible to parliament, was to protect human rights against the excess of the bureaucracy" and "to receive and investigate citizen's complaints against administrative acts of government,"[8] in other words, against the decisions and actions of the members of the public bureaucracy. Thus, strictly speaking, the primary responsibility of the ombudsman is to protect the "rights and liberties" (*i.e.*, human rights in a broad modern sense of the term) of the members of society against bureaucratic wrong-doing and maladministration, and to "redress...grievances of citizens against the administration."[9]

Here it may be noted that in Great Britain aggrieved persons have no direct access to the Ombudsman. All grievances have to be channeled through the Member of Parliament (MP) to whom the findings of the investigation are also reported. Such an arrangement is the outcome of the fact that the MPs in Great Britain want to fiercely safeguard their traditional role as the guardian of the rights of the citizens in their respective constituencies.[10]

Thus, the ombudsman is primarily viewed as a public defender—defender of human rights and also the defender of the public against bureaucracy. The titles of the following two studies of the ombudsman institutions clearly indicate the primary focus of this office: Donald C. Rowat's *The Ombudsman: Citizen's Defender*[11] and Walter Gellhorn's *Ombudsman and Others: Citizens' Protectors in Nine Countries*.[12] They, along with the first Danish Ombudsman Professor Hurwitz and the first New Zealand Ombudsman

Sir Guy Powles, played a significant role in popularizing the ombudsman institution outside Scandinavia.[13] His image has been presented as citizen's defender, champion or protector of human rights and liberties, guardian of law, redresser of public grievances/complaints, and so forth.[14] At the same time it should be noted that the classical ombudsman model was never intended to investigate the people's representatives, *i.e.*, Ministers and the MPs, or to fight bureaucratic and/or political corruption.

An Emerging School of Thought

With the accelerated spread of the ombudsman system across the globe, it has deviated in varying degrees from the Swedish (original/classical) model in several parts of the world. It is not surprising that Rowat indicated in the 1960s that though it was not so desirable, rapid expansion of this system would make it "all too easy to lose sight of...essential features of the original ombudsman system."[15] Hence, as noted above, in the course of the last several decades a number of schools of thought have emerged, with the primary focus or concern of one being to make ombudsmen responsible in varying degrees for fighting and eradicating corruption.

The original school of thought is still strongly in favor of maintaining the classical characteristics or salient features of the ombudsman institution, that is, protecting or defending human rights and redressing grievances or complaints against unfair bureaucratic actions or decisions in order to ensure good governance and transparency, and thus providing remedy and satisfaction to those who have suffered injustice because of maladministration or misuse of power by the bureaucracy. But it strongly opposes the idea of using the ombudsman institution as a weapon for fighting corruption. The emerging school of thought has an almost diametrically opposite view—it considers this institution as a potent weapon against corruption, a relatively recent and evolving trend.

In recent times, donor organizations like the International Monetary Fund, the World Bank, and others have strongly criticized some governments. They argue that political and bureaucratic corruption seriously undermines the development process. They are of the opinion that the office of the ombudsman should be used as one of the tools for fighting corruption.[16] Under pressure from the donor countries and organizations, a number of countries have been inclined to follow their recommendations.

Like the international donor organizations, some other organizations or commissions/committees have expressed views strongly in favor of appointing ombudsmen or providing the existing ombudsman institution with necessary powers to fight widespread corruption in public sector organizations. They want to make provisions for forfeiting unlawfully acquired property by the members of public organizations, and for investigating the actions of elected officials like the Prime Minister, Ministers, MPs, and other public functionaries. For example, Law Commissions in India and Bangladesh strongly feel that

> [i]f acts of corruption of public functionaries are kept out of the jurisdiction of the ombudsman...this institution will be virtually ineffective and will not be able to meet the expectation of the nation. So, in our view, suitable provisions should be made in the Act in order to enable the ombudsman to investigate cases of corrupt practices by public functionaries along with cases of maladministration by them.[17]

In a nutshell, the Law Commissions were in favor of providing the Ombudsman with much wider power in order to utilize this institution for fighting corruption.

The bureaucracy, as well as the political authority, in a large number of countries in the developing world is corrupt, inefficient, and slow.[18] It is also authoritarian and paternalistic in its attitude and behavior.[19] Its public accountability has been minimal or negligible[20] and the people are not politically conscious enough. In recent years there have been increasing demands for adoption of the ombudsman system in some countries as one of the tools for dealing with these problems, especially the problem of corruption.[21]

Whether the office of the ombudsman should be given the responsibility to investigate and deal with corruption is a serious matter that needs to be carefully examined. It is, however, true that with the spread of the ombudsman system to various parts of the world since the 1960s, a number of countries in South Asia (*e.g.*, Bangladesh and many states in India)[22] and elsewhere have given, or are inclined to give, considerable power to their ombudsmen to investigate corruption (although reference is also made to other roles and responsibilities). Rowat has rightly observed that some of India's state ombudsmen have "departed far from the original concept of ombudsman institution and therefore cannot be regarded as genuine ombudsman plans."[23] Although they have not been very successful in dealing with the problem of corruption, they have been geared in varying degrees to fight corruption. He further argues that they "can hardly be classed as a genuine ombudsman plan" because they are concerned with "serious allegation of misconduct or corruption rather than ordinary administrative grievances"[24]—the reason for which the office of ombudsman was originally created in Scandinavia and elsewhere.

As noted above, the ombudsman is an officer or instrument of the legislature. Therefore, an anomalous and contradictory or paradoxical situation will be created if he or she is empowered to investigate elected officials like the Prime Minister, MPs, and the like. Moreover, if he or she is provided with more or different kinds of power, then his or her role becomes similar to that of a police officer, a prosecutor, a bureau of anti-corruption, or other similar institutions, and the very essence of the original concept of the ombudsman as the defender and protector of individual rights and liberties (*i.e.*, human rights in a broad modern sense of the term) against bureaucratic actions and excesses undergoes radical transformation. If he or she is given the power to investigate corruption as well as the decisions and actions of the elected officials, then the focus of this office is lost and its style of operation changes radically. In order to investigate corruption and improper or inappropriate behavior or actions of elected officials, perhaps it is advisable to create separate offices or functionaries with strong and effective prosecutorial powers.

The following examples may be given for further illustration of these points. From 1971 to 1976, the Constitution Commission and the Joint Select Committee of the Parliament in Trinidad and Tobago examined a number of controversial issues concerning the powers and the nature of the office of the proposed Ombudsman. One issue was whether the Ombudsman should be empowered to investigate decisions made at the highest political level, *i.e.*, ministerial decisions. The Commission discussed the pros and cons of this issue in considerable detail: it observed that in Sweden where this office had originated long ago, there was no ministerial responsibility given to Parliament in the strict sense of the term. The Swedish Ministers, unlike the Ministers in the Westminster system, are not directly concerned with the day-to-day administration of Ministries or departments—they are mainly involved in planning and producing regulations and policy directions for the guidance of the members of the civil service:

> They issue and give general directions which are carried out by the civil servants who can be called to account. The civil ombudsman in Sweden is an official appointed by the Parliament to ensure that the civil service works according to the prescribed rules and that any acts of maladministration are corrected. The administrative processes of decision making are quite open.[25]

Therefore, the dilemma was how an Ombudsman would operate in the Westminster type of parliamentary (cabinet) government in Trinidad and Tobago where the Ministers were (and are) responsible and accountable to Parliament for the working of their respective Ministries. If the Ombudsman was given the power to challenge the ministerial decision, then the Minister might seem to be responsible to the Ombudsman and not to Parliament. The Constitution Commission noted that in New Zealand a solution to the problem was worked out. There, the ministerial decision is not subject to the Ombudsman's inquiry, but only the advice by senior civil servants:

> upon which he may have acted. This permits effective inquiry since it discloses whether the Minister acted only after being advised and whether he accepted or rejected the advice he was given; also it permits full investigation of the merits of any advice he may have been given. The principle of ministerial responsibility is thus preserved while at the same time allowing for thorough investigation.[26]

The New Zealand model encouraged the Constitution Commission to recommend that the Ombudsman should not be given the power to question a Minister or Parliamentary Secretary or to "intervene between the Minister and Parliament." It continued to say that:

> if in the course of his investigation it should appear that the action complained of may have resulted from a policy decision at ministerial level, he should be entitled to call for the advice tended to the Minister by his public [i.e., civil] service advisers before the decision was taken. Where the Minister accepted and acted upon the recommendations of his advisers, they can be questioned by the Ombudsman. But where the Minister did not accept their advice or acted without advice, his responsibility would be made plain and the Ombudsman would so report. This procedure preserves the basic principle of ministerial responsibility to Parliament.[27]

Perhaps it is not out of place to indicate that when the Constitution Commission asked various organizations and individuals for opinions, the Trinidad and Tobago Labor Congress went to the extent of suggesting that the Ombudsman should have the power to investigate complaints against Ministers, judges, and even their wives.

However, the Joint Select Committee and later the Parliament accepted the recommendation of the Constitution Commission. Thus, the Constitution of Trinidad and Tobago provides that in "investigating any matter leading to, and resulting from or connected with the decision of a Minister, the Ombudsman shall not inquire into or question the policy of the Minister in accordance with which the decision was made."[28] It also provides that, subject to some of its provisions, "the principal function of the Ombudsman shall be to investigate any decision or recommendation made, including any advice given or recommendation made to a Minister."[29]

Concluding Observations

As noted above, there are some who believe that the ombudsman should be empowered to investigate general "allegations of corruption in public office."[30] The Constitution Commission of Trinidad and Tobago rightly pointed out that this would be a departure from the classical concept and usual or normal role of the ombudsman. It maintained, however, that in the course of his or her investigation of a complaint of a specific injustice to a person or group of persons arising from maladministration, the Trinidad and Tobago Ombudsman "may find proof or evidence tending to provide that corruption was the cause. In such a case, in addition to recommending measures to remedy the injustice he would report his findings on corruption to the relevant authorities for continuation of the investigation and such action as may be appropriate."[31] This is very much in line with the original/classical ombudsman system. Perhaps it is not out of place to indicate that one of the universally accepted principles, as Rowat observes, is that "a genuine Ombudsman institution" is "designed to redress personal grievances" of which corruption may be an incidental or associated factor.[32]

In many developing countries corruption is so pervasive and widespread that it may be considered rather a way of life and is accepted as a part of social, economic, political, and administrative cultures and values. In some of these countries key politicians and top bureaucrats are corrupt to the backbone and rotten to the core. If the ombudsman is expected to deal with corruption, the chances are that he or she is likely to fail in varying degrees. The corrupt individuals' vital interest will be adversely affected and they will fight back tooth and nail, marginalizing the ombudsman's significance and importance and trying to discredit him or her. The ombudsman also will not receive their cooperation in performing other duties or responsibilities. Moreover, investigation of corruption requires special techniques and tools, considerable financial and human resources, and an enormous amount of time and effort. In many developing countries, the governments pay lip service to the significance of this office, but do not provide it with the necessary support and adequate financial and human resources. The following comment made in the 1970s in a developed country has relevance in varying degrees to the present situation in many developing countries:

> I do not think that it is an overstatement to say that an Ombudsman's office not properly budgeted, not properly staffed, not sufficiently independent and not properly backed by those who brought it into being, amounts to nothing more than a front and a facade. The public may well be led to believe that they have a crutch on which to lean when in fact they have nothing at all.[33]

Somewhat similar views were also expressed in the Commonwealth Caribbean.[34] It may be observed that the support and resources that are available to many ombudsmen in the developing world are not adequate to deal with a wide variety of issues like political and bureaucratic corruption.

It should also be noted that the ombudsman approach is, in fact, a different and unique type of grievance management approach. The ombudsman is a facilitator whose principal tool or approach is persuasion or mediation. He or she avoids a confrontational or adversarial relationship with the bureaucracy. Thus, it is an alternative strategy for grievance management.

As indicated above, he or she does not have the power to impose sanctions, reverse or quash an administrative policy, or order any official to that effect. The ombudsman whose "most potent weapon is an expression of his [or her] opinion" heavily "relies upon criticism and publicity rather that quashing of decision."[35] Thus, as also indicated above, the countries that want to deal with political and/or bureaucratic corruption should create a separate office or functionary with a separate name or title and with strong and effective prosecutorial powers.

Endnotes

1. Fritz Morstein Marx, "The Importance of Foreign Institutions" in Donald C. Rowat, ed., *The Ombudsman: Citizen's Defender*, 2d ed. (London: George Allen & Unwin, 1968) [Rowat, ed., *Citizen's Defender*] 256.

2. "The Principle of the Ombudsman" (1971) 52:11 Royal Bank of Canada Monthly Letter 1.

3. Bernard Frank, "The Ombudsman: Revisited" [May 1975] International Bar Journal 48 at 55. These comments by Bernard Frank, then Chairman of the Ombudsman Committee of the International Bar Association, are based on the Resolution passed by this Association.

4. Rowat, ed., *Citizen's Defender*, *supra* note 1.

5. Donald C. Rowat, "Preface to the Second Edition," in *ibid.,* v at xxiv.

6. Donald C. Rowat, "Conclusion" in Rowat, ed., *Citizen's Defender*, *ibid.* at 288.

7. *Supra* note 2 at 3.

8. U.S. Ombudsman Association (USOA), *Public Sector Ombudsman* (Dayton, Ohio: USOA, 1965?) at 1.

9. Donald C. Rowat, "The State Ombudsman in India" (1984) 30:1 Indian Journal of Public Administration 1 [Rowat, "State Ombudsman"].

10. For a better understanding of various aspects of the British ombudsman system, see Roy Gregory & Peter Hutchesson, *The Parliamentary Ombudsman: A Study in the Control of Administrative Action* (London: George Allen & Unwin, 1975) at c. 2-3. Also see Geoffrey Marshall, "The British Parliamentary Commissioner for Administration" (1968) 377 Annals of the American Academy of Political & Social Science 87 and Frank Stacey, *Ombudsman Compared* (Oxford: Clarendon Press, 1978) c. vii-ix.

11. Rowat, ed., *Citizen's Defender*, *supra* note 1.

12. Walter Gellhorn, *Ombudsman and Others: Citizens' Protectors in Nine Countries* (Cambridge, Mass.: Harvard University Press, 1966).

13. Najmul Abedin, "Transplantation of the Ombudsman Institution in Developed and Developing Countries" (1986) 300 The Round Table: The Commonwealth Journal of International Affairs 333.

14. *Supra* note 2 at 1-2.

15. See *supra* note 5.

16. For example, recently in Bangladesh there is a strong and increasing demand for establishing an office of Ombudsman with considerable powers primarily to fight corruption. Donor countries and organizations have also contributed enormously to such pressure. For discussion in detail, see Government of Bangladesh, *Public Administration for 21st Century: Report of Public Administration Reform Commission*, vol. 1 (Dhaka: Government Printing Press, 2000) at xi-xiv, c. 2, 3, 6; A.T.M. Obaidullah, *Bangladesh Public Administration* (Dhaka: Academic Press & Publishers, 1999) at 163-170; Kamal Siddiqui, *Toward Good Governance in Bangladesh: Fifty Unpleasant Essays* (Dhaka: University Press, 1996) at 107-109; Ali Ahmed, "Tackling Corruption in Administration" *The Morning Sun* [of Dhaka, Bangladesh] (March 19-20, 1991) [Ahmed, "Tackling Corruption"]; OMB_GOV@usombudsman.org (March 22, 1999 & April 20, 1999), online: United States Ombudsman Association <http://www.usombudsman.org> (OMB_GOV email provides a wide variety of information on the ombudsman institution all over the world); Nurul Kabir, "LC [Law Commission] for a Powerful Ombudsman, Law to Forfeit Illegal Assets" *The Daily Star* [of Dhaka Bangladesh] (May 8, 2000).

17. Indian Law Commission, as quoted by Law Commission of Bangladesh, as quoted in Kabir, *ibid.*

18. For example, Bangladesh: see Government of Bangladesh, *supra* note 16; Siddiqui, *supra* note 16 at 5, 22-29, 47, 65, 66, 74, 81, 83, 86, 120-130, 145; M.A. Mohaiman, "The All Pervasive Corruption" *The Bangladesh Observer* (June 26, 1991); Ahmed, *supra* note 16. See also Nobel Laureate V.S. Naipaul's account of India in *The Area of Darkness* (London: Penguin, 2001).

19. Najmul Abedin, *Local Administration and Politics in Modernizing Societies: Bangladesh and Pakistan* (New York: Oxford University Press, 1974) at c. 2.

20. For a general discussion on public accountability of bureaucracy, see M.M. Khan "Administrative Accountability in Bangladesh" (1983) 29:3 Indian Journal of Public Administration 682. See also Ali Ahmed, *Ombudsman for Bangladesh* (Dhaka: Academic Publishers, 1993) [Ahmed, *Ombudsman*]; Ali Ahmed, "Concept of Ombudsman and Bangladesh" *The Bangladesh Observer* (July 14-17, 1979) [Ahmed, "Concept of Ombudsman"].

21. Government of Bangladesh, *supra* note 16 at 90-91; Obaidullah, *supra* note 16 at 163-70; Siddiqui, *supra* note 16; Ahmed, *Ombudsman*, *ibid.*, at preface, c. 1, 5, 6; Ahmed, "Concept of Ombudsman," *ibid.*; Ahmed, "Tackling Corruption," *supra* note 16; Kabir, *supra* note 16.

22. In 1972, the Bangladesh *Constitution* made provisions for the Ombudsman institution, and the *Ombudsman Act* was passed in 1980. Since then, there has been considerable discussion concerning the rewrite of this *Act* in order to make provisions for additional powers for fighting corruption. The situation in some states in India is discussed below.

23. Rowat, "State Ombudsman," *supra* note 9 at 1.

24. Donald C. Rowat, "The Need for an Ombudsman in Developing Democracies" (1983) 29:3 Indian Journal of Public Administration 664.

25. Government of Trinidad & Tobago, *Report of the Constitution Commission* (Trinidad: Government Printer, 1974) at para. 360.

26. Constitution Commission (of Trinidad and Tobago), *Thinking Things Through* (Trinidad: Government Printer, 1972) at 95.

27. *Supra* note 25 at para. 363.

28. *Constitution of the Republic of Trinidad and Tobago* (Act No. 4 of 1976), s. 94(1).

29. *Ibid.*, s. 93(1).

30. *Supra* note 26 at 97.

31. *Ibid.; supra* note 25 at para. 364.

32. Rowat, "State Ombudsman," *supra* note 9 at 2.

33. Quoted in Ombudsman, *Fifth Annual Report (1981-82)* (Trinidad: Ombudsman's Office, 1984) at 3. This comment was made by Arthur Maloney, Q.C., a former Ombudsman of Ontario, Canada. Today, the comment may not be accurate in the context of the developed world but, as indicated above, it has relevance in varying degrees to many developing countries.

34. St. Lucia, *The Third Report of the Parliamentary Commissioner* (Castries: Parliamentary Commissioner's Office, 1987) at 3; St. Lucia, *The Fourth Report of the Parliamentary Commissioner* (Castries: Parliamentary Commissioner's Office, 1991) at 1.

35. See *supra* note 6. There is a deliberate repetition of the quote in order to emphasize the point in this context.

CONTRIBUTORS TO AND TITLES IN *THE OMBUDSMAN JOURNAL* AND *THE INTERNATIONAL OMBUDSMAN YEARBOOK* 1981-2004

Professor Mohammed Abdo
"Challenges Facing the New Ethiopian Ombudsman Institution" (2002)

Dr. Najmul Abedin
"What Should Be The Primary Focus of the Ombudsman Institution? Protecting Human Rights and Redressing Public Grievances Versus Fighting Corruption: Emphasis on South Asia and The Commonwealth Caribbean" (2004)

Dr. Stanley V. Anderson
"The Prison Work of the New Zealand Ombudsman" (1981)
"Ombud Research: A Bibliographical Essay" (1982)

Ms. Kerstin André
"The Ombudsman—Meeting Today's Changing Needs" (2003)

Mr. Bruce Aronson
"Elements of a Successful International Employment Exchange" (1986)
"Observations of the Commissioner (Ombudsman) for Local Administration in Scotland" (1986)

Fernando Alvarez de Miranda y Torres
"Human Rights and Their Function in the Institutional Strengthening of the Ombudsman" (1998)

Ms. Daisy de Asper y Valdez
"Maturation Issues for the Ombudsman" (with Gerald Caiden) (1989)
"The Self-Perceptions of the Ombudsman: A Comparative and Longitudinal Survey" (1990-1991)

Dr. Victor O. Ayeni
"The Adoption of the Ombudsman Plan in Nigeria: Background and Aftermath of Decree 31 of 1975" (1984-85)
"The Ombudsman's Periodic Reports—Nigeria's Version" (1989)
"State Complaints Offices in Nigeria—Coping With a Federalized Ombudsman System in the Third World" (1990-91)
"Training for Ombudsman Work in Africa—An Agenda for Recovery" (1992)
"Evaluating Ombudsman Programmes" (1993)
"An Ombudsman for Botswana?" (1994)
"Ombudsman Institutions and Democracy in Africa—A Gender Perspective" (1997)
"The Changing Nature and Contemporary Role of National Ombudsman Institutions in the Commonwealth and Elsewhere: Lessons of Experience" (2000)
"The Ombudsman in the Achievement of Administrative Justice and Human Rights in the New Millennium" (2001)

Dr. Epiphany Azinge
"Code of Conduct Tribunal in Nigeria—A Dormant Institution?" (1993)

Mr. K. Banda
"The Organization and Functioning of the Ombudsman Institution in Zambia" (1994)

Dr. Ina Barrett
"Political Clientelism, Bureaucracy, Administrative Law and the Protection of Citizens' Rights" (1990-91)

Mr. Selby Baqwa
"The Role of the Public Protector Vis-à-vis Other Institutions That Redress Grievances in South Africa" (1999)

Mr. Eugene Biganovsky
"The Experiences of the South Australian Ombudsman: Policy—Administration—Jurisdiction of the Ombudsman" (1993)

Mr. Ivan Bizjak
"The Role and Experience of an Ombudsman in a New Democracy" (1998)
"European Ombudsman and the Rights of People Deprived of Their Liberty" (1999)
"Special Features of the Role of the Ombudsman in Transition Conditions" (2001)

Professor A.W. Bradley
"The Case-Work of the Parliamentary Ombudsman" (1983)

Mr. Gerald Caiden (with Ms. Daisy Valdés)
"Maturation Issues for the Ombudsman" (1989)

Mr. A.J. Callahan
"Maladministration" (1988)

Ms. Marie-José Chidiac
"Administrative Mediation and Ombudsmen: An Encounter With Internormativity" (2004)

Right Hon. Adrienne Clarkson
"Opening Address" (2003)

Professor James G. Coke
Professor John J. Gargan
"Linking Officials and Citizens Through Statewide Information and Complaint-Handling Offices" (1981)

Mr. Luigi Cominelli
"An Ombudsman for the Europeans: Gradually Moving Towards 'Effective Dispute Resolution' Between Citizens and Public Administrations" (2002)

Professor M.J.A. Cooray
"Hong Kong's Ombudsman: The First Decade" (1999)

Ms. Katrine Del Villar
"Who Guards the Guardians? Recent Developments Concerning the Jurisdiction and Accountability of Ombudsmen in Australia" (2002)

Dr. Henri Desfeuilles
"The Control of the Administration in France" (1983) (English & French)

Mr. Ermir Dobjani
"The Establishment and Operation of the People's Advocate: The Ombudsman in Albania" (2002)

Jackson Edokpa
"Strategies for Improving Ombudsman Institutions in Africa" (1999)

Mr. Claes Eklundh
"The Ombudsman Specialized in Judicial Matters" (1998)

Sir Brian Elwood
"How to Harmonize General Ombudsman Activities with Those Related to Specialized Ombudsmen" (1998)

M. Robert Fabre
"The Tenth Anniversary of the Institution of the Mediator of the French Republic" (1983) (English & French)
"For the Revival of the Sense of Good Citizenship" (1984-1985) (English & French)

Mr. Charles Ferris
"Freedom of Information in Canada—The Ombudsman—The Judicial Review Model" (1984-1985)

Mr. Arne Fliflet
"The Historical Development and the Essential Features of the Ombudsman Worldwide" (1994)
"The Ombudsman's Budget, Accounts and Audit—Their Influence on the Ombudsman's Ability to Fulfil His Responsibilities" (1997)

Mr. Hans Gammeltoft-Hansen
"The Ombudsman as a Non-Traditional Tool for Citizen Participation" (1998)

Professor Dale Gibson
"Coping with Quasi-ness: Ombudsmen and Quasi-Judicial Tribunals" (1992)

Dr. Roy Gregory
"Building An Ombudsman Scheme: Statutory Provisions and Operating Practices" (1994)
"The Ombudsman Observed" (1997)
"The Ombudsman: 'An Excellent Form of Alternative Dispute Resolution'?" (2001)

Dr. Walter Haller
"The Ombudsman Idea in Switzerland" (1981)

Professor John Hatchard
"The Institution of Ombudsman in Africa With Special Reference to Zimbabwe" (1986)

Mr. S.M. Hatteea
"The Ombudsman in Mauritius—Thirty Years On" (1999)

Dr. Marc Hertogh
"The Policy Impact of the Ombudsman and Administrative Courts: A Heuristic Model" (1998)

Mr. Graham Hill
"An Exchange of Staff Between the Offices of the Local Ombudsman in Scotland and the State Ombudsman of Alaska" (1986)

Dr. Larry B. Hill
"Institutionalizing a Bureaucratic Monitoring Mechanism: The First Thirty Years of Hawaii's Ombudsman" (2000)

Prof. Edward R. Hill
"The Ombudsman as Mediator: Challenges, Limitations and Opportunities in Vanuatu" (2001)

Mr. Isaac Hochman
"Presentation to the First San Juan Ombudsmanship Congress" (1992)

Mr. Sigvard Holstad
Mr. Sven Borjeson
"The Swedish Parliamentary Ombudsmen and Their Supervision of the Military" (1987)

Human Rights Research and Education Centre University of Ottawa
Ottawa Ontario, Canada
"Ombudsman: Issues and Articles—A Bibliography" (1997)

Dr. Drew Hyman
"Citizen Complaints as Social Indicators: The Negative Feedback Model of Accountability" (1987)

Dr. Mike A. Ikhariale
"Industrial Ombudsman: The Nigerian Approach" (1986)
"The Constitutional Reform of the Ombudsman System in Nigeria" (1989)

Dr. Randall. E. Ivany
"The Theme Address, South African Seminar, Stellenbosch, South Africa" (1982)
"Book Review: *The Ombudsman Plan"* by Dr. Donald Rowat (1987)

Mr. Daniel Jacoby
"The Protecteur du Citoyen du Québec as an Agent of Change" (1993) (with Patrick Robardet)

"Comments on Relations Between Ombudsmen and the Media" (1995) (English & Spanish)
"A Social Contract on Relations Between Citizens and Governments" (1999)

Ms. Roberta Jamieson
"The Ombudsman: Learning From Other Cultures" (1993)
"Ombudsman Investigations: Serving All the People" (1997)
"The Ombudsman's Annual Report: Strengthening the Ombudsman Office in Africa" (1997)

Dr. Rajani Ranjan Jha
"The Lokayukta in Bihar: Expectations and Achievements (1973-1983)" (1984-1985)

Mr. Cedric L. Johnson
"Complaints—Grievance Procedures for Prisoners" (1988)

Mr. Ibrahim S.A. Kajembo
"Helping People Facilitate the Attainment of Fairness and Justice by Government" (1998)

Mr. Frank Kajwara
"Impact of the Ombudsman on Good Governance and Public Service Administration" (1997)

Mr. Jenoë Kaltenbach
"Special Protection Requirements for Minorities: The Parliamentary Commissioner for the Rights of National and Ethnic Minorities of Hungary" (2003)

Dr. Udo Kempf
Mr. Marco Mille
"The Role and the Function of the Ombudsman: Personalized Parliamentary Control in Forty-Eight Different States" (1993)

Mr. Abraham Kiapi
"The Inspector-General of Government: Uganda's Ombudsman of All Trades" (1990-1991)

Mr. Mjemas G.J. Kimweri
"Twenty-five Years of the Permanent Commission of Enquiry (Tanzania Ombudsman Office): Dream and Reality" (1992)

Mr. H.H. Kirchheiner
"The National Ombudsman in a Democratic Perspective" (1987)

Mr. Howard Kushner
"How Do You Know You Are Doing A Good Job?: Strategic Plans, Performance Measures and Surveys" (2003)

Monsieur le juge Louis LeBel
"Démocratie et protection de la diversity culturelle" (2003)

Mr. Gregory J. Levine
"The Engaged Ombudsman—Morality and Activism in Attaining Administrative Justice" (2004)

Professor Douglas Lewis
Professor Rhoda James
"Joined-up Justice: Review of the Public Sector Ombudsman in England" (2000)

Lawyers Committee for Human Rights
New York City, N.Y., U.S.A.
Reprint of "The Price of Independence: The Office of Ombudsman and Human Rights in the Russian Federation" (1995)

Hon. J. Mr. Ulf Lundvik
"The Public's Access to Official Documents in Sweden" (1981)
"A Brief Survey of the History of the Ombudsman" (1982)
"Openness in Government Administration Versus Protection of the Privacy of the Individual, A Legislator's Dilemma in Sweden" (1983)
"The Public as Overseer of Police Activities—Some Recent Trends in Sweden" (1986)

Mr. Niall MacDermot
"The Ombudsman Institution"(1987)

Mr. Jorge Madrazo Cuellar
"New Policies on Human Rights in Mexico: The National Commission for Human Rights 1988-1993" (1994) (Spanish and English)
"The Ombudsman and His Relationship With Human Rights, Poverty and Development" (1998)

Mr. Leonard G. Magawa
"Tanzania's Commission for Human Rights and Good Governance: A Critique of the Legislation" (2002)

Dr. Jorge Luis Maiorano
"The *Defensor del Pueblo* in Argentina: A Constitutional Insitution of Control and Protection" (1995) (Spanish and English)

“The Challenges Facing the Ombudsman in Argentina and Around the World” (1999)

Dr. Barbara Male
“Assessing Ombudsman Performance” (2000)

Dr. Nelson Mandela, Q.C.
“Address” (2001)

Mr. M. Maree
“The Institution of Ombudsman in the Republic of Namibia” (1999)

Mr. André Marin
“Demonstrating Your Value” (2003)

Mr. Zvi Marom
Dr. Shimon Rozevitch
“Israeli Public Administration as Reflected in Citizens’ Complaints” (1989)

Ms. Miria R.K. Matembe
“Human Rights of the Disadvantaged Under the Ombudsman” (1992)

The Hon. Mr. Thabo Mbeki
“Welcoming Address” (2001)

Mr. J.F. Mbwiliza
“The Permanent Commission of Enquiry: For Justice and Promotion of Human Rights in Tanzania” (1999)

Mr. Brian McClelland
“Oversight of Law Enforcement in Northern Ireland” (1987)

Mr. Derrick McKoy
“The Jamaican Contractor-General: An Ombudsman for Contracts” (1990-1991)

Mr. John McMillan
“The Ombudsman and the Rule of Law” (2004)

Mr. Ivan Mifsud
Ms. Cécile Plaidy
“The Roles of Administrative Courts and Ombudsmen in France and Malta: A Review of Two Contrasting Systems (2004)

Mr. Christopher Milton
"The Wider Aspects of Ombudsmanship" (1984-1985)
"The Ombudsman as a Protector of Fundamental Personal Rights" (1988)

Dr. Tore Modeen
"The Finnish Ombudsman: The First Case of Foreign Reception of the Swedish Justitieombudsman Office" (1981)

Ms. H. Gail Morrison
"Decisions by the Ombudsman and Review by the Legislature: Rules, Principles and Policy" (1989)

Mr. Elwyn Moseley
"The New Law Governing the Conduct of Local Authority Members in Wales" (2002)

Mr. Kevin Murphy
"Accountability to the Citizen" (1998)

Mr. William G.F. Napier
"Ombudsman and Authority: A Commonwealth Restatement" (1984-1985)

Dr. Lars Nordskov Nielsen
"The Danish Ombudsman" (1983)

Mr. Vincent M. Okwechime, Jr.
"Policing the Police: The Need for a 'Code of Procedure Ombudsman' in Nigeria" (1988)

Mr. 'Dejo Olowu
"Good Governance and Development Challenges in the South Pacific: The Promise of Ombudsmanship" (2004)

Ombudsman Ontario
"Serving With Equity: Report of a Journey" (1997)

Dr. Marten Oosting
"The National Ombudsman of the Netherlands and Human Rights" (1994)
"The Ombudsman and His Environment: A Global View" (1995)
"The Ombudsman: A Profession" (1997)
"The Annual Report of the Ombudsman" (1998)
"Rights of Persons Deprived of Their Liberty" (1999)
"Rights of Refugees and Asylum Seekers" (1999)
"Protecting the Integrity and Independence of the Ombudsman Institution: The Global Perspective" (2001)

Ms. Emily O'Reilly
"Protecting Rights and Freedoms" (2003)

Ms. Judith A. Osborne
"The Coroner in British Columbia: Ombudsman for the Dead?" (1989)

Mr. Stephen Owen
"Proposal for a Canadian Federal Ombudsman Office" (1992)

Mr. Miguel Padilla
"The Ombudsman and the Mass Media" (1995) (Spanish and English)

Mr. Brent Parfitt
"The Effect of Privatization on Ombudsman Jurisdiction" (2000)

Mr. Brent Parfitt
Dr. Karl Friedmann
"Little Injustices in Institutions" (1986)

Professor Dennis Pearce
"The Ombudsman: Review and Preview—The Importance of Being Different" (1993)

Dr. Ilan Peleg
"The Soldiers' Complaints Commissioner in Israel" (1987)

Ms. Charmaine Pemberton-Carrington
"The Ombudsman and Development: Structural Adjustment and its Effect on the Ombudsman Institution" (1995)

Dr. Viktor Pickl
"Islamic Roots of Ombudsman Systems" (1987)

Dr. Jacob Rang
"Procedures for Handling Police Complaints in Holland" (1986)
"Standards Governing Police Behaviour and the Handling of Complaints in This Area" (1986)

Ms. Margarita Retuerto Buades
"Legitimation Procedures of Ombudsmen for Bringing People's Actions and Class Actions" (1995) (Spanish and English)

Professor Jack E. Richardson
"The Australian Commonwealth Ombudsman State of the Institution" (1984-1985)

"The Commonwealth Ombudsman and the Australian Taxation Office" (1986)

Mr. Patrick Robardet
"The Protecteur du Citoyen du Québec as an Agent of Change" (with Daniel Jacoby) (1993)

Sir John Robertson
"Basis for Remuneration for Ombudsman"(1988)
"Setting Up an Ombudsman Office" (1997)
"The Ombudsman Around the World" (1998)

Dr. Walter L.J. Rosen
"Protecting the Minority: The Ombudsman of Ulster" (1986)

Mr. Michael Ross
"The Ombudsman: A New Court of Chancery" (1988)

Professor Donald C. Rowat
"Why an Ombudsman to Supervise the Courts?" (1992)
"Why a Legislative Ombudsman is Desirable" (1993)

Mr. A. Ruzindana
"Human Rights, The International Bill of Human Rights and the Ombudsman" (1992)
"The Role of the Ombudsman in Enforcing Accountability" (1999)

Ms. Catarina Sampaio Ventura
Mr. João Zenha Martins
"The Charter of Fundamental Rights of the European Union: A Landmark in the European Landscape and the Prospects for a Dynamic Role of the Ombudsman" (2003)

Dr. Ian Scott
"The Ombudsman in Fiji: Patterns of Mediation and Institutionalization" (1982)

Mr. Ross Shamenski
"Judicial Consideration of the Ombudsman in Canada, Australia and England" (1983)

Mr. Stephen Shaw
"A Specialist Ombudsman for Prisoners" (2004)

Mr. Emile Francis Short
"The Development and Future of the Ombudsman Concept in Africa" (2001)

Mr. K. Soremekun
"The Media and Public Opinion As Components of a Successful Ombudsman Experience" (1994)

Ms. Vijayashri Sripati
"A Critical Look at the Evolving Role of India's National Human Rights Commission in Promoting International Human Rights Law" (2001)

Ms. Lisa Statt Foy
"A First Nations Ombudsman: Some Considerations" (2003)

The Hon. J.H. Steyn
"Alternative Dispute Resolution: The Role of the Private Sector Ombudsman" (2001)

Ms. Alice Tai
"The Impact of Social and Political Environments and Their Influence on the Work of the Ombudsman: Hong Kong" (2001)

Professor Richard W. Taylor
"When Germans Complain" (1981)
"The Ombudsman of Rhineland-Palatinate: A Client Oriented Office" (1983)
"Ombudsman Success in the Federal Republic of Germany: The Role of the Specialized and General Ombudsman in a Larger Federation" (1984-1985) (German and English)
"The Position of the Ombuds in Grievance Redress Processes of Britain, Germany and the U.S.A." (1987)
"The Ombud of South Tirol" (1988)

Dr. Bankole Thompson
"Spatial Diffusion of the Ombudsman Institution: African Adaptations of a European Innovation—The Consolidation Problem" (1992)

Mr. Jotham Tumwesigye
"The Role of the Inspectorate of Government in Promoting the Rule of Law in Uganda" (1999)

Mr. Per A. Utsi
"Norway's Military Ombudsman and His Board" (1987)

Mr. Leo Valladares Lanza
"The Challenges Facing the Ombudsman in Latin America" (1998)

Ms. Barbara von Tigerstrom
"The Role of the Ombudsman in Protecting Economic, Social and Cultural Rights" (1998)

Mr. Nii Lante Wallace-Bruce
"Ghana's Ombudsman—An Unusual Breed" (1992)

Dr. Edward Warrington
"The Ombudsman's Oracle: Critic, Counsellor, Champion—A Comparative Study of Ombudsman Reports" (1999)

Mr. Christopher Waters
"Human Rights in an International Protectorate: Kosovo's Ombudsman" (2000)

Mr. Robin Wilson
"The 1988 Official Languages Act: A Renewed Mandate For Canada's Language Ombudsman" (1990-1991)